Eleanor's Teeth, Apawamis' fourth hole.

**Frank Presbrey,
USSGA President and Team Captain.**
Golf Illustrated, 1922

Apawamis clubhouse and eighteenth green.
Painting by Ray Ellis for the USSGA Centennial Celebration.

UNITED STATES SENIORS' GOLF ASSOCIATION

1905–2005

By

William L. Quirin, PhD

The Annual Frolic
of the Veterans

*The Senior Golfers Make Merry in Their
Yearly Meeting at Apawamis*

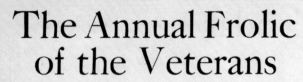

Right, Hugh H. Halsell of Dallas, who regained the championship, which he held in 1920 and 1923, with a score of 161 (Levick)

Left, One of the reasons why Frank Hoyt did not retain the title (P. & A.)

Right, Two of the veterans talk matters over before starting out on their round (P. & A.)

Horace L. Hotchkiss, honorary President, was among those present; he has not missed a single one of these tournaments (P. & A.)

The American Golfer, 1927

4

CONTENTS

INTRODUCTION

ONE HUNDRED YEARS AGO, Horace L. Hotchkiss dreamed of staging a golf tournament exclusively for older men. Although many scoffed at the idea, Hotchkiss eventually convinced enough of his friends and acquaintances to admit their age and forget their infirmities and play thirty-six holes of golf in one day over the hills of The Apawamis Club in Rye, New York. That day, October 12, 1905, marked the birth of senior golf.

After ten years of expansion and reliance on Apawamis' generosity, it was decided that it was time to formally organize, and thus in 1917, the United States Seniors' Golf Association was created, with its primary purpose being to hold an annual tournament on the links of Apawamis. It was the first organization of its kind in the world.

It wasn't long before the existence of a seniors' organization in the United States inspired the founding of similar organizations in Canada, and then Great Britain. Ties between the organizations grew strong, and international team competition began almost immediately: the Devonshire Cup matches between the United States and the Canadian Seniors starting in 1918 in Canada, and the Triangular Matches between all three groups commenced in 1927 in Great Britain. These contests have continued through the years, fostering international good will and fellowship as cherished by-products of very high standard, competitive golf.

Meanwhile, the annual tournament continued to grow, and its format changed, until the present format was adopted in the early 1970s. At the same time, many seniors expressed an interest in getting together more than once each year, and thus were born the Invitational Tournaments, which are held at some of America's finest golf clubs. The Invitationals have become the backbone of the association, and have made membership in the United States Seniors the most desirable way to complete one's golfing career in the later years of life.

Through the years, the United States Seniors' membership has included prominent men from all walks of life, from lawyers and judges to bankers and brokers, from government officials (even presidents) and military leaders to insurance men and teachers. The lasting friendships formed between the members is a hallmark of the association.

In 2005, as the United States Seniors celebrates its centennial, this book records its story in words and pictures.

P R E F A C E

THE UNITED STATES SENIORS' GOLF ASSOCIATION has been fortunate through the years to have had its history recorded and preserved in three primary sources. Horace Hotchkiss himself was the first to "write it down" when he penned *The Origin and Organization of the Seniors' Tournament* in 1922. A fiftieth anniversary book was prepared in 1955, with Henry Flower and Gordon Hill supplementing Hotchkiss' work. At the seventy-fifth anniversary, the "Red Book" was published, with Flower and Hill extending the chronological history, William Ward Foshay discussing the International Matches, and Sydney Stokes the Invitational Tournaments. The three clubs hosting the annual tournament, Apawamis, Round Hill, and Blind Brook, were portrayed by Richard Pinkham, John Gates, and Lewis Lapham, respectively, and Gates also wrote an essay about the United States Seniors' "Hall of Fame." Finally, Everett Fisher updated the "Red Book" in 1995.

This book brings the history forward through 2004, with the dedicated assistance of the Centennial Book Committee, chaired by Jonathan M. Clark and including Everett Fisher and Bill Souders, thereby commemorating the first one hundred years of the United States Seniors. The words of the previous authors have in large part been preserved in this tome, although on the surface the book appears to have been written by one person. Changes in content in light of the passage of time have also been made when warranted.

Substantial portions of the supplementary materials found primarily in the sidebars come from other sources. The United States Seniors has Minute books dating back to the year of its organization. The Seniors' Annual Bulletin was first published in 1933, and its name was changed to the Yearbook in 1966. It has provided a wonderful source of information, anecdotes, and pictures through the years. In the years prior to World War II, the annual tournament and the international matches received regular coverage in the newspapers (the *New York Times* is the primary source used in this book) and magazines. The latter are on file at the United States Golf Association's Golf House in New Jersey, and also were the source of detailed information about the annual tournaments, anecdotes, and pictures.

This book is a compendium of all of these sources, and offers a complete and enhanced history of the United States Seniors' first one hundred years.

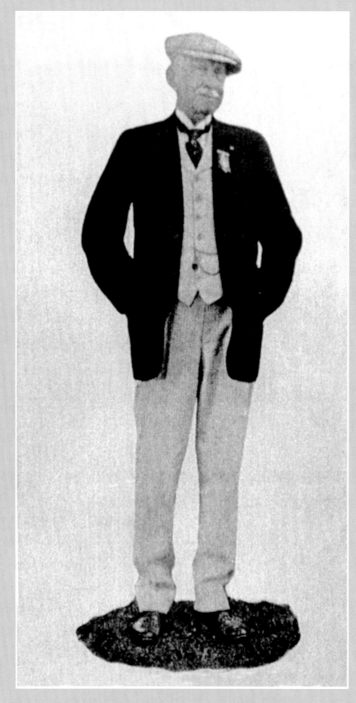

Horace L. Hotchkiss, founder of the US Seniors.

Setting the Stage

THE GAME OF GOLF TOOK FIRM ROOT IN THE UNITED STATES during the 1890s after the initial seeds were planted in the late 1880s at such fabled clubs as St. Andrew's in Yonkers, Newport Golf Club, The Country Club in Brookline, the Tuxedo Club, Shinnecock Hills Golf Club, and the Chicago Golf Club.

Golf's early proponents were generally not young men, but rather wealthy businessmen with leisure time on their hands. The list of early US Amateur champions includes Charles Blair Macdonald (1895; architect of the National Golf Links of America and Blind Brook), Findlay Douglas (1898, later a US Seniors' president), and Walter Travis (1900, 1901, and 1903; designer of Round Hill and Ekwanok). Macdonald and Travis were forty at the time of their conquests, definitely "senior" by today's US Amateur standards.

> *The courts of law can now resume their interrupted activities, the "Street" will once again feel the hand of the mighty, and the Ship of State should glide more smoothly in the near future, for the great annual seniors tournament at Apawamis is over.*
>
> *— New York Times, 1919*

It is estimated that there were approximately five thousand golfers in the United States at the turn of the twentieth century. Many of the finest of these lived in the suburbs of New York City, Boston, Philadelphia, and Chicago. Indeed, all national championships (US Amateur, US Women's Amateur, and US Open) from 1895 through 1906 were held at clubs in or near Chicago or in the Northeast corridor between Washington and Boston.

US Senior Findlay Douglas, the 1898 US Amateur champion.
Golf Illustrated, 1930

The America they knew was emerging from an extended period of social depression following the Civil War, and idle time was a novelty. The typical work week included at least Saturday morning.

The average life expectancy for a male in the United States in 1900 was 46.3 years, demographics that clearly were skewed by the high death rate in the first year of life. However, those reaching 50 in 1900 had a life expectancy of 70.76 years. By comparison, those same numbers in 1930 were 58.1 and 71.51 years, in 1950 were 65.6 and 72.83 years, and in 2000 were 74.7 and 78.2 years.

Into this setting stepped Horace L. Hotchkiss, a member of The Apawamis Club in Rye, New York, which itself dated to 1890. Quoting from a "classic writer" in his own memoirs, Hotchkiss included the following about the game of golf:

Golf is probably the most scientific of all outdoor games, requiring as much accuracy of stroke as tennis and far more judgment than cricket or baseball. The fascination which makes it the game of all games is that the mental as well as the physical makeup of the player enters into it; no man excells at it no matter how mechanically correct he may play, unless his personal characteristics are a part of every stroke he makes.

No other game requires such a variety of physical and mental adjustments, and no other game gives so complete a measure of the whole man.

The Apawamis Club's anniversary book, *100 Years of Apawamis*, includes the following passage:

The Apawamis golf schedule for the 1903 season presented a most ambitious program, including an opening day competition that included a special prize, offered by James McCutcheon of New York, for the player handing in the lowest score whose age was not less than fifty. Mr. McCutcheon reserved the privilege of asking a few intimate friends and some strangers to take part. This unusual event may have been the prelude to the idea that inspired what we now know as "the Seniors."

Hotchkiss at work in the bunker at Apawamis' eighteenth hole.
Golf Illustrated, 1916

CHAPTER 2

Horace Hotchkiss' Dream:
"Recapture the Spirit of Youth"

HORACE L. HOTCHKISS inspired the founding of the United States Seniors' Golf Association, and with it senior golf. He dreaded retirement. He loved to be with his friends but couldn't just sit around, smoke his pipe and listen to them talk. He knew that if he had no office, Mrs. Hotchkiss would think of a thousand things for him to do around the house. He didn't mind jobs but be did mind unnecessary jobs. He found the answer in golf. It was only natural, therefore, that after his return from Europe in 1903 he thought he would try to organize a senior tournament at Apawamis the following year. He sent invitations to all of his friends over sixty who owned a set of clubs, inviting them to join him in a tournament in 1904. The response was so meager that the age limit was dropped to fifty-five and the tournament postponed to 1905.

> In September 1905, invitations were sent out to various clubs in the district to send representatives for a tournament to be held over The Apawamis Club course, at medal play of 36 holes, the winner to be known as the first champion of the "Senior Golfers." And so it came to pass that on a very sparkling day, October 12, 1905, some fifty men appeared to contest the richly deserved title, "Champion Golfer Ancients."
>
> — *Fifty Years of Apawamis*

Thus began senior golf; the only logic there is to it is that the most important day in any golfer's life is when he becomes fifty-five and thereby old enough to be designated a senior.

Regarding the origin and organization of the Seniors' Tournament, it is a simple story, and it can be said of it that, like Topsy in *Uncle Tom's Cabin,* it "growed up."

Horace Leslie Hotchkiss

Horace L. Hotchkiss was an important figure in Wall Street's early days. According to his obituary in the *New York Times* on May 11, 1929, he was "largely responsible for revolutionizing business methods in the world's financial centres."

Horace L. Hotchkiss, the golfer.
Golf Illustrated, 1914

Horace Leslie Hotchkiss was born in 1842 in Auburn, New York, and in 1857 at age fourteen left home to take a clerical position for the American Exchange Bank. After service in the Civil War — he was with Farragut's fleet at Mobile Bay — he returned to Wall Street. In 1867 he became associated with E. A. Callaghan, inventor of the stock ticker. Together with four others, they founded the Gold and Stock Telegraph Company, of which Hotchkiss was the secretary and treasurer. The company introduced the stock ticker to Wall Street, making it possible for brokers everywhere to get the quotations in real time as they were made on the floor.

In his capacity as treasurer, Horace often advanced $5 or $10 on the salary of a telegraph operator by the name of Thomas A. Edison, money that helped the young inventor finance the purchase of the "doodads" Edison needed for experiments that resulted in important inventions such as the multiple telegraph, the incandescent light, and the phonograph.

Hotchkiss was one of the founders of the New York Stock Exchange. He bought his seat for $5,200 in 1874 (and eventually sold it for $300,000 in 1927). Also in 1874 he established the first branch office of a Stock Exchange firm, running a private telegraph wire from its Broad Street offices "over the house tops" to the Fifth Avenue Hotel on Twenty-third Street.

Hotchkiss was part of a syndicate that planned to build a canal across Nicaragua, and lost a great part of his fortune when the canal effort failed.

Hotchkiss was always an optimist and an enthusiastic sportsman. He was an officer of the Union League Club, and a life member of the New York Yacht Club. He was a Long Island Sound commuter, making the daily trip by yacht from Mamaroneck to his office.

Horace's first wife, Clara, died after fifty-four years of marriage. He married his second wife, Lucy May, in 1927 at age eighty-five.

Horace died of a cerebral hemorrhage in San Antonio at age eighty-seven in 1929.

Horace Hotchkiss and wife Clara.

The original idea of such a tournament started from a discussion at the "nineteenth hole" at The Apawamis Club in the winter of 1904. The following is taken from the book, *Fifty Years of Apawamis*:

They Came To Play

John W. Griggs (facing page) graduated from Lafayette College in 1868 and was admitted to the bar in 1871. After serving terms in the New Jersey assembly and senate, he became in 1895 the first Republican governor of the state in twenty-five years. In 1898 Griggs was appointed attorney general of the United States. He was a close friend of Vice-president Garret Hobart – both were among the founders of the Paterson Golf Club (now North Jersey Country Club). Griggs was quick to point out that the real difficulties with the war against Spain would begin when the United States was asked to decide issues that would arise after the conquest.

Judge Horace Russell was born in upstate New York in 1843, then graduated from Dartmouth College before attending Harvard Law School. Russell was an active Republican leader in the state, and served on the New York State Supreme Court. He served as general counsel to the A. T. Stewart estate, developers of Garden City, and was a founding member of the Garden City Golf Club.

John D. McDonald, who hailed from County Cork in Ireland, was the general contractor who built New York City's subway in the early 1900s.

Little is known about James Dwight Foot, winner of five of the first seven Seniors' tournaments. Foot joined Apawamis in 1899, and was relatively new to golf when he won the inaugural Seniors' event in 1905.

One afternoon during the winter of 1904, a group of a half dozen elderly men were gathered in the little old dark 19th hole at Apawamis. They were more or less neophytes at golf, and were discussing what this new pastime had in prospect for them.

Some radical views were being expressed in regard to the future of golf in the United States – that the game would be played by young men, and that it would only be on rare occasions when men of fifty to sixty years of age would be seen on golf links. As he was at that time over sixty years of age and also very much interested in golf, Hotchkiss challenged this view of the future of golf in America and declared that a field of golfers could be arranged in the near future, sufficient in number to make up a tournament on the Apawamis links, and all the players would be fifty-five years of age and over.

The problem of arranging a tournament seemed difficult, as the general impression existed that the moderate skill acquired at that time by the "old men," as they were called, would discourage many who might wish to enter the competition, by the possibility that it might prove a spectacular exhibition of old age and poor golf.

Later on, in the same winter, after a conference with his colleagues on the Apawamis Board, and notwithstanding the false start with a field of players sixty and older the prior year, Horace was encouraged to undertake, with full authority, and as the only member of the Committee in charge, the work of trying to create a field of golfers made up of those who were eligible for the coming event, to be held in September or October, 1905.

The following quote is taken from the minutes of the Apawamis Board meeting of July 17, 1905:

The Chairman of the Golf Committee read a letter from Mr. Horace L. Hotchkiss suggesting that the club offer its course for a three days' tournament to be held on October 10th, 11th, and 12th open to all men of 55 years of age or over who are members of clubs in the Metropolitan district, and the Secretary was instructed to write Mr. Hotchkiss and say that the Club would be glad to acquiesce in such a tournament.

Having passed much of his adult life on Wall Street, Hotchkiss was particularly knowledgeable of those of his associates who were golf players and eligible for the competition. He corresponded with them and many others, and invited them to take part in a golfing competition to be arranged on the Apawamis links. Horace received many interesting and amusing replies, and was soon satisfied that a field of fifty or more golfers could be depended upon to make up the first tournament.

From the very beginning, Hotchkiss found the term "Old Men's Tournament" to be quite distasteful to some of those who played, as this title was being continually used when talking about the tournament. He discouraged the use of this title and christened the event the "Seniors' Tournament," which distinguished title has from that time identified the annual at Apawamis as one of the important amateur golfing fixtures of the United States.

In arranging for a tournament composed of a field of golfers who were to be drawn from professional, commercial, and industrial life, men busy in their various vocations, it was impossible to plan for a schedule based upon "match play." It was therefore decided to have a competition of one day's medal play of thirty-six holes, with four prizes to be awarded as follows:

Best Gross	36 Holes
Second Best Gross	36 Holes
Best Net	36 Holes
Second Best Net	36 Holes

Attorney General J. W. Griggs.
Golf, 1910

The first Seniors' Tournament did not have a national flavor. Quite the opposite, actually, the first field came almost entirely from the New York area. Invitations were sent out for the first tournament to be held October 12, 1905, and the hospitality of The Apawamis Club was extended to all who entered, including a bountiful luncheon provided by the club as a part of the program.

Many of the Seniors who responded to Hotchkiss' initial invitation declared that this was their first appearance in public in a golfing competition. A spirit of good fellowship was quickly established between all competitors.

Arrangements were made in advance for pairs, and old rivalries were renewed in these individual matches, with the understanding that each player's score was to be returned as against the whole field.

The fact that the schedule of play was for 36 holes made this a real test of endurance, for two rounds over the Apawamis links represented a distance of about nine miles.

The inaugural tournament of 1905 was won by James D. Foot of Apawamis with a score of 179. Foot was the winner again in the second year, this time with a score of 184. Over thirty seniors started in 1905, and twenty-five of them completed the 36 holes.

After the first and second tournaments, it became fashionable among golfers to wish to be fifty-five, and thus the augmented numbers annually participating in this event continued to prove the truth of the early adopted motto, "Once a Senior Always a Senior, Sometimes Venerable but Never Aged," that was coined by *New York Sun* sportswriter George Trevor.

The Competitions

The *New York Times* reported briefly on both the 1905 and 1906 tournaments, each time under the headline "Age Limit Golf Match." Both events were played on Thursdays.

On October 11, 1906, the *New York Times* had the following to say:

Wintry winds and a snow squall or two failed to diminish the ranks of the army of aged golfers yesterday on the links of The Apawamis Club at Rye. Forty-six contestants drove off in the morning from the first tee, and all completed the entire 36-hole match.

The prize for the low gross score for the 36-hole round was won by J.D. Foot of the home club with a card of 184 strokes. J.D. Goodsell won the net score prize with a score of 202, 36 – 166.

One of the interesting incidents of the first tournament was the spectacular drive from the eighth tee when Judge Horace Russell saw the ball land on the green, and roll up near the cup, thus enabling him to make the hole in two.

The *New York Times* article reporting on the 1905 tournament.

AGE LIMIT GOLF MATCH.

Ex-Judge Horace Russell Leads Notable Field at Apawamis.

A golf tournament conducted under novel and interesting conditions was played on the links of the Apawamis Golf Club at Rye yesterday. The contestants were limited to men who would admit an age of 55 years or over. Notwithstanding this apparent handicap there was no lack of entries. They came from New Jersey, Long Island, and other neighboring resorts. The game was a 36-hole handicap, and prizes were offered for both gross and net scores.

Ex-Judge Horace Russell led the field of over thirty starters, winning the first net score prize with a score of 177 from 20 handicap. Ex-Attorney General John W. Griggs of New Jersey was a close second, finishing but one stroke behind, although his gross score was a point better than Judge Russell's.

James B. Foot, one of the veterans of the home club, came third, but he was the only player rated at scratch, and turned in the low score of 179, which won the gross score prize handily. The second gross score prize went to R. H. Robertson, ex-President of the United States Golf Association.

John B. McDonald, the man who built the Subway, earned a special prize for the best net score of the afternoon, his figures being 94, 11—83. George P. Sheldon was well up among the leaders, but J. Rogers Maxwell showed his golfing friends that he knew more about yachts than golf, as his place was close to the bottom of the list. E. C. Converse, S. Ward Doubleday, Judge F. M. Scott, and L. J. Buzby were among the old timers who enjoyed the sport.

The players who completed the double round were:

	Gross.	Hdcp.	Net.
Horace Russell	197	20	177
John W. Griggs	196	18	178
James D. Foot	179	0	179
John D. McDonald	202	22	180
R. H. Robertson	189	8	181
George P. Sheldon	200	18	182
Hugh D. Eddy	210	26	184
H. L. Hotchkiss	210	26	184
J. B. Hall	216	32	184
Goodwin Stoddard	221	36	185
Henry Stoddard	204	18	186
Alfred Craven	206	20	186

Other scores were: H. W. Brown, 105, 8—187; James McCutcheon, 215, 28—187; C. E. Gedney, 202, 14—188; S. Ward Doubleday, 200, 12—188; E. C. Converse, 209, 20—189; Robert Goodbody, 211, 20—191; William Runkle, 211, 18—193; William Jarvie, 213, 20—193; Judge F. M. Scott, 222, 26—196; L. J. Buzby, 237, 36—201; James Rogers Maxwell, 237, 36—201; S. W. Brown, 244, 36—208; T. T. Slevin, 253, 36—217.

James D. Foot (left), winner of five of the first seven US Seniors' Tournaments, and Maturin Ballou, Apawamis member and co-designer of the original golf course. *Golf Illustrated,* 1914

Judge Henry Gildersleeve putting on the first green, with Morgan O'Brien looking on.
Golf Illustrated, 1914

The Early Years: 1907–1916

THE FIRST DECADE OF THE SENIORS' TOURNAMENT was a time of remarkable growth. Changes became necessary. The first important one came in 1909 when it was decided that 36 holes in one day were too much to expect of golf's senior citizens, and so the tournament was expanded to two days, with 18 holes played each day.

The number of participants increased from over thirty in 1905, then forty-six in 1906, to well over two hundred in 1915, by which time it had become evident that the number of participants was already too great for a two-day tournament. The Apawamis Club, through its special committee in charge of the Seniors' Tournament, announced that the event would be extended to four days, with half of the entries to play on the first two days, and half on the last two days. This plan relieved the former congestion and proved so satisfactory that it was used for many years thereafter.

> *Golf steadies the nerves, improves the circulation, clears the vision, and strengthens the intellect.*
>
> *— New York Times,*
> *September 30, 1911*
>
> *I obtained tips of more value on form by watching a skillful elderly player swing than through any other source.*
>
> *— Chick Evans*
> *1916 and 1920 US Amateur champion*

In addition to dividing the field, the players were split into classes on the basis of age, and special prizes were added with the provision that a winner could take but a single prize. All this made the selection of the official prize list a formidable affair, one that could not be completed coincident with the close of the tournament.

The *New York Times* provides the actual numbers for the 1916 tournament:

One hundred and twenty two started in the first half of the tournament, and a like number in the second, making a new high water mark for entrants in this tournament, and also establishing a record entry for any tournament in this country.

Veteran senior Simeon Ford spoke tongue-in-cheek about the group's growing numbers, as reported in the October 1914 issue of *Golf Illustrated*:

Simeon Ford solemnly testified: "Our committee finds that golf prolongs life – a little too long. No one of the Seniors, unfortunately, has passed away since we started this affair nine years ago (in fact, they are getting hardier every year), and they are coming to be fifty-five years of age with astonishing, overwhelming rapidity. We will soon have to accommodate five hundred aged aspirants for our clocks, tea sets, cake baskets, and inkstands – and how they will manage to limp around our somewhat hilly course in two days, is more than I can imagine. We sent them out in foursomes this year, and though they played gaily along with each other's balls, and violated all known rules of the Royal and Ancient, they took so much time that many had to finish by moonlight and the help of auto lamps. I thought that by forcing them to buy an old time $1.50 Grand Union lunch each day, many would stay away, but they brought their own sandwiches, cold tea and hard-boiled eggs, and picnicked along the course.

But we fear that nothing that we can do will be able to stem the tide. It is giving our committee the nightmare – we see nice genial old gentlemen swearing hard and hacking out of bunkers in our dreams; and thousands of dear old grandpas made peevish by fishing balls out of our pond, or wading about in our brook. We had charitable hopes that many would be sunstruck in the ninety-five degrees of heat last Wednesday, but they all came in smiling, and many asked for hot tea. Having seen the inability of heat to decimate the Seniors, our Committee has about decided to set the date of the 1915 tournament for March 12, as the great blizzard occurred on that date – and may occur again – and many might possibly pass away in the snowdrifts. But if we do decide on that date (with a cold lunch at $5.00 per), I haven't a doubt that we will find over four hundred old gentlemen on the first tee with a bottle of hot soup, ready to start. Really it is a serious matter, and the Committee is badly stumped."

The Boston Bowl

The Boston Bowl was presented to Apawamis in 1913 by a group of Seniors from Boston. It was to be presented annually to the Apawamis member with the low net score in the annual tournament. In 1984 Round Hill and Blind Brook members were included as eligible contestants.

Herbert Jacques and Daniel Chauncey, both former USGA presidents.
Golf Illustrated, 1914

"I can't play," said one man, "I'm on the wrong side of 55. I'm 53."

— Golf, 1909

Many who were there last year were competitors now, and they seemed to have grown younger, perhaps because golf has the faculty of renewing one's youth.

— Golf, 1909

It seemed the mental capacity of the players reduced the handicap of years from which most of them suffered.

— Golf, 1910

A Gift To Apawamis

The Seniors who entered the 1908 tournament presented to The Apawamis Club a beautiful testimonial for hospitality extended. This artistic bronze tablet lies imbedded in granite on the western side of the clubhouse overlooking the first tee, a symbol of loyalty to the game of golf and a valued treasure for the Club.

As a boy in Scotland, the late Alexander Milne, of Scarsdale, New York, played golf on the Montrose links, the town in which he was born. He is said to have won an open medal in Montrose as far back as 1847. He learned the steel business in Sheffield before coming to this country in 1869, and brought with him his old love for the game.

Milne could be seen at the Annual Seniors' Tournaments up to the eighty-third year of his life, when he won a prize in Class D. Alexander Milne passed away in the summer of 1915, and his loss as a comrade and golfer was felt by a large circle of the devotees of the game.

Alexander Milne of Scarsdale, 81 years old, who has played golf for more than sixty years, led the field in the first day's play at the annual Seniors' tournament over the links of The Apawamis Club at Rye yesterday, Next on the list came Wilson P. Poss of Deal, who gained fame as an international amateur billiards player some years ago.

There is no more notable tournament in the history of golf than the annual gathering of the seniors, and the idea originated nine years ago by Horace L. Hotchkiss has spread to other parts. But there is only this event which attracts men of renown in other fields than golf. Such men as Darwin P. Kingsley, Justice Mahlon Pitney of the Supreme Court of the United States, William S. Gummere, Chief Justice of the New Jersey Supreme Court, Judge Henry A. Gildersleeve of New York, Ralph Peters, President of the Long Island Railroad, Simeon Ford, Morgan J. O'Brien, and E.C. Converse were competitors.

— New York Times, 1913

To prove that the weight of more than 70 years' judicial cares and white hairs is no handicap to the follower of the royal and ancient game of golf, Judge Henry Stoddard of New Haven led the field of 172 seniors with a net 18-hole score of 72 in the first day of play of the 12th annual Seniors' Tournament at Apawamis.

— New York Times, 1916

It will be hard going for any Class D golfer over 70 who tries to equal the record left by Colonel S.A. Worthington of Chevy Chase, who lost his leg on a battlefield in the civil war, and yet retains enough courage, grit, and skill to limp around the links with the aid of a cane, and to capture the low net in his class with a card of 209-60 = 149.

J.V. Christi of Forest Hill has left an imperishable memory at Apawamis, though he failed to win a prize of any kind. His regular golfing outfit, ready for exhibition at any time, no charge, consists of a brassie and an iron. The iron club, however, is not what it seems to be, rather it is a great deal more than it appears to be at a casual glance, and it performs a variety of services which is remarkable in these

Simeon Ford.
Golf Illustrated, 1933

days of specialization. In its ordinary condition, it is a midiron, a twist of a screw and the insertion of a new face, which the owner abstracts from his pocket, makes it a mashie at a moment's notice. Another turn of the screw with the insertion of a triangular block of wood, and the club becomes a straight-faced putter capable of sending the ball into the cup from any angle at any time.

The club is the innovation of Christi, but he has a still more remarkable club in his putter "de luxe,"which he carries on special occasions, such as the Seniors' Tournament at Apawamis. After holing a sizable putt on the home green with it, the Forest Hill golfer slid the leather grip down the shaft, unscrewed a brass top piece, and disclosed the fact that the handle was an up to date, melodious-toned flute, on which he proceeded to play a Highland Fling. He explained that with this instrument he could soothe his own and other savage breasts in wild moments on the links, and its ability to express sorrow at a missed putt was only equaled by the triumphant paean that it sent forth when a long one clinked into the cup.

— New York Times, 1916

Back in 1866 George Wright was playing shortstop for the Cincinnati Reds of those days, and to show that he survived even this terrible experience, he tied for first net prize in class C yesterday."

— New York Times, 1916

One of the queer cases that came up before the committee was that of Gage E. Tarbell of Garden City, who wished to play Tuesday and Wednesday in class A, 55 to 59 years. Informed that it would be necessary for him to play in the second division yesterday and today, he changed his class and announced that he would play in class B, 60 to 64 years as he had just turned the threescore milestone yesterday. He finished in a tie for fifth place."

— New York Times, 1916

Dr. Walter Fairbanks was born in Scotland and learned to golf there. He was a sportsman of the first rank, indeed, the "Babe Ruth" of nineteenth-century cricket in England. Fairbanks spent his winters in Southern California, honing his golf game. In 1899 he played in and won his first club championship at the Denver Country Club — despite being more than forty years of age.

Fairbanks won numerous regional golf titles, and qualified for match play at the U.S. Amateur in both 1899 and 1901, reaching the round of 16 in 1899 after winning a 40-hole match. Dr. Fairbanks remained a member of the Denver Country Club until his death in England in 1924.

Simeon Ford is remembered in golf history as the friend who gave Walter Travis the Schenectady putter he used to win the 1904 British Amateur. He owned the Grand Union Hotel in Manhattan from 1881 to 1914, when it was demolished.

Good Fellows All

The mystery that is the game of golf, with its thousand and one charms, with its lure for Youth and solace for Age, with its myriad problems and its soul-satisfying rewards, was never before so well exemplified as at the tenth annual Seniors' tournament at Apawamis last week. The powerful financier that a King might summon in vain, the aging but never aged scholar deep in his studies, the clergyman in the pulpit, the lawyer in the court, the jurist on the bench, all these and more answered respectfully to the call of the starter at Apawamis and dutifully received and did their best to follow the instructions given them by ignorant little caddies for several hours on two consecutive days.

Each and every golfer had a tag affixed to his cap or his coat with his name printed thereon, not to aid in their common recognition as good fellows all, for the very fact of their presence was sufficient testimony on that point, but that they should know even the least important thing about their fellow guests at Apawamis — their names.

It was not in the quality of golf that was played, nor in the fact that it had the largest entry list ever recorded in this country, that the seniors' tournament is to be regarded as such a success. Rather is it a striking fact that the poorest players had the best time and contributed most to the jollity of the occasion . . . . In the world of golf this tournament is an annual triumph of the spirit over the flesh, and it proves to the satisfaction of the players at least that neither ideals nor idylls are the happy possessions of Youth alone.

The Seniors at Apawamis played golf not for a score, but for the pleasure found in playing, the spirit of honest rivalry going hand in hand with good fellowship.

— New York Times, 1916

The only way to tell the age of the contestants is to look at the scoreboard, for the demeanor of all concerned in this golf event, their jaunty steps, bubbling humor, and their care-free attitude could give the impression that the oldest player was about 20, with all the others in their teens.

— New York Times, 1916

The object is ostensibly to play golf — the real object is to sit around under the trees — talk diseases and swap stories."

— Golf Illustrated, October 1914

And finally, a quote from a famous, unnamed golfer of the time:

To the golfer of the younger set, a visit to Apawamis at the time of the annual Seniors' Tournament would be a liberal education as well as a privilege. Men gathered from all parts of the country, and from all walks of life, the players in this tournament demonstrate what golf may hold for the man who cherishes the spirit of youth even in the bones of age. It is much to be regretted that each player who takes up the game cannot undergo a novitiate at the hands of the Seniors' Golf Association in the lack of manner and the abundance of good manners; in the good fellowship that is found and the prejudices which are lost; in the spirit of youth that tempers the wisdom of age. The Seniors' Tournament may serve to bring home the truth of the game to the thousands who play it over American courses. If the spirit that animates these older golfers in any way leavens the great mass of golfers, then what the game has done for the Senior golfers will be little in comparison with what the Senior golfers have done for the game.

Golfers, Are They??

No, I didn't hear of or see any scraps during the tournament — but I saw many novel ways of driving as I sat on the tee. One old gentleman raised his club up three times, and bowed low, as if kowtowing to some heathen god of Luck, before striking the ball. Another took a running leap at his ball, and hit as he went past.

Another teed up on one of the white discs — but was told he was not obliged to do so. One pair both sliced into the woods and disappeared with their caddies hunting for their balls, until six or seven other pairs had started out, then reappeared suddenly, to the surprise of everyone, and the blocking of the course.

Another old-timer teed up with at least four inches of sand, then hit a sky ball or species of foul into the long grass. All were nervous of course, with the gallery behind them, and one player teed up a hard-boiled egg by mistake, which he was carrying to sustain him on the tenth tee. I did not see this myself, but was told it on good authority.

Another teed up in front of the disc line, and when called back said, "I always play that way in Cincinnati." Another swung and missed the ball, turned gravely to the Committee, and asked if the stroke counted. He was told that it surely did. Another gentleman asked the loan of a ball.

— Golf Illustrated, October 1914

Darwin Kingsley, the first president of the USSGA.
Golf Illustrated, 1918

Formal Organization

THE ENTRIES TO THE SENIORS' TOURNAMENT for 1915 exceeded 200 and for 1916 they were about 240. It was felt by some of the leading Seniors who were members of The Apawamis Club that the time had come for the Seniors to organize as an association, to take over the work of running their own tournament, and to relieve The Apawamis Club of this labor, which had grown far beyond what was contemplated when these tournaments were started.

This thought, which was suggested by Walter Brown, proved an instantly popular one, and through the initiative of Frank Presbrey, then chairman of the Seniors' Tournament Committee of The Apawamis Club, an informal meeting of the more prominent and active Seniors was called and held, at which it was decided to organize such an association, to select a proposed board of governors, to prepare a proposed constitution and bylaws, and to call a general meeting for permanent organization at Delmonico's in Manhattan on January 29, 1917, a dinner for those attending to be a part of the program.

> *In reviewing these past years and going back to the early days of the inception of this tournament, I now fully realize that my labor of love would have been fruitless had I not received the loyal and hearty support of all those who were invited and who were willing to join and make up a field of golfers brave enough to come out in the open and acknowledge that they were fifty-five years of age.*
>
> — Horace L. Hotchkiss

Darwin Kingsley

Darwin Kingsley was born in Vermont in 1857. After working his way through the University of Vermont, he moved to Colorado and became the editor of a local newspaper, and began his career in insurance there as an auditor.

In 1899 he was hired by New York Life as inspector of Agencies for the North Eastern States, a big job for a forty-one-year-old. He was named president of New York Life in 1907, and chairman of the Board in 1931. Kingsley passed away in 1932.

On January 12, 1917, the *New York Times* carried the following report on this seminal meeting:

After twelve years of happy reunions at The Apawamis Club, the senior golfers have reached a point where in their estimation the time has arrived for the formation of a Seniors Golf Association, and with that end in view, it is proposed to organize at a meeting to be held at Delmonico's on Monday evening, January 29, at seven o'clock.

The idea of forming a Seniors Golf Association was first suggested in a casual way by Walter Brown, the Essex Fells and Montclair golfer, while in a conversation with George H. Barnes. The latter thought well of it, and took up the matter with Frank Presbrey with the result that a preliminary meeting was called at which a number of men of prominence gathered.

Matters progressed to such an extent that names were proposed to constitute a board of governors, and a tentative constitution and bylaws were drafted. The names of those proposed to serve on the board are as follows: George H. Barnes, New York; Daniel N. Bates, Worchester, Mass; T.B. Boyd, St. Louis; Walter Brown, Essex Fells, NJ; James F. Fahnestock, Philadelphia; Judge H.A. Gildersleeve, New York; Judge W.O. Henderson, Columbus, Ohio; John Hertsler, Lancaster, Pa.; Horace L. Hotchkiss, Rye, NY; G.H.N. Johnson, Bridgeport, Conn.; Darwin P. Kingsley, New York; Henry W. Lamb, Brookline, Mass; Robert W. Lesley, Philadelphia; Judge Morgan J. O'Brien, New York; Rollo Ogden, New York; Justice Mahlon Pitney, Washington, D.C.; Frank Presbrey, New York; William H. Reed, Boston, Mass.; Winthrop Sargent, Haverford, Pa.; Judge Henry Stoddard, New Haven, Conn.; James A. Tyng, New York; Thomas H. Watkins, New York; Fred J. Wessels, Chicago; and George Wright, Boston, Mass.

The growth of the tournament, both in its importance and in number of participants, has therefore reached a point where it is considered advisable to form a self-sustaining organization of permanent character to assume the general conduct of the annual event in connection with The Apawamis Club, which has so generously for all these years not only given its course for the event, but paid all the expenses, besides providing the variety of trophies offered as prizes.

It is proposed to have an initiation fee of $5 , with annual dues of $2. There will be a charge of five dollars for playing in the annual tournament.

Invitations to join the proposed Seniors' Golf Association were mailed to all who had participated in previous tournaments, and the responses were very gratifying.

On January 29, the *New York Times* reported:

About 200 linksmen who play in the annual seniors' tournament at Apawamis will dine tonight at Delmonico's and form an association to be known as the Seniors' Golf Association. This tournament has grown to such proportions that nothing except a regular organization can carry on the work now. More than 250 golfers, all at least 55 years of age, teed up and played over the Apawamis course in this event last September, making it the largest tournament ever held in this country.

In actuality, about one hundred and forty attended the meeting and dinner at Delmonico's. The meeting was chaired by Frank Presbrey, and the preliminary work of the voluntary board was ratified unanimously. Both the Constitution and the Bylaws were approved. The Seniors' Golf Association became an actuality, with its purpose declared to be:

The *New York Times* headline announcing the formal organization.

The objects of this Association are to encourage friendly competition in golf among senior players and to hold an annual golf tournament at The Apawamis Club, Rye, NY, each autumn.

A twenty-four man Board was established, as was the position of honorary president, to which Horace Hotchkiss was elected. At this meeting, officers for 1917–18 were elected as follows:

President: Darwin P. Kingsley, New York.
First Vice-president: Justice Mahlon Pitney, Washington, DC.
Second Vice-president: Judge Morgan J. O'Brien, New York.
Secretary-Treasurer: Walter Brown, New York.

All those attending the dinner signed the roll as charter members, and before the time limit had been reached within which entrants could become charter members, there were a total of three hundred and eighty signatures. Applications for membership began coming in to the secretary thereafter so rapidly that it was soon seen that the contemplated membership limit of four hundred must be exceeded or a large number of applicants be left upon the waiting list. In consideration of this matter a special meeting of the Association was called and held at the office of the president, on July 9, 1917, at which it was voted to increase the membership limit to five hundred.

Despite this increase, the number of waiting applicants, and new applications immediately thereafter received, brought the membership up to the new limit before the date set for the 1917 tournament, and a new waiting list was started.

The year of formal organization coincided with this country's involvement in World War I. The Seniors were not deterred, as the *New York Times* reports on April 28:

The Seniors' Golf Association has decided to hold the annual seniors' tournament at Apawamis despite the unsettled condition of all sports. It is not expected that any recruiting Sergeants will attempt to interfere with the proceedings.

The annual tournament was held, as the *New York Times* reported, on September 19, 1917:

The 1919 dinner at Delmonico's honoring Horace Hotchkiss. The founder is at the "Putter" table facing the photographer.

In his own words, Horace Hotchkiss recalled the dinner honoring him on the occasion of his seventy-seventh birthday:

The next event of importance in Senior golfing annals was the midseason dinner of the Seniors' Golf Association, held at Delmonico's, New York, on April 24, 1919, which took the form of a testimonial to myself as Founder of the Seniors tournaments and Honorary President of the Association, the occasion being in celebration of my seventy–seventh birthday.

About one hundred and thirty were present, including a delegation from the Canadian Seniors comprising W. R. Baker, V. V. O., President of the Canadian Seniors' Golf Association; Hon. Wallace Nesbitt, K. C.; Lieut.-Col. J. B. Miller of Toronto; Ralph H. Reville, Hon. Secretary of the Canadian Seniors' Golf Association; Frank A. Rolph, President of Canadian Amateur Golf Association; and C. H. Peters, St. John, N. B., who came as invited guests of the United States Seniors. Mr. William H. Conroy, President of The Apawamis Club, also was present as the guest of the Association.

As the proceedings at this dinner were largely laudatory of myself, and as my natural modesty might lead me to say less about them than an impartial chronicler should, I shall take the liberty of quoting from the Secretary's minutes such portions of his records as will give an outline of the principal happenings.

"President Kingsley made an eloquent address, felicitating the guest of honor, which was liberally applauded. At the close of his remarks Mr. Kingsley proposed a toast to Mr. Hotchkiss, which was drunk standing.

In response Mr. Hotchkiss spoke very feelingly at considerable length, in the course of which he reviewed the early history of the Seniors' Tournaments, thanked his assembled friends for their expressions of esteem, and complimented the Canadian Seniors' Golf Association and their delegates present for their enterprise as well as for their affiliation with and friendship for the Seniors' Golf Association of the United States.

Following the speeches of Mr. Kingsley and Mr. Hotchkiss, the President introduced Mr. W. R. Baker, President of the Canadian Seniors' Golf Association.

At the close of his interesting and forceful address, Mr. Baker turned his attention to Mr. Hotchkiss, handed to that surprised gentleman a handsome silver humidor, and told him that he had been deputized by the Canadian Seniors' to present it to him as a token of the esteem which that association had for the founder of Senior golf tournaments, for the interest he had shown in their own organization, and because of their great personal regard for him."

The inscription upon this humidor, which, needless to say, I shall always cherish as one of my choicest treasures, reads as follows; "To Horace L. Hotchkiss, Esq., from the Governors of the Canadian Seniors' Golf Association, on his 77th birthday, as a slight token of their appreciation of his assistance and encouragement in the formation of the Canadian Association, April 24, 1919."

This dinner was also made the occasion for the presentation of an elaborately engrossed testimonial and a superb silver service to Mr. Frank Presbrey in recognition of his distinguished services for three years as chairman of the tournament committee. This testimonial had been under way for more than two years, the delay in presentation being due to the fact that Mr. Presbrey had positively declined to accept any testimonial as long as the war lasted.

A considerable portion of the judiciary, War Department, and business brains of this country came to a full stop yesterday and threaten to remain dormant for the rest of the week. No strike of our leading citizens caused the temporary check in handling the affairs of the nation, but rather the call of nature proved irresistible to some 175 men, all over 55 years of age, who begin their annual four days' tribute to golf in the Seniors' Golf Association tournament at The Apawamis Club.

At the first tournament of the Seniors as an association, there were altogether three hundred and twenty-six entries representing one hundred and six different clubs. One hundred and seventy-nine players participated in the first two days, and one hundred and forty-seven in the second.

At the first annual meeting of the new association, which was held at The Apawamis Club on Wednesday evening, September 19, 1917, the board of officers chosen at the organizational meeting was elected for the full year. Mr. Frank Presbrey, however, who had been a very active and efficient chairman of the Tournament Committee for three years, stated that he would be unable to continue in that position and asked to be relieved. He was succeeded by Frederick J. Wessels, who had already served with Mr. Presbrey on this committee.

At the annual dinner that year, the members drank a silent toast to the late James D. Foot, winner of the first Seniors' Tournament in 1905 and four more thereafter. Former US President William Taft wrote a letter expressing his regrets at being unable to attend the annual meeting.

At this annual meeting, Walter Brown, the secretary-treasurer, urged that the association had now grown to a size where these two offices should be separated in order not to impose excessive work upon one official. Amendments covering this change were offered and referred to a later meeting for action. This meeting was held at the office of President Kingsley on November 13, 1917, and the amendments were adopted. Following this special meeting, Mr. Brown was continued as treasurer, and Mr. W. H. Hale, who had ably assisted the Tournament Committee for several years, was appointed secretary for the association at a salary to be fixed by the Board of Governors annually.

Golf Illustrated carried the following jocular comments on the new association at the time of the 1917 annual meeting:

The Seniors Association has the longest waiting list of any association in the world – 55 years.

The unworded motto of the association: golf before business.

And, on a more serious note, the same magazine reported on the annual dinner in 1917, which was held on the second night of the four-day event:

There happened two events that perhaps meant more to those present than all the eloquence that preceded or followed. The first was the singing of the Battle Hymn of the Republic by Judge Gildersleeve, the 300 veterans standing and joining lustily in the chorus. The second occurred after Justice Pitney of the United States Supreme Court had made a stirring speech in which he declared that he would never have entered the tournament if "younger men had not gone in heart and soul for the liberation of the world." He then called upon all those who had sons or grandsons in the service to stand, and three-quarters of the members rose to their feet.

In 1918 it was proposed that an annual dinner be held in New York City in the winter, and consequently the first "mid-season" dinner was held on April 24, 1919.

At the 1918 annual meeting, Morgan J. O'Brien led the "company" in the singing of "The Golfer's Hymn," and President Darwin Kingsley gave a long, humorous speech explaining how certain Shakespearean characters were acquainted with the game of golf. Clearly, US Seniors' President Kingsley was a man of letters and wit. Apparently, former US President Taft made an appearance at the annual tournament in 1918, as the following passage from Kingsley's speech suggests:

During this year we have dug up a rare specimen, one we call "Big Bill" Taft. He is really "a" if not "the" missing link in golf. For persistence with which we take our eye off the ball even after years of play has made it clear to many of us that there must have been a time when keeping the eye glued to the ball wasn't necessary. Until this specimen was placed in a museum, we were not quite sure. Now we are. He has shown us that looking at the ball is entirely unnecessary, because he hits it when it is entirely below the line of the horizon." (Kingsley used the term "museum" to refer to the Seniors' Tournament.)

At the annual meeting of the association, held at The Apawamis Club on Wednesday evening, September 10, 1919, and at which members of the Canadian Seniors' team were present as guests, there were numerous excellent speeches by Seniors from both sides of the border.

President Kingsley expressed his wish to lay down the burdens of office and retire from the presidency. This wish was respected by the Seniors present and Frank Presbrey was chosen in his stead. The full ticket elected for 1919–1920 was as follows:

President:	Frank Presbrey, New York.
First Vice-president:	William O. Henderson, Columbus, Ohio
Second Vice-president:	Robert W. Lesley, Philadelphia.
Treasurer:	Joseph A. Flynn, New York.
Secretary:	W. H. Hale, New York.

Later at this meeting a committee was appointed to draft a set of resolutions to be presented to Mr. Darwin P. Kingsley, the retiring president.

Because the association was the parent senior golfing organization of this country, because it was national in scope, and because of the necessity of differentiating in title between the United States Seniors and those of Canada, it was decided at a special meeting of the Board of Governors, held at the office of the president on November 12, 1919, to recommend incorporation under the name of the United States Seniors' Golf Association (USSGA). At a special meeting of the association called to ratify this action, which was held at Delmonico's on December 3, 1919, it was unanimously voted to incorporate. The president appointed Judge H. A. Gildersleeve and John W. Herbert as a Committee on Incorporation. Through the efforts of this committee the application for incorporation was put through, and the certificate was issued by the Secretary of State of the State of New York, under date of May 14, 1920.

Another important action taken at the special meeting of December 3rd was the vote to increase the membership limit to six hundred. This was a very popular move, as there was a waiting list approximating one hundred and fifty, some of whom had been awaiting election for nearly two years.

The Competitions

The chief prize winners at the 1917 tournament were W. E. Truesdell of Fox Hills, with a low gross for 36 holes of 172, and T. P. Anderson of Siwanoy, who had the best net 36 holes of 193–44 = 149.

John H. Duffy of Knollwood furnished the principal amusing incident at this tournament. Bunkered at the twelfth hole, and after four frantic strokes in the sand without result, Mr. Duffy, it is said, with a silent prayer for guidance and direction, and his eyes shut to keep out the sand, made one more mighty swipe and was rewarded by having his ball land on the green, roll up to the cup, and drop in.

Champion Canadian golfer George Lyon attended the 1919 annual dinner, and sang "My Wild Irish Rose," which was wildly applauded and encored.

Frank Presbrey

Above: A "notable fourball," including Frank Presbrey, James Tyng, Mahlon Pitney, with Darwin Kingsley driving. *Golf Illustrated,* 1914

Frank Presbrey. *Golf Illustrated,* 1922

Frank Presbrey was born in Buffalo and raised on a farm in upstate New York. He graduated from Princeton in 1879, in the same class as Woodrow Wilson and Supreme Court Justice Mahlon Pitney (also a member of the USSGA). Presbrey began his career in the publishing business, but in 1896 started his own advertising agency, which he headed until retiring in 1930.

Presbrey was regarded by many as the "dean of American advertising." His *The History And Development of Advertising,* first published in 1929, provided a comprehensive chronology of advertising in England and America, and was considered a standard reference work for those interested in the history of advertising.

As Pinehurst's "advertising counselor," Presbrey created a young boy who appeared in the resort's early advertising, and was called "The Golf Lad" or "The Golf Boy." In 1912 sculptress Lucy Richards used the lad as the model for a bronze statuette and sundial that stood on the clubhouse lawn between the two putting greens for many years. The statuette was originally called "The Sundial Boy," but in the 1970 the name "Putter Boy" caught on.

Presbrey was a strong advocate of professional ethics in advertising. In the late 1920s he foresaw the role television would play as an advertising tool. He was in charge of Red Cross advertising in New York during World War I, and was deeply interested in the Boy Scouts of America. In 1921 Presbrey published the "Philosophy of Golf For Young and Old," and in 1915 he helped organize the annual Father and Son Golf Association and related annual tournament.

Frank Presbrey passed away on October 10, 1936, at the age of 81.

Mahlon Pitney was born in New Jersey in 1858, and was a classmate of Woodrow Wilson's at Princeton. He was elected to Congress in 1894, then after serving two terms there, was elected to the New Jersey Senate in 1898, aspiring to the governorship. However, he was appointed to the New Jersey State Supreme Court in 1901, where he served for twelve years before being appointed to the United States Supreme Court by President Taft in 1912. He was a strong supporter of due process jurisprudence. Pitney remained on the Supreme Court until suffering a stroke in 1922, and died in 1924. Pitney was a member of the Chevy Chase Club in the Washington suburbs.

A Philadelphia group including F. L. Bailey, J. F. Fahnestock, E. C. Felton, Robert Lesley, C. F. Quincy, and Winthrop C. Sargent.
The American Golfer, 1916

Morgan J. O'Brien was a justice in the New York Supreme Court (1st District) from 1900 to 1903. He also was a delegate from New York to the Democratic National Convention in 1912, 1920, and 1924. He was a member of the old Oakland Golf Club in Bayside, Long Island, where Walter Travis got his start as a golfer.

Frederick Wessels (1860–1948) was the manager of the Chicago Symphony Orchestra from 1899 until his retirement in 1926.

James F. "Sunny" Fahnestock was president of the Pennsylvania Railroad. Born in Gettysburg in 1859, his family tree traced back to the early German settlers in Pennsylvania on one side, and the Mayflower and the early Colonial governors of New England on the other. Fahnestock moved to Philadelphia shortly after the Civil War Battle of Gettysburg, and eventually worked with various steamship lines before taking a position as assistant treasurer of the railroad in 1908, and worked his way up the corporate ladder. He was a member at Merion.

Fahnestock reportedly carried the following pass:

Pass No. 31.
U.S. Seniors Golf Association
To Sunny J. Fahnestock, Prof of Elocution,
and all Members of the U.S.S.G.A.
Over all Railroads of the United States
(on payment of tariff rates)

Judge William O. Henderson

Robert W. Lesley of Merion played a role similar to that of Horace Hotchkiss, donating a cup and thereby starting the inter-city Lesley Cup Matches, which also are celebrating their centennial in 2005.

Judge William O. Henderson, a member of the Scioto Golf Club in Columbus, Ohio, is remembered as a true sportsman and a close observer of golf etiquette. He was a member of the first Yale football team in 1872, and a member of the first football team in this country ever to play eleven per side. He served on the USSGA Board of Governors, and was vice-president for three years.

The great rivalry, Snare vs. Lyon.

The Start of the
International Team Competitions

AS THE US SENIORS GREW IN POPULARITY AND NUMBERS, regional organizations of senior golfers were formed. In particular, the phenomenon spread to Canada.

The idea of sponsoring matches with other seniors' organizations undoubtedly came early to the founding United States Seniors but at that time comparable organizations able to provide opposition were non-existent. As word of the success in the United States spread, seniors in other countries became enthusiastic, moved to establish associations on the United States model, and in so doing sought the help of the founders of the US Seniors. In responding, their advocacy featured the prospects of international team matches.

Credited with providing initiative north of the border, an editorial in the *Canadian Golfer* for November 1917 spoke admiringly of the United States prototype, "which included among its members Supreme Court judges, leading educators, bankers, doctors, authors, journalists, manufacturers, in fact, prominent men in every branch and phase of activity," and urged a similar organization in the Dominion. Mentioned in support was a letter from Frank Presbrey, chairman of the United States Seniors' Tournament Committee, offering assistance and adding:

If you form an association it would be a particularly nice thing to arrange a match, in Boston, or some convenient place, between a team from your association and one from the association in the United States. A great deal of interest could be aroused in this and it would be a notable affair.

The principal match was between Truesdell and Lyon, champions of the two associations, and was won handily by Lyon, who was 8 holes and 11 strokes better than Truesdell. Lyon shot a fine 76.

After the match the United States representatives were entertained at a luncheon by the Canadian Seniors, at which occasion numerous congratulatory speeches were made and Lord Richard Nevill, representing the governor general, presented His Excellency's cup to George S. Lyon, captain of the winning team. The cup, which is a large and beautiful example of the silversmith's art, bears the following inscription:

Presented by
His Excellency, The Duke Of Devonshire, K. G.
To The Seniors' Golf Associations
Of The United States and Canada,
To Be Played For Annually
As An International Trophy

The 1919 match, the first to be contested on American soil, was played at Apawamis the day after the annual tournament. Teams of fifteen competed this time, once again at 18 holes match play (Nassau scoring), and the US Seniors won handily, 21 to 7. In the lead match, Lyon defeated William Clark, who had won the Seniors' championship the day before. Lyon shot 79 over the rain dampened course.

The third international match between the United States and Canadian Seniors took place on the Royal Ottawa Golf Club's course at Ottawa, Canada, on Friday, September 10, 1920, the week before the annual Seniors' Tournament at Apawamis. The visitors, seventeen strong this time, arrived in Ottawa on Thursday morning and were taken at once to the Chateau Laurier, where they were quartered as guests of the Canadian Seniors' Golf Association. After getting into their golf togs, they were escorted to the Royal Ottawa Golf Club, where, after a special luncheon served on the clubhouse verandah, they spent the afternoon familiarizing themselves with the course over which the match was to be played on the following morning.

In the evening at the Royal Ottawa golf clubhouse the annual dinner of the Canadian Seniors' Golf Association was held, and the United States Seniors' players were made the special guests of honor. The dinner was a most enjoyable occasion and was carried through with great spirit.

The match between the two teams, which took place on the following morning, was under lowering skies with frequent dashes of rain, but it was sharply contested and, while the Americans won for the second time, it was anybody's match until the finish. A motion picture cameraman was kept busy filming the interesting features of the contest, the film being shown at the United States Tournament at Apawamis the following week.

New York Times headline concerning the 1919 Devonshire Match.

OUR OWN SENIORS CARRY OFF MATCH

Even George S. Lyon Is No Terror to U. S. Linksmen and Canadians Lose, 21 to 7.

International Senior Team Match.			
UNITED STATES.		CANADA.	
W. Clark	0	G. S. Lyon	8
W. E. Truesdell	3	G. C. Helmtzman	0
Mgr. M. M. Sheedy	0	J. H. Cauldwell	0
C. G. Waldo	0	C. A. Bogert	1
G. P. Hart	3	G. T. Brown	0
I. R. Prentiss	3	C. S. McDonald	0
Col. J. E. Smith	2	P. S. G. Pepler	0
H. Revell	3	P. D. Ross	0
F. A. Wright	3	Alfred Wright	0
E. J. Hasse	0	Col. M. Hamilton	3
D. P. Kingsley	0	W. G. Ross	0
J. A. Tyng	0	J. A. Machado	0
G. H. Barnes	2	J. L. Weller	0
H. Wendell	0	F. M. Delafosse	0
Frank Presbrey	2	W. R. Smyth	0
Total	21	Total	7

The box score for the 1919 Devonshire Cup Match.

Team Play

The veterans on this side of the border will be represented in a team match with the Canadian Senior Golf Association at the Royal Montreal Golf Club on Wednesday next. At the annual meeting held at the clubhouse Wednesday night, the challenge from the Canadian golfers was read and a motion of acceptance was made. Frank Presbrey was appointed Captain, and he is to round up a team to go to Montreal. The competition will be for a cup presented by the Duke of Devonshire, Governor General of Canada.

— New York Times, 1918

In the leading match of that first Devonshire Cup, George Lyon won the maximum three points from W. E. Truesdell, twice champion of the United States Seniors and frequent winner at Pinehurst and other tournaments in the States. In another match D. P. Kingsley, President of the United States Seniors and of the New York Life Insurance Company, gained the maximum from Hon. Martin Burrell, the Canadian Secretary of State. The score remained even when Mr. Justice Pitney of the United States Supreme Court halved with a Dr. Ruttan of Montreal. Through their successes in the remaining matches, the Canadians won the Cup 23 to 19.

At a luncheon afterward Lord Richard Nevell representing the Governor General, presented the Cup to Captain Lyon, and in so doing, expressed hope that the competition would be the means of creating much good feeling and friendly rivalry between the members of the two Associations. In accepting, Lyon said he was very glad Canada had won the trophy the first time because he knew the calibre of the golfers in the States and was afraid that once they got the cup over there it would never come back.

— New York Times, 1918

George S. Lyon was the bright particular star of the heavy going yesterday. Three score and one years have no terror for this ex-cricketer, and he has been holing long putts since Chick Evans and Francis Ouimet were wrapped in swaddling clothes. Nothing would content him yesterday except breaking 80, and he did it with a fine 79. When it is considered that the recent rains have made the fair greens heavy, this is a creditable score for the low handicap star forty years his junior.

— New York Times, 1919

Waxing Poetic

The *New York Times* never simply "covered" the Seniors' Tournament. They sent out their best reporters who, time after time, waxed poetic over the achievements of golf's "old-timers." Witness the following taken from the 1918 and 1919 coverage:

Although long since removed from the draft age, there will be no lack of vim, vigor, and virility in the army of golfers that will be represented on the links of The Apawamis Club this week. For years, the sires and grandsires, all of whom have passed the fifty-five year mark in life's journey, have shown a contempt for Father Time. (1918)

There was that in their mien that laughed time to scorn, those links warriors who gathered nearly 200 strong to start the second annual tournament of the Senior's Golf Association at The Apawamis Club yesterday. (1918)

What has always distinguished the meeting of the "oldsters" at Apawamis is the unqualified good fellowship that ascends the throne at the outset and reigns supreme until the last putt is sunk and the players are parting with faithful promises of attendance the following year. The cares that weigh heavily on the mighty men of affairs are cast aside for a few days, judicial dignity is ruled out of court, legal motions are superseded by a fair swing and good follow through, and Par takes a better and sweeter meaning for those who rule "The Street." (1919)

Under new regulations for the match, the presidents of the two associations
(Frank Presbrey and W. R. Baker) were to be de facto members of the respective teams
and to lead off, playing on their handicaps (Presbrey won the closely-contested
match). They were to be immediately followed by the team captains and then by the
other contestants in the order of selection. The score of this match, which included
singles play only, was 20 for the United States' team and 15 for the Canadians.

The presentation of the Duke of Devonshire's cup to the winning team took
place after the match on the eighteenth green, and the beautiful trophy was brought
back to Apawamis for a second year.

Apropos of the second winning of the cup, the following incident will prove
interesting. Shortly after the cup was first won by the Canadian Seniors in 1918, the
United States Seniors received from them a large and handsomely framed photograph
of the trophy which was hung in The Apawamis Clubhouse. One Senior looking at it
and espying nearby one of the members of the unsuccessful team, asked the latter
facetiously, "Is this all you got? Why didn't you bring back the cup?" To which the
team member merely replied, "Wait till next year."

Sure enough, the next year in 1919, when President Baker of the Canadian
Seniors displayed the cup itself at the annual dinner of the United States Seniors in
the Apawamis clubhouse, he said that while he had fully expected to take it back with

They Came To Play

Horace L. Hotchkiss, familiarly known as the "father of the seniors," was one of the starters. He is now the Honorary President of the Seniors' Association, the president being Darwin P. Kingsley, years ago a St. Andrew's frequenter, but latterly identified with the Sleepy Hollow Country Club. Kingsley again proved that he was a golfer by making a round in 89, the second best gross of the day.

— New York Times, 1918

Fred Snare receiving the Devonshire Cup from the Canadian captain.
Golf Illustrated, 1928

Fred Snare driving from the first tee at St. Andrews in the 1929 Triangular Matches.

him, he had misgivings that the American Seniors had fallen in love with it and determined to retain it themselves. Whatever the cause, the cup remained at Apawamis after the 1920 match.

In 1923 the USSGA donated a cup, called the United States Seniors' Trophy, to be awarded to the player with the low gross score during the Devonshire Cup Matches. George Lyon won the first US Seniors' Trophy in 1923, then captured it again three years running from 1930 to 1932. The first US Senior to win the cup was Hugh Halsell in 1928.

About ten years after the inception of the Devonshire Cup matches, history repeated itself on the other side of the Atlantic. After a game at Stoke Poges in June 1926, Frederick Snare, captain of the United States Seniors, and Clarence A. Bogert, president of the Canadian Seniors, interested their British hosts, Frederick W. Ashe and Lt. Col. Francis J. Popham, D.S.O. in organizing a seniors' organization in their country. In October Snare sent Ashe a follow-up letter saying:

At a dinner given to the United States and Canadian Seniors competing at The Apawamis Club, I mentioned to them the possibility of the formation of a Senior Golfers' Association in Great Britain and the hope that this happy event might be followed by a match between teams of Americans and British. If you had heard the Canadians enthusiastic response to the thought, I am sure that you would be encouraged to take up seriously the formation of a Seniors' Association as suggested. Picture a three-cornered team match between, say, fifteen Britishers, fifteen Canadians and fifteen Americans, representative men over fifty-five. Seems to me it would be worthwhile.

Reassured, Popham interested others, including Arthur C. "Crumbo" Croome, golf correspondent of the *Morning Post,* who was particularly intrigued by the prospect of soon "having old gentlemen working for their International Caps." The project advanced apace so that in November 1926 at a meeting in London forty enthusiasts formed the Senior Golfers' Society with the Earl of Balfour, K.C., its first president.

Immediately after its organization the new British Senior Golfers' Society moved to add a three-cornered contest. As reported by F. B. Lloyd, its distinguished and long revered secretary and later captain: "Almost the first act of the Committee of our new society was to send an invitation to the United States and Canadian Seniors to send teams to this country in the summer of 1927 to take part in the first Triangular International Tournament." The invitations were promptly accepted and the match was played over the Old Course at Sunningdale on July 6 and 7, 1927, for a trophy presented by the Earl of Derby, the first vice president and later successor to Lord Balfour as the president of the Seniors' Society.

Reporting on the second day's play of the first Triangular Matches, the *New York Times* commented:

The singles of the senior golfers tournament were disastrous for the Americans, who lost ten to the British and won only three. Against Canada the Americans fared better, winning six and losing seven.

The Americans entered the oldest player in the person of General J. E. Smith, aged 77, who has become something of a fixture at Sunningdale.

It is hoped that the three teams will play the next match in the United States. This year England was able to put a strong team in the competition, but the question is being asked, what will happen thirty years hence when Bobby Jones, Jess Sweetser, and other present American stars qualify as veterans?

The fourteen-man US Seniors' team competing at Sunningdale in 1927 included Fred Snare, W. E. Truesdell, C. D. Cooke, Joshua Crane, J. E. Smith, C. F. Strout, Frederick S. Wheeler, F. L. Woodward, Alex Revell, Jerome Peck, Dr. W. S. Adams, R. C. Mitchell, A. B. Jenks, and C. M. Hart. Strout was the most effective of the Americans, winning in both singles and sixsomes play.

In the Triangular competition's early years, the format quickly became teams of twelve competing in one round of three-ball sixsomes and another of three-cornered singles with one point to be awarded for each victory and one-half for each halved match.

Prior to World War II an annual schedule was adhered to with the match being played on each side of the Atlantic in alternate years and Canada and the United States taking turns serving as host on their shores. In the late 1950s, the competition became a biennial played in odd numbered years, and in 1973 the rotation was changed so that each country was host every six years.

The International team matches have brought senior golfers together in head-to-head competition over venerable courses on both sides of the Atlantic. Both on and off the course, the players have enjoyed the usual pleasures of congenial competition and experienced as well the lift which comes from representing one's country. In the process the matches have served well their objective of fostering the cause of international friendship.

One of the great rivalries in the international matches started almost at the very beginning of the team competitions.

Captain of Canada's team was her already legendary athlete, George S. Lyon. Born in 1858 and settled in an insurance business in Toronto, Lyon excelled in any number of sports, baseball, football, rowing, pole vaulting, tennis and other racquet games, curling, and especially cricket in which as a batsman he

George Lyon.
Golf Illustrated, 1930

established the Canadian record of 238 not out. At the age of thirty-eight he took up golf and only two years later won his first of eight Canadian Amateur championships between 1898 and 1914.

In 1904 at St. Louis golf was part of the Olympics and drew a field of eighty-four golfers from Europe and North America. The forty-six-year-old Lyon was among them and eventually won the Gold Medal. In the 36-hole final he defeated the twenty-three-year-old United States champion, H. Chandler Egan, who had eliminated Walter J. Travis in the semi-final. At the dinner following the victory, Lyon gave a demonstration of his exceptional physical prowess by walking the length of the room on his hands. For the next Olympiad, Lyon was the only golfing entrant (the Americans and British he had defeated in 1904 were so upset they boycotted the event), and he declined to accept the medal by default. He thereby became the only Olympic golf champion ever, the game never again being an Olympic sport.

In 1906 Lyon was the runner-up in the United States Amateur, losing to E. M. Byers two-up in the final after meeting and defeating in the semi-final none other than the then twenty-year-old J. Ellis Knowles. After World War I, Lyon at sixty turned to senior golf, and in the remaining twenty years of his life won the Canadian Seniors' championship ten times. He established numerous records in international team matches.

Described as Canada's "grand old man of golf," George Seymour Lyon captained two Canadian teams in matches against the United States in 1919. In the earlier unlimited amateur contest his team ran into an array of amateur talent most formidable indeed: John G. Anderson, W. C. Fownes (captain), Max R. Marston, Francis Ouimet, Robert A. Gardner, Jerome D. Travers, Robert T. Jones, Jr. and Charles Evans, Jr. The Devonshire was played later at Apawamis and as Lyon had predicted the United States took away the Cup 21-7. *The American Golfer* noted, however, that Lyon won from his opponent the full three points with a fine 78, notwithstanding four putts on the eighth and three on three other greens.

George Lyon died on May 11, 1938, at the age of seventy-nine. A trophy was put into play that same year in his memory. Called the George S. Lyon Memorial Trophy, it is awarded to the player with the low net score in the medal round of the tournament.

Frederick Snare, the first United States Senior to achieve preeminence as a senior internationalist, was born in 1862 in Huntingdon, Pennsylvania. He achieved success in the international construction business he founded. A natural athlete, he came to golf in his early thirties at Hot Springs, Virginia, joined the USSGA in 1920 and was its champion in 1922 and 1925. For twenty years he never failed to win some senior event and had the remarkable record of leading his age category sixteen times. He served as president in 1923 and 1924, and was elected honorary president of the USSGA in 1945. On the international front Snare was the great evangelist of the gospel of international senior golf. A most thoughtful recognition came in 1936 when the British tendered Snare a dinner in New York and gave him a cane inscribed "In Happy Remembrance."

Snare was designated team captain in his first year as a member of the Association and was continued in the office over a period of more than twenty years. The 1924 match marked the beginning of a head-to-head rivalry unique in its intensity, excitement, and longevity. As opposing captains, Lyon and Snare played one another, usually in lead matches, at least once a year in virtually every one of the next twelve years. Fortunately Snare had his team victories to look back upon because against Lyon it was uphill all the way. Of the first ten encounters, Lyon won eight and halved two, or to put it the other way, only after eleven years trying did Snare succeed in his determination to beat Lyon. The victory came in the Triangular at Sandwich in 1933, with difficulty. Snare was one up with two to go, but at the seventeenth he was 40 yards from the cup in two while Lyon appeared stone dead with a magnificent second. Snare

got his four, Lyon uncharacteristically missed and with a half at the home hole Snare achieved his ambition. But the taste of victory lasted only about two months for in the Devonshire Cup later that year Lyon won. To complete the story, the two giants were to square off only twice again, Lyon winning in 1935 and Snare in 1936.

In the early 1900s Frederick Snare founded an engineering company that helped build Cuba's infrastructure. The company built bridges, schools, and the National Baseball Stadium in Havana. He was decorated by the Cuban government for his contributions to the economic growth of that country and for his work in developing social and cultural relations between the United States and Cuba. Residents of Havana knew him affectionately as "Father Snare."

Eventually many steamship terminals in Latin America were constructed under his supervision, and his efforts contributed to better understanding between the United States and the Latin American countries.

In the New York area, Snare's company helped build the Whitestone, Triborough, and Goethals Bridges, the Outerbridge Crossing, Rip Van Winkle Bridge, West Side Highway, East River Drive, and Chelsea Pier.

Snare founded the Havana Country Club in 1911, and was its president until his death in 1946. His portrait hung over the mantel in the reception room of the clubhouse until the revolution. Snare served on the USGA Green Section. He also helped organize the British Seniors in 1926.

A heart attack curtailed his physical activities in 1940. In 1945 he was elected honorary president of the US Seniors.

Fred Snare. *Golf Illustrated,* 1931

The novelty event this year will consist of a driving competition, each contestant to be entitled to two drives, which will be his efforts from the first tee. In other words, when the first man swings off on Tuesday morning, a flag will be placed in the ground opposite his ball. That will be the longest drive until someone gets a better ball, then the flag will be advanced to the new spot. On the second day, the same players will have their second chance to better their original distances.

— New York Times, 1918

Interest in the driving competition, new this year, was maintained throughout the day. The best early drive was 198 yards by Alexander Revell of Chicago. Later W.E. Truesdell hit a 218-yard ball and that remained supreme until the far-driving Joseph P. McFadden of Deal hit the rubber core for 219 yards.

— New York Times, 1918

J.F. Morrill, the Wollaston golfer, showed that there was little wrong with his short game by winning the putting competition with a score of 36 for 18 holes.

— New York Times, 1918

Edward Hasse of the Philadelphia Cricket Club only missed duplicating Truesdell's winning score by the narrow margin of a stroke. An approach shot to the home green that stopped within an inch of the cup but failed to drop shows how closely Hasse came to tying for the Seniors' title.

— New York Times, 1918

The 1919 annual tournament brought out the usual large and enthusiastic gathering of seniors, the interest in the occasion being augmented by the fact that the second international match between the United States and Canadian Seniors was to be contested at Apawamis during the Seniors' Tournament week. This match was held on Thursday, September 11.

Left: Monsignor Morgan M. Sheedy, a US Senior who played on the 1919 Devonshire Cup team.

Seniors' Associations Worldwide

As the first senior golf organization, the success of the USSGA has, indirectly at least, stood as a shining example leading to the formation and proliferation of senior golf associations throughout the United States and the rest of the golfing world.

The numerical membership limitations of the US Seniors' Golf Association and the rapidly increasing interest in senior golf resulted in the burgeoning of new senior golf associations. British Senior Guy Burnett, in his *The Story of Senior Golf,* says of the founding of the USSGA ,"Thus was started the movement which has spread amongst all the English speaking races, and beyond."

As for the British Senior Golfers' Society, some forty members were enrolled at the seminal 1926 meeting and by 1927, there were nearly five hundred members, including Field Marshal Haig and Admiral of the Fleet Jellicoe of World War I fame.

Starting in 1935 seniors societies were formed throughout South Africa and Rhodesia. Only a year later Australia followed and finally Kenya in 1950.

In the United States, the success of the USSGA inspired the organization and proliferation of regional senior organizations. The first of these was the Pacific Northwest Senior Golf Association in 1923. Its By-laws give credit to the USSGA for advice and assistance. The New England Seniors followed later in the same year.

Today, early in the twenty-first century, there is hardly a state without its own seniors' organization and there are larger regional associations including the following:

Eastern Seniors' Golf Association
Desert Seniors' Golf Association
Middle Atlantic Seniors' Golf Association
Southern Seniors' Golf Association
Three Score and Ten Club
Western Seniors' Golf Association

In 1924 the USSGA resolved that there would be no formal affiliations with any of the state or regional senior associations.

From 1935 to 1950 an invitation tournament for seniors was conducted by a Florida hotel. The popularity of this tournament led to the formation of the American Seniors' Golf Association in 1951. This Association started with a winter stroke-play competition and a match-play tournament in the spring, both in Florida.

The "Three Guardsman of Senior Golf," W. E. Truesdell, Frank Hoyt, and Hugh Halsell.
Golf Illustrated, 1928

The 1920s
Golf's Golden Era

ON THE HOME FRONT, as American golf enjoyed its "Golden Era" during the 1920s and Bobby Jones became a household name, the Seniors continued to flourish, and the annual tournament continued to grow.

Any history of the Seniors' Tournaments would be incomplete that did not give due credit to several prominent features in the practical management of these events. The success of these tournaments has been largely due to the skillful, experienced and thorough work of its Tournament Committees. The work of these committees was well-nigh perfect, indeed it had to be so, for when there was a field of one hundred pairs of players to be started off between 8.30 A.M. and 3.30 P.M. there could be no delays anywhere. And there were none. For many years, it was the rule rather than the exception at these Seniors' Tournaments that, with a scheduled headway of four minutes between pairs of players, the starters continually kept well ahead of their schedule. This would become a greater challenge in later years.

The securing of a sufficient number of experienced caddies for such large fields of players was another problem that called for much thought, but which was finally solved most satisfactorily.

> *Someone has said that to know how to grow old is the masterwork of wisdom, and one of the most difficult chapters in the art of living. To see the Seniors cavorting about the links at Apawamis makes a profound impression. They seem to have thoroughly learned this lesson. In their play they are twenty again. The frost is upon their brows, but their hearts are still joyfully exuberant.*
>
> *– Golf Illustrated, 1923*

Scoring was a feature of great importance as well as intricacy, but was developed to a remarkable degree of perfection by the well-known Apawamis professional, "Billie" Potts. Twice Potts had to enlarge the Apawamis scoreboard to accommodate the increasing Seniors' lists, and during the early 1920s, it became a mammoth affair some eight feet in height by twelve feet in length, this size being required for the twelve full-size sheets of cardboard needed to post the detailed scores for two days. An entirely new set of cards went up for the second two days, and a subsidiary scoreboard was often necessary for the classification, the summarizing and the list of winners.

In 1920 the *New York Times* reported as follows regarding the scoreboard:

> *Those old-timers having their annual gambol at The Apawamis Club yesterday put in a harder day translating Bill Potts' hieroglyphics on the scoreboard than they did shooting their snappy little 105s, even their 134s. It wasn't Bill's fault, understand, for he did all he could in scurrying around a dozen stationers' stores to find a green crayon to supplement his red and blue ones, but the composite tout ensemble was a treat for sore eyes.*
>
> *Here was a line of blue figures. Fair enough. That was the card for the first eighteen holes played Monday. Then underneath it was a line of red marks for yesterday's second eighteen holes. But no one could begin to decipher the rest without help. Out in one column to the right were totals for the gross aggregate. Then was a column for the handicaps, which ran as high as 60 for the two days. Still another column was the net aggregate, but there were still two more columns for those who weren't already color-blinded. One was the handicap allowance for the kickers handicap, picked at random, and the other for the kickers net total. And then underneath all this was a row of fancy green marks for the selected*

card of the two days. The seniors did a fine thing in providing an adding machine so that the scorers needn't try to add in their heads. But they didn't go far enough. What they really need is a Chinese counting board like the laundry man has and in addition to this some smoked glasses.

Some day the Seniors will know definitely just who won prizes, but at a late hour last night, the half of the field which played Tuesday and yesterday remained in the dark.

According to the metes and bounds of the tourney, one man can win only a single prize. But how about Addison B. Colvin, the upstate publisher from Glens Falls? He had low net Tuesday, and low net for the two days. It looked as if Colvin slipped one over on the tournament committee for, despite a highly respectable gross of 192 for two days, he

Getting Younger

What a spirit, and how true of the senior golfers in general. They have come to the years, most of them, when philosophy is a predominating factor. They realize that, for most of them, ability to play in low figures is forever denied. The best they can hope for is to get around in figures gratifying to them, even if well removed from the par of the course. They are ambitious, but not grasping. They have acquired golfing poise.

Watching some of these men of 70 to 84 years of age step on to the first tee, some of them with a real spring in their step and a lusty zip in their swing, was enough to make a man many years their junior say to himself, or at least think "Would that at the same age I could be in the same physical condition they are today, and be so well fitted to enjoy the declining years as they appear to be." If golf has such a beneficial influence, it is the elixir which Ponce de Leon sought in vain.

Judge William O. Henderson of Columbus, Ohio, who, at the age of seventy-six, found an attack of neuritis too much for him, but wrote a cheerful letter expressing his regrets at having to forego the trip, jokingly remarking that he presumed the tournament would have to be postponed, but in the event of its going on, warned his brother seniors against "excessive pivoting."

— Boston Transcript, 1926

had an aggregate handicap of 46 to give him a winning net of 146. He is a fat man, and when he laughs, it is a signal for all around him to join in. There was a lot of laughing yesterday.

– New York Times, 1920

From 1915 Mr. Potts had the assistance of Mr. W. H. Hale, the secretary of the Seniors, who introduced in 1920 a counting machine for quickly and accurately adding and checking the scores turned in.

The sterling quality of golf displayed by the seniors during their early tournaments was a matter of constant surprise to younger players of the game. Yet this was by no means the chief feature of these tournaments. The fraternal feeling that existed among this body of seniors was most remarkable. Their sportsmanship was of a high order. They played the game as it should be played and they returned each year to Apawamis to renew their old friendships, and to take part in rival competitions that kept their hearts and spirits young.

In 1921 the age classifications "E" through "A" were established; class "A" was created at this time, and the order was reversed from previous usage, placing the oldest of the seniors in the "A" classification.

The future of the United States Seniors' Golf Association looked bright indeed, but its ability to take in all the worthy seniors who aspired to join the ranks presented a continually unsettled problem. The Association had a membership of six hundred in 1922, which was the maximum number to be contemplated because of the impossibility of caring for a greater number of players at the annual tournament.

Regrets From the President

The motto of your organization has inspired me with a special wish that I might be able to accept your invitation (to play) so graciously conferred. Unfortunately, for me, my public duties have been so heavy that I have been compelled to relinquish all hope for such pleasurable indulgence.

I suppose I can't help qualifying as a senior, but I should like to meet up with your members and give them a demonstration that I am not yet venerable, and, like the rest of you, have no intention of ever being aged.

Please convey my thanks and best wishes to the members.

Very sincerely yours,
Warren G. Harding

– New York Times, 1921

And again in 1922, Harding wrote apologizing for his absence:

Please extend to the members my greetings and good wishes. You may add in my behalf, if you care to do so, that I have spent a long and hot summer here in Washington with substantially nothing to do but work, at rather uncertain intervals play a round of golf; and as the season nears its end, I am able to congratulate myself on the fact that the golf has contributed a good deal to my comfort and condition. I am more than ever convinced that the Seniors' Golf Association has precisely the right idea.

After losing the first match in 1919, the US Seniors' team enjoyed success in the Devonshire Cup Matches with victories at Royal Ottawa in 1920, Apawamis in 1921 and Scarboro, Toronto, in 1922.

Charles D. Cooke, a prominent international team player.

Instead of returning to the United States the next year, the Devonshire was played at Royal Montreal so that it could be part of the observance of that club's jubilee year. The match proved one of the closest ever, with all hinging on the result between W. G. Ross of Canada and Martin J. Condon of Tennessee. According to *Golf Illustrated*, "They were all square at the home green and here Ross sank a long putt to win the hole, 9 and match." So the jubilee was celebrated most fittingly by an 18 to 13 victory for Canada and the recapture of the Devonshire Cup. Victory at Apawamis the next year returned the trophy to the United States, where it was to remain many years.

Of the Devonshire Cup matches in 1924, *Golf Illustrated* noted that the Canadians held their own in the top brackets but lost in the lower brackets. The United States victory at St. Andrews, New Brunswick, the next year, was reported most graciously by the *Canadian Golfer:*

Always welcome to Canada and Canadian links are these representative golfers from across the Border, keen of eye and lithe of limb, with a wonderful game in their bags.

Fresh from winning the United States championship, Snare "found once again in Mr. Lyon a foeman with a wee bit keener blade, and had to acknowledge a 3 point defeat."

In the first decade, when the Devonshire Cup Matches alone were played, the United States won eight and Canada two.

We turn to the *New York Times* for some additional details about early Devonshire Cup competitions:

The international match quite overshadowed the doings in the regular event in spite of the fact that a newcomer in the ranks of the old fellows, a mere lad of 56, shot a 79 and looms up as a possible champion. H.H. Redfield of Hartford, Conn., was the player to make this sterling score.

Mr. Cooke added to the lustre of his golfing performances by registering the initial victory over the Canadian captain Lyon. The Arcola man made two points for his team in the

Nassau system of scoring under which the contest was played. This marked the first time the redoubtable Canadian champion has been forced to lower his colors

— New York Times, 1921

George S. Lyon of Toronto, the perennial seniors champion of Canada, and leader of the Dominion's forces in today's lost cause, registered a two point victory over Frederick Snare of New York, the former champion.

— New York Times, 1924

The best golf of the day was played in the 18-hole round for the international individual honors. This annual event, played each year after the international team matches, is open only to those with club handicaps of ten or better.

— New York Times, 1924

Captaining the British in the first Triangular was Edward B. H. Blackwell, a giant Scot who in Bernard Darwin's terms hit the ball "malignantly hard." At St. Andrews in 1892 he drove a gutta percha ball a record 366 yards. His counterparts were, as usual, George S. Lyon and Frederick Snare. It was Blackwell whom Walter Travis defeated in the final match of the historic 1904 British Amateur.

In the foursomes, H. E. Taylor and Sir Alfred Mays-Smith for Britain beat the United States 3 and 1 but lost to Lyon and J. Dix-Fraser for Canada by one hole. After seesawing back and forth, the latter match came to the eighteenth all square and was resolved when Lyon holed a putt of over three yards for a winning 4. By winning his singles match as well, the redoubtable Canadian garnered the maximum 4 points for his side. J. Beaumont Pease, the British champion, and his partner completely overwhelmed their opposition, never permitting either to win a hole. Commenting in the *Morning Post,* "Crumbo" Croome was moved to surmise that Pease must have been in a hurry to get back to Lloyds Bank. Victorious in both foursomes and singles, the British won that Triangular with a total of 38 points to 28 for the United States and 12 for Canada.

More interested in the technicalities, the *Daily Telegraph* observed that all golfing tradition had been defied in three particulars: the playing of three-ball matches, the elimination of stymies though recognized as imperative in the circumstances, and the use of steel shafted clubs which were then barred by the Royal and Ancient Golf Club of St. Andrews. But none of this mattered, it was conceded, because the enjoyment derived by these bankers, financiers, and merchants clearly justified the open defiance of rules and regulations.

The first Triangular on this side of the Atlantic was played at Blind Brook in 1928. Now on home grounds, the United States team, captained by Snare and including such veterans as Jerome A. Peck and Hugh Halsell, newcomer Frederick H. Ecker, and the earliest of the putting cripples, Joshua Crane, scored a decisive victory with 42 points against 19 for Canada and 16 for Great Britain. At a concluding lunch, to commemorate their first visit the British Society presented to the USSGA a goodwill silver trophy which now stands in the display case at Apawamis.

Over the Old Course at St. Andrews in 1929 "under waterlogged conditions," the British won as impressively as had the United States the year before. *Golf Illustrated's* commentator, Bronlow Wilson, opined that "although the United States heads us in the skill of the younger players today, our men last longer and retain their form longer . . . because their swing is more natural," and went on to predict quite logically that "when the present US crack amateurs reach the veteran stage, we shall still find that our seniors of that day are better on average."

A Seniors' Toast

When Anglo-Saxon golfers meet
For golf's great recreation
It matters not what flag they fly
Nor what may be their nation
One annual "link" unites them all
And grips above all others —
Bond most true that binds anew
And brands all golfers brothers
As through the world, unconsciously,
Their wandering steps they wend
To meet good golfers everywhere
Rare spirits of fine blend
One race in fact, in speech, in creed
In spite of outside scoffers
And what is more, both "far and sure"
They stand as brother golfers
So gentlemen, a toast we'll pledge,
To our great recreation
To golfers all who play the game
No matter what their station
May we "hole out" when we "play dead"
And win what Heaven offers
United still, come will or nil
A "well up" brand of golfers.

The above was penned by W. Hastings Webling, a competitor on Canadian teams in international matches. It was published in *Golf Illustrated* in 1924.

The Hotchkiss Memorial at Apawamis.
Golf Illustrated, 1930

The Great Depression

WITH THE 1930s came the most debilitating depression the world had ever known, followed by a world war whose manpower demands and social restrictions seriously impacted club life. The Depression and subsequent war years were especially difficult for golf and country clubs, which were considered luxuries. It's impact on the USSGA seemed minimal, however.

Although the Great Depression was precipitated by the Stock Market Crash of October 1929, it was not until 1931 that it began making serious inroads into American life, reaching its depths in 1932. In fact, 1930 was a fair year. The crisis deepened in 1931 when a number of banks collapsed. From a bank's perspective, the takeover of a financially ailing country club during the Depression years was not considered a prudent investment, and this fact extended the existence of any number of clubs during this period.

The Depression and subsequent war years, however, strangled many clubs financially, and forced a number of clubs, including such prominent ones as Lido and Salisbury on Long Island, to close their doors forever.

H. S. Redfield watching Hugh Halsell swing.
The American Golfer, 1932

Several enhancements to membership in the Association were made in 1933. The first annual Bulletin (predecessor of today's Yearbook, the name change taking place in 1966) was published that year. A scarlet jacket was authorized as the official coat of the Association, to be worn at the annual dinner and the dinners associated with the team matches; it was abandoned a few years later. The By-laws were amended to establish the Member Emeritus class, with sixteen eligible immediately. Emeritus status was granted any member over eighty years of age with at least ten years of membership, and with it came full privileges and no dues. And in 1940 all members were sent the first official tie, which was quite similar to the Canadian tie.

Commenting on the annual meeting and dinner at Apawamis in 1939, the Bulletin commented that "a colorful picture resulted as the red coats of the Canadian Seniors' team and officers were scattered throughout the more somber-outfitted black tuxedos worn by our Seniors."

The four-day format for the championship at Apawamis, established in 1915, proved troublesome. The weather often changed during the four days, giving an unfair advantage to those who played in the good weather. Also, many who played on Tuesday and Wednesday were not available for the annual banquet on Thursday night; the annual meeting and dinner were moved to Wednesday evening in 1933.

Entertainment at the 1935 annual dinner was provided by the Radio Corporation of the United States, and included an address by Governor Al Smith, singing by a Metropolitan Opera star, and impersonations of various radio announcers.

Triggered by the hurricane in September 1938, the tournament was transferred to four days in late June of 1939, even though the Association's charter has never been amended to reflect this change.

A fixture at every international match has been a team dinner memorable for its ambiance, toasts, and, on occasion, ad-libbing. Speaking for the hosts in 1934 at Royal Montreal, the Honourable Martin Burrell, a farmer who rose to become Canada's minister of agriculture and later secretary of state, noted the ominous clouds of war over Europe and concluded that "we should agree that the greatest guarantee of peace and security is that good relationship which now exists between the British Commonwealth and the United States." Next Major General James G. Harbord, president of the USSGA, after some well chosen humor and compliments to the Canadians on weathering the depression with such quiet efficiency, concluded with the hope that the yearly meeting of English, Canadian, and United States golfers would continue far into the future "until even England's Mr. Shaw and America's Mr. Mencken can find no fault with their countries and their countrymen."

Inspired, General Sir Harold Fawcus for the British looked to the Triangulars, where there were no axes to grind, to do more to cement relationships than the League of Nations. In keeping with established custom, George Lyon followed his programmed remarks with his always fresh song "My Wild Irish Rose." Not to be outdone, Findlay Douglas countered with "Loch Lomond."

In 1934 an individual medal competition was added to the Triangular Matches, emulating the United States Seniors' Trophy competition in the Devonshire Cup Matches. The event's purpose was to commemorate the inauguration of the matches in 1927, and those responsible therefor; namely, Great Britain's Frederick S. Ashe, Arthur C. M. Croome, and Lt. Colonel F. J. Popham; Canada's William G. Ross and Clarence A Bogert; and the United States' Frederick Snare. The Founders' Cup was presented in 1934 by Popham, Bogert, and Snare, and put into play that year. The first winner was J. W. B. Pease of Great Britain, whose score of 74 led the field by eight strokes.

Jerome Peck, S. C. Mabon (USSGA secretary), and Fred Snare.
The American Golfer, 1935

Findlay Douglas

Writing in 1957 in the USGA Journal, John P. English, then assistant executive secretary of the USGA, had the following to say about Findlay Douglas:

It is fairly common knowledge that Findlay Douglas, who soon will be 83, is the oldest living Amateur Champion, having won in 1898. In the five years from1897 through 1901, he was the Champion once, runner-up twice, and semi-finalist twice. He also won the Metropolitan Amateur in 1901 and 1903. In his only appearance in the Open Championship, in 1903, he tied for eighth and won the amateur gold medal.

Even now he looks the part of a golfer — tall, erect, with the twinkle in his eye which bespeaks his enjoyment of the sociability of golf and with the burr in his speech which reveals his Scottish birth. He continues to play regularly at the Blind Brook Club in Port Chester, N.Y., with hickory-shafted clubs.

One of the two Amateur Champions who have risen to the presidency of the United States Golf Association (the late William C. Fownes, Jr. was the other), he came up through the Metropolitan Golf Association to that office in 1929 and 1930 in time to present to that other great amateur golfer, Robert T. Jones, Jr., the Open and Amateur trophies which formed a part of the immortal "Grand Slam" of 1930.

When he passed into the ranks of the seniors, he pursued the Championship of the United States Seniors' Golf Association until he won it with a record score of 74-74=148 in 1932. The record endured for eleven years.

As a senior, also, Findlay Douglas started again up the administrative ladder and became president of the USSGA from 1937 to 1941, as long a tenure as any president has had.

Born in St. Andrews, Scotland, on November 17, 1874, Findlay Douglas was, of course, a player first. When he went on to St. Andrews University, which he attended from 1892 to 1896, he was a member of the University golf team, and its captain in 1896.

Having established himself as a golfer of promise in the homeland of the game, he decided upon graduation to visit his oldest brother, who had emigrated to the United States. On March 20, 1897, he landed in New York, a set of clubs grasped hopefully under one arm.

Despite his quick success in golf, Findlay Douglas was anything but a career golfer. The only time he could give to golf in his early years here was on week-ends and during his two-week vacations, which he saved for championships.

After playing his first round of golf in this country at Van Cortlandt Park in 1897, Douglas joined the Fairfield County Golf Club (now the Greenwich Country Club), the Nassau Country Club on Long Island, and The Apawamis Club. He later was among the founders of the National Golf Links of America and the Blind Brook Club. Incidentally, National never held a championship tournament until 1934, when Douglas was sixty years of age. Nonetheless, he won it with an 81 in high wind.

Writing of him in 1931, Bernard Darwin, the dean of British golf commentators, observed that:

> *"Mr. Douglas, for all he has lived so long in America, is still a Scottish golfer through and through. No steel shafts for him; no imperceptible waggle and gentle swing, but the exuberant flourish and slashing dashing swipe, as the old books used to call it, of his St. Andrews boyhood."*

Findlay Douglas was a mainstay of the international matches for years, as he had been in the Lesley Cup Matches decades earlier.

The hurricane of 1938 did not completely halt play, According to the 1938 Yearbook:

Although they were the only competitors to finish, Findlay S. Douglas and Richard S. Francis were not the only contestants to tee off. Another pair of hardy club swingers, Frederick Snare, Captain of the Team and Chairman of the Executive Committee, and Secretary S. Clifton Mabon, set out a few minutes earlier.

Thoroughly drenched after playing three holes, they allowed the Douglas-Francis twosome to pass through with pleasure and hastily made their way back to the clubhouse.

Douglas and Francis had the good fortune to finish before high winds swept over the course, blowing down trees. They and their caddies embarked on wading expeditions frequently. Traps were miniature swimming pools, and more than half the fairway leading to the first green was transformed into a lake.

After taking a 7 on the initial hole, Douglas never fared as badly on any subsequent one. He was out in 45 and duplicated that figure on the inward route. The high spot of the round was a birdie 4 on the 585-yard ninth, the biggest hole of the layout, where he sank a long putt after reaching the green in 3. Douglas equaled par on five holes, while Francis accomplished the feat on four. The latter, who, like his playing partner, had only a single 7, toured the outgoing nine in 50, then returned in 43.

The hurricane of 1938:
(above) swinging through a puddle and
(below) the lake at the twelfth hole.

Some day, somebody with time and snoopiness to spare is going to check the roster of the USSGA against WHO'S WHO IN AMERICA. *The result, we are sure, will reveal that the Seniors present a larger array of distinguished men than can be boasted by any other sport.*

Scarcely a page of the Seniors' yearbook fails to carry several names of men noted in American business, science, and the arts. It's a great old guard that golf can assemble.

— New York Times

Jerome Alvord Peck of Port Chester, New York, was a veteran of the earliest matches. Peck was born in Greenwich, Connecticut, and earned his degree from NYU Law School. "Uncle Jerry" to his associates, Peck was a leader of the Bar in Westchester County, and a "firm friend and reliable mentor" to hundreds of struggling young lawyers. He also was a devoted member of Apawamis and the Seniors. He died of a heart attack at the age of seventy-five in November 1938 while putting on the fourteenth green. In a eulogy, a State Supreme Court justice said: "He was a perfect type of sportsman. I will wager that one of his last conscious acts was to concede a putt to his opponent." He was chairman of the Tournament Committee for fourteen years (1923–1936), and vice president from 1936 to 1937.

The 1930 winner George Gregg putting.
Golf Illustrated, 1930

**Left:
Jerome Peck**

Rodman E. Griscom was a pioneer in Philadelphia golf, having brought over from Great Britain some of the first clubs used in the region. Griscom was a member of a Philadelphia shipping and banking family. His daughter Frances was an early winner of the US Women's Amateur, and later donated the Griscom Cup for inter-city matches between teams of women. Griscom served as vice-president and on the Executive Committee of the USGA.

Team Play

In 1931 at Swinley Forest, London's equivalent to Blind Brook near Ascot, the British again defeated the United States with the Canadians unavoidably absent. In the lead foursome R. H. de Montmorency partnered by Major W. G. M. Sarel, taking the place of J. Beaumont Pease, the Lloyds Bank chairman "who was detained in London by reason of the German financial crises," would have lost to Snare and Crane but for the latter's putting eccentricities and difficulties. According to the press:

As a putter, Crane has always been a marked individualist. For many years he used an implement so tiny that the player had almost to go on his hands and knees in order to get at the ball. The toothpick putter has now been replaced by one with a shaft of ordinary length but with a blade nearly as long as a carving knife. At impact the sound is not dissimilar to that of the striking of a dinner-gong. The new love did not behave quite so well as the old, but any errors which Crane made in the putting were more than balanced in his short game, more particularly the pitch-and-run shot, of which he is a masterly performer.

Specifically, Crane's missing a putt of no more than a yard at the fifteenth and the pair taking 3 putts from seven feet at the sixteenth caused an apparently safe lead to be lost and the match halved.

In a remarkable match in the singles that year, the Rev. H. A. Tapsfield won the first 6 holes and was 7 up at the eighth. According to the press account:

This was great, and it looked as if Tapsfield would polish off his victim with merciful dispatch. But in some mysterious and inexplicable way, Tapsfield collapsed like a house of cards. His own words were that "I cracked completely," the main cause of which was a breakdown in driving. In attempting to correct a slice Tapsfield went to the other extreme, landed his drive at the last hole in a private garden.

Meanwhile, the holes had slipped away until Tapsfield's credit account had not only vanished, but had been turned into a debit. Coming home in 37, the American, who at one time had practically given up the ghost, won an amazing match on the last green. Golf is like life: you never know what is waiting for you round the corner.

Swinley Forest appears to have been the first Triangular viewed and written about by Bernard Darwin, who characterized the event as a "carnival of age." In "Seniors at Play," his article in *The American Golfer*, he said it was "the jolliest and most cheerful international match at any game I have ever seen," and "the best and friendliest of days, and to be a member of such good company is something to look forward to." Which is precisely what he then proceeded to do, noting that "the seventh of September, if I live so long, will be my fifty-fifth birthday, and it will be at least some consolation for being so old, that I shall be qualified to belong to the Senior Golfers' Society. Perhaps," he went on, "I may even play once more in an international match between the Seniors of Great Britain and of the United States."

Those wishes came true in the 1933 Triangular at Royal St. George's in Sandwich. Bernard Darwin not only played but contributed points to an easy recapture of the Derby Cup which had been left at Apawamis the year before. Afterward in "Seniors at Work" in *The Field,* Darwin was moved to consider the home course advantage:

Joshua Crane

The only thing to be said against this match, which takes place every year on one side or other of the Atlantic, is that in the nature of things the home team has too good a chance of winning. It is not humanly possible for the visitors to be at anything like their full strength: business and wives and families, and rates and taxes and other inevitable things of life will always prevent several of the strongest players from making the journey. On this last occasion at Sandwich the British side had no fewer than seven players who had, in the pride of their youth, played in real internationals for either England or Scotland: and, if necessary, it might have had more. Such a team, in its own country, was almost sure to win, and it did win decisively; but when our guests of this year become our hosts, the position will doubtless be reversed.

In 1934 both the Devonshire Cup and the Triangular Matches were played during the same visit to Montreal, and each ended in a tie. In the Triangular it was Great Britain and the United States 22 to 22. In the Devonshire it was 22½ to 22½.

Making his first appearance in 1934 was Robert M. Gray, another great Canadian player from the Rosedale Club in Toronto. While destined to make history by winning four of his first five Canadian Seniors' Championships, Gray's team debut failed to live up to the advance billing. By 1938 the blot had been erased so completely, however, as to move *Bridle & Golfer* to acclaim Gray as "worthy of shouldering Mr. Lyon's mantle and carrying on for the Canadian Seniors," and to predict "that in all probability he will continue his record of victories and eventually tie or surpass Mr. Lyon's great record." As team member and captain for a time, Gray carried on with distinction through fifteen campaigns.

Prestwick entertained the 1935 Triangular, and there the British continued their home course winning ways notwithstanding strong opposition. The Canadian side combined the talents of George Lyon, Bobby Gray, and I. Rankin among others; and the United States had such veterans as Fred Snare, Findlay Douglas, Raleigh W. Lee and Morton Fearey, the Wall Street lawyer from Garden City.

Again in action, Bernard Darwin furnished the British side two points in the sixsomes and one in the singles. Afterward he published some impressions in *Country Life:*

At Turnberry I plunged into a mass of old gentlemen — in a golfing sense only, of course — some of them old friends and some new ones. The tripartite international match between the Seniors of the United States, Canada and Britain was this year played at Prestwick at the rate of one round a day, the foursomes on Monday and the singles on Tuesday. We are too old to dare more than one round a day, but, apart from the fear of our falling down dead, the provision is perhaps a wise one, because a sixsome, if

The 1931 US team.
Golf Illustrated, 1931

that be the right term, does take a very long time, and even an ordinary three-ball match, played with a friendly blood-thirstiness, does not go quickly. Britain began by making a grand slam in the foursomes, and after that we could dine with minds tolerably at ease. In fact, we won, as the Americans would say, "handily," and so did the United States against gallant Canada.

Prestwick was in lovely order. It was rapidly getting very fast in the wind and sun, and, though this made the senile drives run farther, I thought it also made the golf exceedingly difficult, for the ball seemed always to be trickling into a bunker at its last gasp. The opinion of all the visitors was that the course was "well trapped," and it certainly is. I never realized before that there were so many bunkers there. I think everybody enjoyed himself, and, though everybody wants to win, victory is not the point of the match. The point is friendliness, and that is attained by all. I fancy we shall generally win this match

at home until there comes a generation of American Seniors who have begun the game as boys, and then it will be another story. I suppose the great Bobby himself will play in it some day, but it is a painful thought that I shall be hovering on eighty by that time and my watching powers, if any, will be strictly limited.

While not opposed in the Triangular, Lyon and Snare met in the Devonshire later that year, where the "grand old man" of Canadian golf was acting captain due to the illness of his successor. At age seventy-seven he extracted two points from the seventy-two-year-old Snare and averted what otherwise would have been a complete shutout for his team.

At the National Golf Links in September of 1936, the Triangular and the Devonshire were combined. Due to an accident that summer, George Lyon first decided not to appear but at the last moment was persuaded to join up. As the odd man he did not play in the Triangular, which the United States won by the relatively close margin of 24½ to 20½ for the British and 9 for the Canadians. In the Devonshire, however, Lyon and Snare had their last go and this time Snare captured all three points.

On home grounds again in 1937 at Royal Lytham—St. Anne's the British scored another decisive victory in the Triangular. Afterward a "Coronation Dinner" was held at Dorchester House in London. A British editor who was there later commented in his publication:

We have seldom attended a happier evening or one where the worthwhile spirit of golf was so wholly captured. Our views about international golf contests are well known. We would be prepared to alter them if the spirit which the Seniors play their international matches could be transferred to all such encounters. The game is the thing and the Seniors always remember this.

The Household Brigade

After the 1931, 1933, 1935, and 1937 Triangulars, the United States played challenge matches against golf teams of the Household Brigade, an association of present and former officers of military units closely connected with the Throne. The United States won in 1931 and 1935; in each of the other two years both the singles and the foursomes were halved. As a member of the Brigade, H. R. H. The Prince of Wales participated in the foursomes in 1933, losing to Fred Snare and W. H. Conroy.

At Toronto in September 1938 both the Triangular and the Devonshire were won by the United States. Matters were fairly close in the sixsomes but not so in the singles, for according to the local press:

The Americans were "hot" today — but they took their triumph and honors in a modest manner as they always do.

On hand to play in the singles, Captain Snare defeated his opponents, but the occasion was saddened for all and most of all for him by the absence of George Lyon, who had passed away the preceding winter. In 1938 a presentation was made to the Canadian Seniors of a silver trophy to be known as the George S. Lyon Memorial Cup, to be competed for annually.

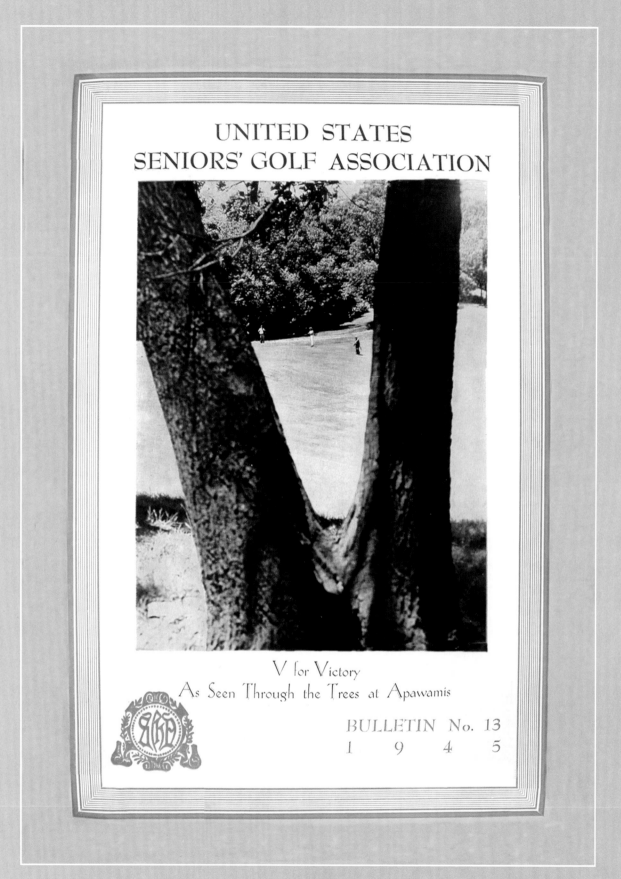

The Victory Tree at Apawamis.

War Years

AFTER A BRIEF RESPITE IN THE LATE 1930S, the world plunged into an even deeper abyss – World War II. Club life went on, albeit on a subdued scale. Gas and tire rationing took its toll, limiting travel to and from the clubs. Golf continued on a lesser scale, and the preservation of golf balls became a concern. The manufacture of golf balls was prohibited during the war and those available were rationed. Old balls were reconditioned.

In 1941, before the United States entered the War, $2,500 was contributed by the USSGA to the British Seniors to provide a mobile canteen. The response from the British was appreciative and enthusiastic.

In spite of the Depression and war years the number of entrants in the annual championships increased from about three hundred to four hundred, more or less, although the number who actually played at Apawamis dropped from about 310 in 1939 and 1940, to 240–250 during the war years. Because the membership of the US Seniors was nationwide (thirty-five states were represented in the membership in 1944) and entries were thus from all parts of the United States, the annual championship maintained its status as the most important tournament limited to senior golfers in the country. The winner was widely accepted by the press as the senior champion of the United States.

> *They're rationing our gasoline.*
> *They're rationing our tires.*
> *They're rationing most everything*
> *humanity requires.*
> *Our incomes too they're cutting off*
> *in a manner that appalls*
> *And now, begad! I understand*
> *They're cutting off our balls.*
>
> – 1942 Bulletin

Wartime transportation from Rye railroad station to Apawamis.

Team Play

At Blind Brook in 1939, Canadian Captain George Robinson defeated Fred Snare in his final appearance as captain and player. Before another match could be played Snare died in 1946 at his winter home on the grounds of the Havana Country Club which he had founded and which he had served as president until his death.

The annual championships were continued through the war years. In both 1942 and 1943, however, there was concern that a sufficient number of seniors would attend to warrant the use of four days, rather than just two. And so it was decided that early in the season each member be sent a postcard asking whether he planned to attend. Enough did attend each year to maintain the four-day status of the tournament.

In April of 1942 it was decided to move the annual tournament from the third to the second week in June, and to donate entry fees to some war relief fund chosen by the USSGA president and treasurer. The Red Cross was the choice in 1942, but in the remaining years (1943–1945) the fees were divided between the Red Cross and the National War Fund. In fact, in each of 1943, 1944, and 1945, a check for $1,500 was donated to the National War Fund. Many members contributed even though they did not play. Instead of trophies, the winners were awarded prize certificates by the Red Cross.

In 1944 the Tournament Committee decided to put into play a special rule recognizing wartime conditions. That rule allowed the players to lift any ball on a fairway or green, then replace it as near as possible to its original position, as long as the original stance was maintained. The intent of this special rule was the preservation of golf balls.

Henry Sutphen and his "Tak-It-Easy"
in 1943.

Many of the regular Apawamis caddies served during the war, and consequently most of the caddies during the war years were schoolchildren from Rye. Since school was still in session, special permits had to be obtained, and school authorities cooperated. Over two hundred caddies were on call to take care of the Seniors' requirements. In 1943, however, the tournament coincided with the Regents' exams, and the USSGA had to enlist the services of firemen, policemen, truck drivers, and war workers on night shift.

The International matches did not fare as well. The plan was to play the 1939 Triangular in the summer at Hoylake, but in May a cable from Sir John Simon, president of the British Seniors, advised against sending teams. And so, the Triangular was suspended for the duration of the war.

Of the twelve prewar Triangulars, all six played in the United Kingdom were won by the British; five of the six on this side of the Atlantic by the United States; and the sixth tied. Evidencing some frustration, the Bulletin opined that "until more of our strong players can find it convenient to cross the water, it will be difficult for the United States team to make a better showing or at least to the extent of winning against the British as they have so many golfers available and of high calibre."

The United States won the Devonshire Cup in 1939. At the team dinner Findlay Douglas, again in rare form, told a number of Scottish stories. The Canadians responded in kind and added a rendition of "Alouette." The mayor of Rye, Livingston Platt, later a USSGA president, extended the keys of the town to the Canadians and closed with a recitation of "Turn On Those Harbor Lights."

From 1918 through 1939, the Devonshire Cup was played annually without interruption. Before another year could roll around, Canada was in the thick of World War II and the Devonshire joined the Triangular in suspension.

A relatively treeless Eleanor's Teeth.

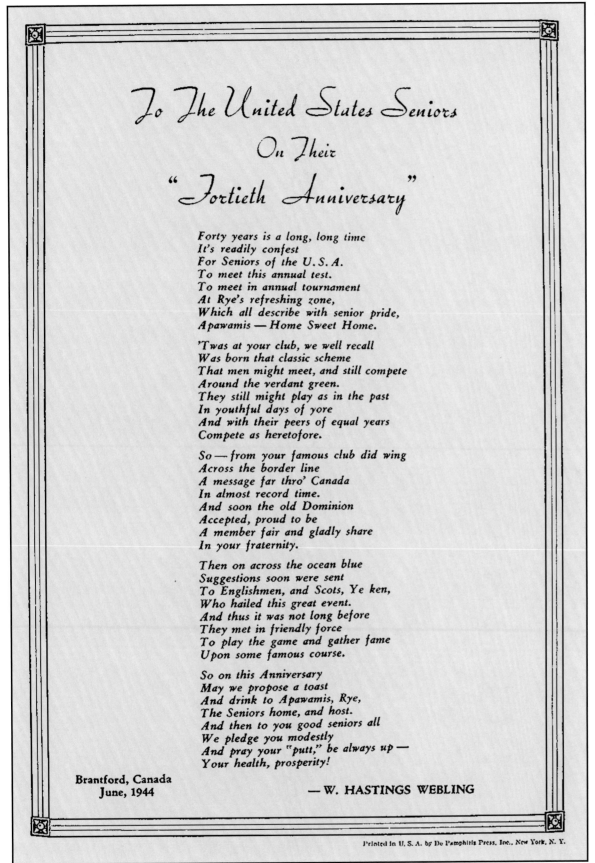

To The United States Seniors
On Their
"Fortieth Anniversary"

Forty years is a long, long time
It's readily confest
For Seniors of the U. S. A.
To meet this annual test.
To meet in annual tournament
At Rye's refreshing zone,
Which all describe with senior pride,
Apawamis — Home Sweet Home.

'Twas at your club, we well recall
Was born that classic scheme
That men might meet, and still compete
Around the verdant green.
They still might play as in the past
In youthful days of yore
And with their peers of equal years
Compete as heretofore.

So — from your famous club did wing
Across the border line
A message far thro' Canada
In almost record time.
And soon the old Dominion
Accepted, proud to be
A member fair and gladly share
In your fraternity.

Then on across the ocean blue
Suggestions soon were sent
To Englishmen, and Scots, Ye ken,
Who hailed this great event.
And thus it was not long before
They met in friendly force
To play the game and gather fame
Upon some famous course.

So on this Anniversary
May we propose a toast
And drink to Apawamis, Rye,
The Seniors home, and host.
And then to you good seniors all
We pledge you modestly
And pray your "putt," be always up —
Your health, prosperity!

Brantford, Canada
June, 1944

— W. HASTINGS WEBLING

Printed in U. S. A. by De Pamphilis Press, Inc., New York, N. Y.

A poem sent to the US Seniors from a Canadian colleague on the occasion of the USSGA's fortieth anniversary.

They Came To Play

John G. Jackson

John G. Jackson, USSGA president from 1941 to 1945, was born in Middletown, Connecticut, in 1880, and played golf for the first time there in 1894. He graduated from Columbia, playing on the golf team in his senior year, then for two more years while at Columbia Law School. He was general counsel to the USGA from 1929 to 1937, and served as USGA president in 1936–1937. He also succeeded Fred Snare as USSGA team captain.

John K. Wadley took up golf at age thirty-nine, left-handed in his first year, right-handed thereafter. He served as president of the Texas and Arkansas Golf Associations in the same year, and also was a director of the Western Golf Association.

After graduation from Yale, Julian Wheeler Curtiss took a job with A. G. Spalding and Brothers, and later became the firm's president. He is believed to have designed one of the first basketballs with Dr. James Naismith. Curtiss loved to tell the story of how he bought $1,500 worth of golf equipment in London on Spalding's account, only to be told there was no market for it in the United States. Curtiss sold some of the equipment to his neighbors, and that led to the founding of the Fairfield County Golf Club (known today as the Greenwich Country Club). A member of the Yale crew team, Curtiss later in life enjoyed participating as a regatta referee.

Major General James G. Harbord, USSGA president from 1933 to 1937, enlisted as a private in 1889 and rose through the ranks. He was a major during the Spanish-American war, fought in Verdun and Belleau Wood during World War I, helping stop the German advance on Paris. He was appointed major general in charge of the Second Division in the Soissons Offensive. Later deputy chief of staff, he retired in 1922, and three days later became president of RCA.

Major General Robert C. Davis, a West Point graduate in 1898, was cited for gallantry during the Spanish American War and the war in the Philippines. As an adjutant general during World War I, he organized and directed the greatly expanded war activities of the Red Cross.

Admiral William Harrison Standley, USSGA president 1945–1947, was born in California in 1872, and graduated from the Naval Academy in 1895. He served in the Asiatic fleet during the Philippine insurrection. In 1933 he was appointed commander, Battle Force, US Fleet, chief of Naval Operations at the rank of admiral. He later served as acting secretary of the Navy, was a member of the Roberts Commission investigating the facts relating to the attack on Pearl Harbor, and ultimately became US ambassador to Russia.

George Nicol

George A. Nicol was the USSGA secretary for ten years (1938–1947). His life was one of service to golf. He was the president and treasurer of the Westchester County Golf Association, president and secretary of the Metropolitan Golf Association, founding member of the Westchester Seniors, and four-term president of Wykagyl Country Club. As a Lesley Cup player, Nicol is remembered for his vision in bringing the Canadian team into the competition.

Sherrill Sherman of the Yahnundasis Club in Utica, New York, was a son of former US Vice-president James Sherman (1909–1912 under Taft). He was a semi-finalist in the US Amateur in 1915.

Left: A military trio: Colonel J. C. Montgomery, Brig. General Robert C. Davis, and Major General James G. Harbord.

United States Seniors' Golf Association

The Competitions

Italy declares War. Duce's Troops Invade At Riviera.

Italy At War, Ready To Attack; Stab In Back,
Says Roosevelt; Government Has Left Paris.

Nazis take Paris and sweep south.

— New York Times, June 11–14, 1940
during annual tournament

The 1941 annual tournament concluded on Friday the 13th, with the newspapers carrying the fore-boding news that a German U2 boat had intentionally sunk an American ship. Heavy rains made matters worse, and only 104 brave souls teed off. William Ryan of Detroit, whose 74 on Thursday was the lowest score of the week, soared to a 91 in the rain. Charles H. Jennings of Garden City, attempting to become the first to make it three championships in a row, shot 85 following a first-round 77. The winner was Alvah H. Pierce of Boston, who carded 157 playing on the first two days of the week.

In 1942 Ellis Knowles first surfaced with a new record of 143 for 36 holes and the first sub-par round in the history of the Association. Knowles scored a two-stroke victory over George V. Rotan of Houston, who played in the fog and rain on the second two days.

And then in 1943 Knowles established a new 18-hole record of 33-34=67 while again winning the championship. His round included five birdies and thirteen pars, and he lipped out three additional birdies. Heavy rains marred the second day, and Knowles soared to 80, but his 147 nonetheless spread-eagled the field.

In 1944 Knowles shot a first round 71 that he called "one of the toughest rounds he had played in modern times, carved out by might and main, and some superb putting." Knowles noted that as a busy office man, he could only indulge in weekend golf. He had no regrets about the passing of golf years, declaring that he was several strokes better now than as Intercollegiate champion. Knowles 71-74 was best by four strokes.

Knowles started with 71 again in 1945, then faded to 78 in the winds of an approaching tropical storm, still good enough to win his fourth consecutive by two strokes over Sam Graham of Greenwich.

Charles Jennings

The 1942 Ellis Knowles scorecard.

United States Seniors' Golf Association

	Yards	Par	1	2	3
1 The Meadow	377	4		4	
2 Fairview	350	4		4	
3 The Dipper	315	4		4	
4 The Knoll	325	4		4	
5 The Dell	150	3		3	
6 Sunnyside	323	4		4	
7 The Gorge	405	4		4	
8 Woodside	335	4		3	
9 Broadway	585	5		6	
Total Out	3165	36		36	

Players

2 *Ellis Knowles.*

Date, June **9th** 1942

	Yards	Par	1	2	3
10 Lands End	502	5		4	
11 The Bridge	340	4		4	
12 Bunker Hill	203	3		4	
13 The Loch	321	4		4	
14 Waterloo	435	4		4	
15 Mount Hope	415	4		4	
16 Consolation	179	3		3	
17 Sl'py Hollow	505	5		4	
18 Home	295	4		4	
Total In	3195	36		35	
Total Out	3165	36		36	
18 Holes	6360	72		71	
Handicap					
Net Scores					

THIS CARD MEASURES SIX INCHES STRAIGHT ACROSS

United States Seniors' Golf Association

	Yards	Par	1	2	3
1 The Meadow	377	4		4	
2 Fairview	350	4		4	
3 The Dipper	315	4		4	
4 The Knoll	325	4		4	
5 The Dell	150	3		3	
6 Sunnyside	323	4		5	
7 The Gorge	405	4		4	
8 Woodside	335	4		4	
9 Broadway	585	5		5	
Total Out	3165	36		37	

Players

2 *Ellis Knowles.*

Date, June **10th** 1942

	Yards	Par	1	2	3
10 Lands End	502	5		5	
11 The Bridge	340	4		4	
12 Bunker Hill	203	3		3	
13 The Loch	321	4		4	
14 Waterloo	435	4		4	
15 Mount Hope	415	4		4	
16 Consolation	179	3		3	
17 Sl'py Hollow	505	5		5	
18 Home	295	4		3	
Total In	3195	36		35	
Total Out	3165	36		37	
18 Holes	6360	72		72	
Handicap					
Net Scores					

THIS CARD MEASURES SIX INCHES STRAIGHT ACROSS

THE CARDS THAT WON THE 1942 UNITED STATES SENIORS' CHAMPIONSHIP

The largest annual dinner to date, Apawamis, 1960.

The Postwar Era: 1946–1961

WITH WORLD WAR II OVER and living conditions getting back to normal on the world stage, the United States Seniors entered a period of change, especially regarding host clubs for the annual tournament, the nature of the membership, and the formats of the international matches. So, too, did the United States, which entered the baby-boom era, a time that saw many families move to the suburbs. Country club life, which had been "on hold" for more than a decade, would soon flourish.

For almost a decade, there had been complaints about the climb up to the second green at Apawamis, especially for cardiac sufferers. Ellis Knowles, then president of Apawamis, arranged for a subscription to add an alternative green, swinging it to the right to make for an "elbow" hole. The second shot now called for a well-played high pitch to a narrow saucer-like green. The third tee was moved to the left and to a lower level. The US Seniors contributed $500 to help Apawamis defray the cost of the changes.

> *What advantage does the young, enthusiastic par-shooter have over the older man save the ability to pound the living daylights out of the ball. The older men putt as well, they pitch as well to the greens, and they have been known to hold their tempers and play more coldly and calculatingly.*
>
> *— John P. English*
> *USGA Journal, June 1953*

Governor Thomas E. Dewey (center)
at the 1946 annaul tournament,
with (left to right) USSGA Secretary
George. A. Nicol, Candian Seniors'
Secretary H. P. Baker, USSGA
President Admiral William H. Standley,
and USSGA champion Ellis Knowles.

At the same time, the bunkers surrounding the eighteenth green were removed, and replaced for a time by one gorge-like depression at the left front corner that was nicknamed "Knowles' Abyss."

A NATIONAL MEMBERSHIP

In 1947 to make the organization truly national was a major priority, and the need to attract members from west of the Mississippi was discussed. In 1953 the USSGA adopted a new policy for the election of members – 50 percent were to come from the New York Metropolitan Area, the other 50 percent from outside that area. Of the ninety-eight members elected in 1958, for instance, only twenty-three were from the New York area. Elaborate plans were made to elect new members from each of the five "districts" nationwide, twenty from each for a total of one hundred annually until the desired balance was attained.

THE ANNUAL TOURNAMENT

To speed up play for the 1948 tournament, it was recommended that the championship flight, for those with handicaps of nine or under, be played on Tuesday and Wednesday at Apawamis, starting before the rest of the field, playing in threesomes with each player having his own caddie.

In 1948 the Board also began discussing the possibility of a two-day tournament

at two clubs, with the second club most desirably being Blind Brook. Apawamis agreed on both counts, and Apawamis president Stewart S. Hathaway brought the proposal to Blind Brook President I. J. Harvey, who also agreed.

Apawamis' new second green.

And so the Board of Governors approved the change on a trial basis. Starting in 1949, play was on two days only, with one round at Apawamis and one at Blind Brook for each entrant. This format made the annual banquet and other functions readily available to all entrants.

However, in 1950 the membership voted 394 to 146 to restore the four-day format in 1951. Apparently the membership felt it was being divided among two clubhouses and courses, and that an appropriate opportunity was not being provided to renew the many friendships and memories that in the past had made the tournament successful. And so in 1951 the championship flight (and others) played on the first two days, the rest of the field on the second two days, and in 1952 both Apawamis and Blind Brook were used on the first two days, and just Apawamis the second two days. The four days at Apawamis format was re-adopted in 1953.

Action in the putting contest.

At the same time a resolution was adopted that "deepest appreciation be expressed to the Blind Brook Club for its kindness and courtesy to the United States Seniors' Golf Association for use of the Blind Brook links for the Seniors' Tournaments for the past two years."

The Seniors' treasury was low in 1951, and it was suggested that each member voluntarily contribute $10 to replenish it. That request resulted in the collection of $4,317. A similar request was made in 1953.

Franklin "Fritz" Clement

Because of the summer heat at the end of June in 1951 and 1952, the 1953 championship was rescheduled, again with the cooperation of Apawamis, to the first week in June.

In 1955, as a result of the pressure of those wishing to enter, the championship was divided into three sections –– all at Apawamis – and the play was over six days. Those living nearby were requested to play Sunday and Monday, and the remainder of the field was split evenly between Tuesday and Wednesday and Thursday and Friday. Also in 1955 play was started on first and tenth holes at ten-minute intervals – not just the first tee as had been done for fifty years. In 1955 this practice cut the time for a round to four hours. The use of six days, however, was a one-year-only experiment, and the four days at Apawamis format was back in place in 1956.

In 1959 Vice-president Franklin G. Clement suggested a change to the two-day format again, so that "all contestants could encounter the same weather conditions." The matter was referred to the Tournament Committee, who were asked to discuss the matter with Apawamis first. In 1960 the two-day format was adopted again, this time with the South Course at Westchester Country Club as the second course. This format remained in place until 1970, when pressures on membership play caused by the Westchester Classic prevented the Westchester Country Club from allowing an outside group use of its facilities for two consecutive days.

The popularity of the annual championships placed increasing pressure on the membership. From 1922 to 1933 the membership limit was increased from six hundred to seven hundred, and then to seven hundred fifty. Then in 1951 it went to eight hundred, and in 1953 to eight hundred fifty. These limits were tailored to the number who wished to play and could be comfortably and adequately accommodated in the championship. This represented nearly 50 percent of the active membership each year, a proportion that has remained valid into the twenty-first century.

THE INTERNATIONAL MATCHES

The early fifties witnessed a number of significant developments in the Devonshire Cup. The practice of playing informal foursome matches in conjunction with the Devonshire Cup was revived in 1950, but a plan to make them part of the match in 1951 was rescinded.

Postwar currency problems having continued to deny the British travel to Canada or the United States, the Triangular was played temporarily at Mid-Ocean, Bermuda, in 1953 and again in 1956, the first two on this side of the Atlantic following the war. The problems were answered by an expense sharing arrangement under which each host provided the visitors' living accommodations and tournament expenses at the competition. The voluntary contributions from the US Seniors were used for a time solely to defray the costs of this hospitality when the matches were played in the United States.

Lasting changes in the Triangular's format had their origins about this time. Since churning the lineup could make it difficult to establish lasting friendships, it was agreed that there should not be more than six changes from match to match. For initiating further measures to perpetuate friendships, credit goes to Ellis Knowles and to Britain's super-senior and later captain, Rear Admiral C. H. G. Benson, D.S.O. The two of them got together at St. Andrews in 1958 and decided it was high time they played in the Triangular again. The next year at Pine Valley the teams had been increased to sixteen players and both "The Admiral" and Ellis were aboard. In 1961, however, the number reverted to twelve and any special dispensation for age was left to the future.

USSGA officers (left to right): James D. Miller, Franklin G. Clement, Mason B. Starring, President Isaac B. Grainger, and James H. Ackerman.

In 1954 the US Seniors also decided to limit the captain's role to arranging the order in which the team will play; the Tournament and Executive Committees were to select the team members. Presently, the team captain selects the players, then reviews his selections with the president and team secretary.

With the Devonshire still on the annual basis and the Triangular now convening every odd year and on these shores alternately, the two competitions were played in combination at Pine Valley in 1959. Again on the British side was T. A. Torrance, who, after a notable international career for Britain, including five of the first eight Walker Cup matches and captain in 1932, became one of the most highly revered of all seniors, and an honorary member of the US Seniors. Aided by this seasoned campaigner, the British led after the first day's sixsomes but in the end the United States, captained by Ellis Knowles, won both cups and narrowed to one the British margin in the Triangular series.

On November 5, 1959, a dinner was held at which Isaac B. Grainger, the president of the United States Seniors, was master of ceremonies. Talks were called for from John Hadden, Ellis Knowles, and Sir Cecil Carr in which good will, wit, and reminiscence overflowed. Before the close of a wonderful evening, to everyone's surprise, including his own, Ike Grainger even recited some "poetry" written years ago on the provisional ball rule of golf.

With their numbers large and their pace of play not quite fast enough, the Seniors began experimenting. Electric carts were allowed for the first time in 1959, when thirty-eight members used them, all of whom regularly used carts at their own clubs for medical reasons.

The AA class, for members eighty years of age and older, was established in 1962, when ten venerable seniors played.

Former USGA President Ike Grainger.

Among the first golf carts to be used in the annual tournament.

A Visit To Sweden

As an ardent golfer, H.R.H. Prince Gustaf Adolph Bertil of Sweden made a visit to Philadelphia in the late forties an occasion for playing Pine Valley. While there he learned from John Arthur Brown that the Triangular would bring the international team to England in the summer of 1949. Believing his country-men's interest in golf would be increased, the Prince suggested a visit to play informal matches against a number of the clubs in Sweden.

The invitation was accepted and following the Triangular a seven-man team traveled to Sweden. The first match was played at Goteborg and won by the visitors. The second, which was against the Bastad Golf Club team, was a different story. The proceedings started with lunch, merged into open-ing ceremonies, and finally moved to the business at hand, all graced by the presence of the Crown Prince. In the words of the Bulletin:

The international team with the Crown Prince of Sweden (center).

We were honored at luncheon, given by the President of the Golf Club, to have present HRH Crown Prince Gustaf Adolph. It was a delightful informal luncheon with general conversation and no formal program. At this luncheon the Secretary pinned upon the lapel of HRH The Crown Prince one of our new United States Seniors pins. On the porch of the club, at the practice putting green, The Crown Prince pleasantly posed with different members of our team. Later at the first tee, he was photographed with different pairs of contestants as they started their rounds. For more than four hours he walked about the course. With his sleeves rolled up, he was as democratic and friendly as one could possibly be.

Whatever the cause, the match was won by the hosts 4^1/$_2$ to 2^1/$_2$. In the third and fourth matches, at Falsterbo and Stockholm, the United States team redeemed itself.

Their missionary zeal aroused, the travelers returned with visions of converting the Triangular to a Quadrilateral. As reported by the Bulletin:

"It is the unanimous wish of those who visited Sweden that the Swedish Golfers will organize a Swedish Seniors Golf Association and that we can in the United States return to the best of our ability their courte-sies so happily extended to us in July, 1949. There is a possibility of creating a Quadrilateral league with British, Canadian, Swedish and United States Seniors forming teams and meeting in rotation.

In 1958 it was decided to limit international competition to the two already in existence.

Ellis Knowles' famous bunker shot iin 1954.

Ellis Knowles won his fifth straight Seniors' championship in 1946. There was a six-man 18-hole playoff (one picked up after a rocky front 9), and Knowles won easily with a 70, the best round of the tournament.

The following description of the conclusion of the 1948 annual tournament is taken from the Bulletin:

A birdie on the 13th was the first glimmering of light in the gathering gloom. That left John Riddell with the task of playing the last five holes in par to tie with Knowles. To win, he had to get a birdie some- where along the route. Fortunately in Rocco Calandrill, one of these sagacious caddies for which Apawamis has been noted since Al Ciuci carried the clubs of Fred Herreshoff in the historic battle against Harold Hilton, Riddell had a backer who never failed.
"I let him hand me the irons," Riddell commented, "I never questioned his judgment."
Riddell made his pars at the 14th and 15th, hitting No. 2 irons at both. Still that birdie had not shown up. It came at the 179-yard 16th, where Riddell hit his trusty No. 2 iron into a cross wind twelve feet from the pin. The player had to figure out a roll, but he made the putt for a 2.

Ellis Knowles' sixth USSGA championship on June 11, 1954, came in dramatic fashion at age sixty-seven. After a front-9 score of 34 that left him a likely winner, Knowles faltered on the back 9 with five bogies to leave him one stroke behind coming to the eighteenth. When he bunkered his approach, the sit- uation appeared desperate, but he told his caddie. "I still have one shot left." Using a twenty-year-old remodeled wedge, he holed out on one hop to tie Joseph M. Wells. Knowles carded rounds of 74-74=148 to Wells' 73-75=148. Knowles won the playoff on June 30, the day before the team sailed for England, becoming the winningest US Senior ever. Knowles' wedge is now on display in a trophy case at Apawamis.

In 1958 George and John Dawson shot 73s on June 4. Both brothers were USSGA champions, John three consecutive years 1958 to 1960 and George in 1962. Although he never lived up to his promise as "the next Bobby Jones," Johnny Dawson did win the Bing Crosby National Pro-Am in 1942 with a 36-hole score of 133. He was runner-up in the 1947 US Amateur, also at Pebble Beach.

In 1953 Frank Ross, the Connecticut Amateur champion in 1926 and 1930, started 3-2-3-3 (5 under par) on the second day and finished with a 69 to win the annual tournament. He had played hockey, baseball, and basketball while a student at MIT.

The annual tournament has often been plagued by rain, but very seldom by snow. There was a play-off in 1955 in which John W. Roberts of Columbus, Ohio, had a snowman on the eleventh hole, then birdied the twelfth and matched par the rest of the way to win. His opponent, Roy Moore of Maine, was four strokes ahead standing at the twelfth tee, but then took a very costly 8 at the seventeenth hole.

John Dawson

Press Coverage

Until the latter part of the 1950s, the terrace at Apawamis was covered with equipment furnished to or installed by the wire services (Associated Press, Western Union, and United Press) and their sports reporters. News of the tournament was distributed daily to newspapers throughout the country.

On Wednesday in 1951, Prescott Bush shot a round of 31-35=66 during which he made eight birdies, had fourteen birdie putts, and missed an ace at the tough sixteenth hole by 18 inches. He also hit his approach in the stream on the eleventh, and drove out of bounds on the fifteenth, taking one-stroke penalties for both mistakes. Eventual winner Tom Robbins of Winged Foot had yet to start when Bush finished, and so knew exactly what he had to do. Bush was in at 142, and Robbins shot 67 for a new Seniors' record 140. Robbins finished with birdies on the last three holes, holing out a recovery on the eighteenth to end with a flair.

Prescott Bush and his scorecard.

Thomas Robbins and his scorecard.

PRESCOTT S. BUSH

UNITED STATES SENIORS' GOLF ASSOCIATION

Hole	1	2	3	4	5	6	7	8	9	Out	10	11	12	13	14	15	16	17	18	In	Total
Yards	377	325	315	325	150	323	405	335	555	3110	480	340	170	321	410	415	179	475	295	3085	6195
Par	4	4	4	4	3	4	4	4	5	36	5	4	3	4	4	4	3	5	4	36	72
PLAYER *Prescott S. Bush.*																					
	4	4	4	4	4	5	5	5	5	39	5	4	3	3	4	5	4	6	3	37	76
	4	4	4	3	3	3	3	4	3	31	4	5	3	4	3	5	2	5	4	35	66
																					142

THOMAS C. ROBBINS

UNITED STATES SENIORS' GOLF ASSOCIATION

Hole	1	2	3	4	5	6	7	8	9	Out	10	11	12	13	14	15	16	17	18	In	Total
Yards	377	325	315	325	150	323	405	335	555	3110	480	340	170	321	410	415	179	475	295	3085	6195
Par	4	4	4	4	3	4	4	4	5	36	5	4	3	4	4	4	3	5	4	36	72
PLAYER *Thomas C. Robbins.*																					
	4	3	4	5	3	4	4	4	5	36	5	4	3	5	4	4	3	5	4	37	73
	4	3	4	3	3	4	4	4	5	34	5	3	3	4	5	4	2	4	3	33	67
																					140

The US Senior Amateur Championship

When in 1954 the United States Golf Association proposed its own Senior Amateur Championship, the USSGA was somewhat taken aback. At a meeting of the Executive Committee on June 1, 1954, the USSGA's thoughts on the matter were formalized, as follows:

. . . regarding the proposed US Senior Amateur in 1954, the USSGA resolved that:

> *1. It was not within the province of the United States Seniors' Golf Association to make any recommendations or objection to the USGA as to whether it should or should not organize a Senior Section or hold a USGA Senior Tournament;*
> *2. it most sincerely wished and hoped that the USGA would not undertake such a course, particularly at this time.*

Nonetheless, the USGA Senior Amateur was born in 1955, in part because of the US Seniors' private membership policy and a long waiting list. The senior division of the USGA gave an opportunity for all amateur golfers fifty-five or over to compete, and determine the real champion — not the best player among the USSGA members. However, the members of the USSGA have distinguished themselves in the prestigious national senior championship of the United States Golf Association.

This difference in opinion in 1954 notwithstanding, the USSGA and USGA have had a harmonious relationship through the years. Numerous US Seniors have served on USGA committees, including the Executive Committee, and a majority of USGA presidents have been US Seniors. In 1998 the two organizations entered into an agreement under which the USGA will protect the United States Seniors' trade name and the USSGA service mark against third-party infringement.

A number of US Seniors have won the US Senior Amateur, including three of the first four winners of the event (J. Wood Platt, 1955; Frederick J. Wright, 1956; and Thomas C. Robbins, 1958).

Bill Campbell won in 1979 and again in 1980 (the same year he was runner-up in the US Senior Open) beating Ed Updegraff in the semi-finals and USSGA member Keith Compton in the finals. Updegraff defeated USSGA member Dale Morey in the finals in 1981.

Lew Oehmig won three US Senior Amateur titles (1972, 1976, and 1985) over a span of fourteen years. Several other members have also won twice, including Curtis Person (1968–1969), Dale Morey (1974, 1977), Bill Hyndman (1973, 1983), Gordon Brewer 1994, 1996), and Bill Shean (1998 and 2000). One other US Senior, Robert B. Kiersky in 1965, won the US Senior Amateur.

US Amateur champions who later in life became USSGA members include Findlay Douglas (1898), Bob Gardner (1909, 1915), William C. Fownes, Jr. (1910), Francis Ouimet (1914, 1931), Jess Sweetser (1922), Max Marston (1923), William Turnesa (1938, 1948), Jack Westland (1952), Bill Campbell (1964), and Marvin "Vinny" Giles III (1972). Giles defeated Ben Crenshaw in the finals to win his title, while Campbell defeated Ed Tutwiler in his finals match, with Vinny Giles co-medalist that year.

Several members of the USSGA have been honored by the USGA with the "Bob Jones Award" for distinguished sportsmanship, the highest honor given by the USGA. Francis Ouimet was the first honoree in 1955, and was followed by William C. Campbell (1956), Findlay Douglas (1959), Charles Coe (1964), Richard S. Tufts (1967), Joseph C. Dey, Jr. (1977), Billy Joe Patton (1981), Jess Sweetser (1986), Isaac B. Grainger (1988), Lewis Oehmig (1994), Fred Brand, Jr. (1997), and Dr. Edgar Updegraff (1999).

Lew Oehmig

Bill Hyndman

Francis Ouimet, Frank Craven, and Elmer Ward.

General Dwight D. Eisenhower was elected an honorary member in 1950, and General Omar Bradley was elected to membership in 1959.

On November 19, 1950, US Senior Francis Ouimet was elected captain of the R&A. Ouimet is best remembered as the twenty-year-old amateur who put American golf on front pages worldwide by defeating Harry Vardon and Ted Ray in a playoff for the 1913 US Open title at The Country Club. He also won the 1914 and 1931 US Amateur championships, was a member of eight Walker Cup teams, including two as captain (1932 and 1934). He served twice as vice-president of the USSGA, and was honored with the Bob Jones Award in 1955. His fellow US Seniors remember him for his "sportsmanship and warming personality."

Nathaniel Vickers, the grand old man of American golf, died in 1949 at age one hundred three. Born in England in 1846, he came to the United States in 1885, and took up golf a few years later at age fifty, tennis and cricket having become too strenuous. Vickers played golf for fifty years, giving it up at age one hundred one. He was the USSGA's oldest playing member; elected in 1930 at age eighty-four, he played through 1943 (at age ninety-seven), when he carded a 130. When he played, Vickers walked the course vigorously, erect as a West Point cadet, and completed his 18 holes in one day (rather than splitting it over two days, as was customary among the older members at that time). He had a youthful viewpoint on life, and believed in moderation towards all things.

As a young man, Vickers worked on the restoration of several English cathedrals, and later did similar work at St Patrick's Cathedral and the Cathedral of St John the Divine in New York. At age one hundred he designed dwellings for several of his friends.

In 1951 brothers Milton R. and Stewart R. Brown both moved into class A after twenty-one years as members.

In 1956 Timothy F. Allen became the first Senior to play with his son, Timothy, Jr.

John Arthur Brown, president of the Pine Valley Golf Club from 1926 until his death in February, 1977 at age ninety-two, was educated at the University of Pennsylvania and the University of Pennsylvania Law School. He was a member of the USGA Executive Committee, president in 1947–1948, and vice-president of the Philadelphia Golf Association for fifteen years. In his own words:

After some twelve years of college and club rowing, that manly sport which puts a premium on a strong back and a weak mind, by accident I became interested in golf, a game which I first believed to be simple and easy of mastery. That was in 1919, and since then I have unsuccessfully endeavored to substantiate this belief.

In 1919 I joined the Pine Valley Golf Club, and since that time I have been a constant source of income to my opponents and despair to my partners.

Nathaniel Vickers

Left: John Arthur Brown of Pine Valley.

Ellis Knowles and Livingston Platt.

Livingston Platt's first sporting interest was squash-tennis, which he played at the Ardsley Casino and was runner-up in the national championship. An attorney and Yale alumnus, he moved to Rye in 1913 and joined Apawamis, where he served on the Board for eighteen years (1921–1938) and as club president for twelve years (1927–1938). Platt also served on the Executive Committee of both the MGA and USGA, and was general counsel to the USGA. In his spare time, he served fourteen years as mayor of Rye (1930–1943).

John F. Riddell took up golf after graduating from college in 1913, and became a "serious" golfer after World War I when he moved to Garden City. He once reached the semi-finals of the Met Amateur, and played in the 1936 US Amateur at Garden City Golf Club, advancing to the quarter-finals, where he lost to eventual runner-up Jock McLean.

Former US Amateur champion Bob Gardner (left) with William Hunt and John Riddell.

Midwesterner Robert A. Gardner was a two-time US Amateur champion (1909 and 1915) and a member of the first four United States Walker Cup teams, playing captain the last three times.

Experience *vs.* Enthusiasm

The champions of thirty years ago are not, generally speaking, the senior champions of today.

There is, of course, no single explanation for the emergence of new champions with the passing of years. Several factors are involved.

First, many men are not so circumstanced as to begin the game until their contemporaries are already tournament golfers.

The second point is enthusiasm. An older man may find he loves the game. He gets his pleasure making the ball behave. The younger star may well find his enthusiasm waning as he gets older.

Thirdly, the older man must keep his health. How few senior golfers look their age! Time inevitably weeds out many of those who were splendid golfers in their younger days but who have succumbed to arthritis, misplaced sacroiliacs, or any of a score of nature's handicaps.

Finally, we find much of the answer in the nature of the game itself. After all, what advantage does the young, enthusiastic par-shooter have over the older man save the ability to pound the living daylights out of the ball. The older men putt as well, they pitch as well to the greens, and they have been known to hold their tempers and play more coldly and calculatingly.

— John P. English
USGA Journal, June 1953

Safaris In Europe and East Africa

From St. Andrews in 1954, the British, Canadian, and United States teams all journeyed to Deauville for matches with teams from France, West Germany, Switzerland, Belgium, and Italy. The teams were drawn into a flight of eight and played off over three days with foursomes each morning and singles each afternoon. By eliminating Switzerland, Great Britain, and Belgium, in that order, the United States team, captained by John Riddell, won.

That autumn a different five man team representing the USSGA visited "Kenya Colony" at the invitation of the senior society there. Two official matches were played, one at Muthaiga which the United States won and the other at Karen Golf Club where the hosts prevailed. The British and Canadians also competed. Following some seventeen unofficial matches, the team went on thirty-day safari in Uganda and the Belgian Congo, which was found "thoroughly delightful, interesting, and sometimes exciting." They returned looking forward to a proposed return visit by the Kenyan team the following year.

Perhaps the busiest of all years was 1956. After the second Mid-Ocean Triangular, in which the British were captained by Bill Tweddell, there were informal matches against Bermudian seniors and others. Then came Deauville again where the United States after a bye and a victory over the Swiss succumbed in the final to the French 5 to 4. Next came the visit to Canada for the Devonshire Cup where 4½ inches of rain caused the foursomes to be abandoned and the singles and individual championships to be played together. Finally, the Kenyan team arrived and were entertained in a month's travel and play around the country. The Kenyans golfed at Pine Valley, National, Maidstone, and, of course, at Apawamis. They visited the White House along the way, and concluded their visit with a one-day match against a team of US Seniors at Apawamis.

Team Play

The Devonshire Cup was revived in 1946 at Apawamis, and the United States team won decisively. Due to the passage of time the faces in the line-ups were all new or nearly so. The teams consisted of just twelve men per side.

There was a tighter match in 1947 at Rosedale, near Toronto. Only a hole or two separated the winners and losers but in the final reckoning the United States won 26 to 19. Findlay Douglas reappeared but lost three points to Bobby Gray, and so the victory must be credited to Ellis Knowles, who won three points, and even newer arrivals such as Col. Martin S. Lingrove, Duane L. Tower, Joseph M. Wells, John F. Riddell, Jr., Gardiner White, August F. Kammer, and US Senior's President John Arthur Brown, the patriarch of Pine Valley. At the team dinner following the match, Canadian Secretary H. P. Baker placed the insignia of the Canadian Golf Association in the lapels of the coats of the members of the United States team, thereby designating them as honorary members of the Canadian Association.

The team selected by Captain John G. Jackson for the 1948 Devonshire Cup at the National Golf Links was reported to be the strongest ever chosen. Francis Ouimet was expected but could not play due to a back sprain a few days before, but the lineup was embellished by another former United States Amateur Champion, Robert A. Gardner. The team won impressively $36\frac{1}{2}$ to $8\frac{1}{2}$, with each member contributing at least $\frac{1}{2}$ point; Ellis Knowles, Martin Lindgrove, Sam Reynolds, John Arthur Brown, Joe Wells, John Riddell, Gardiner White and August Kammer – 3 each; Bill Hunt, Harrison Smith and Dr. E. B. Sullivan – $2\frac{1}{2}$ each; Bob Gardner and Fred Riggin – 2 each; and Duane Tower and Sherrill Sherman – $\frac{1}{2}$ each.

Although invitations were received from the British in 1946 and 1947, resumption of the Triangular Matches was not possible until 1949 when the United States sent over a team of eight with John G. Jackson as non-playing captain. The Canadians having declined due to transportation difficulties, the match was a two-sided affair. Meeting the British on their home course at Woking in July, the United States achieved its first victory on British soil 7 to 5. Interestingly enough the singles were halved and the United States' victory was won in the foursomes.

In 1952 Ellis Knowles being president of the Seniors and John Arthur Brown the immediate past team captain, the Devonshire Cup was played at Pine Valley, where record temperatures, 95 degrees with humidity over 90 percent, forced the players to resort to selective drives. Material aid in forgetting the heat was provided at the dinner by mint julep toasts back and forth. The resulting temporary exhaustion of supply was remedied by raids upon the mint beds of resident members, and a United States team member reportedly slept with the swans in the bunker fronting No. 18.

The fifteenth Triangular was played over the Old Course at St. Andrews in July 1954, the year of the Royal and Ancient's bicentenary. Appropriate to the occasion, the British won handily, though that could hardly be said of the beginning of the lead match, which pitted C. J. H. Tolley and Dr. William Tweddell, both former British Amateur title holders and Walker Cup players, against Ellis Knowles and J. L. Brumley for the United States and Colonel Chipman and James Stewart for Canada.

As one writer described it, Tolley teeing off at the first topped his drive and Tweddell promptly put him in the Swilcan. "With admirable patriotism, but doubtful wisdom" Tolley waded in but left the ball in the burn and the hole was conceded; then at the long fifth Tolley hooked the drive and "unfamiliarly routed his ball into the Hell bunker" whence it was trouble all the way to an 8; but rousing themselves the British veterans proceeded with pars on every hole through the fourteenth to the eventual victory.

Knowles meanwhile found difficulty on the double greens; by aiming at the fifteenth flag en route to the fourth he required of Brumley a putt of over 40 yards, his longest ever. The next day's three-ball singles produced more of the same. Playing out the round following defeat, Knowles and Chipman saw their opponent, Brigadier W. H. H. Aitken, drive the eighteenth green 356 yards away. Later J. M. Wells of the United States and James Stewart of Canada fell to T. A. Torrance who, at the age of sixty-four, went round in 70. This was in the face of a hard southwest "Guard Bridge Wind" which the press described as "no respecter of grey hairs or thinly thatched heads," and prompted one Canadian to observe "that it was a new experience for him to see the balls blown about on the greens." The final point count gave the British 32, the United States 17½. and Canada 5½..

Afterward in a ceremony in the Big Room, the Derby Cup, which had been held by the United States since 1938, was returned to the victorious British. Adding to the occasion Ellis Knowles and Charles Cowie presented gifts from their Associations to the Royal and Ancient to mark the anniversary, four silver candelabra from the United States and from Canada, a George II silver coffee pot bearing the London date mark 1754. Moved by all this, Sir Guy Campbell epitomized the audience reaction:

As one very old golfer remarked to me, "Sometimes in the last few years I have wondered why I had to live so long. Now I know. And it has been so worthwhile that I hope to go on living long enough to see another such meeting here, whatever else may happen." and concluded— "A goodly gathering of friends at St. Andrews; good weather; good golf and green memories. What could be as good?"

In June 1955 the Devonshire Cup was at the National Golf Links for the third time, and there E. F. ("Eggs") Quittner and John W. Roberts made their respective bows. A month later a team of five was off to Deauville to defend the informal "international title." Captain of the team was Maurice R. Smith, who had played in Devonshire and Triangular Cup Matches on occasion in the fifties, sixties, and seventies. With Canada and Italy absent, the United States retained the team title by virtue of a bye and victories over Switzerland and France. The award was a new trophy, the "Coupe Internationale des Seniors."

The US and Canadian teams at the Devonshire Cup at the National Golf Links in 1955.

The 1957 Triangular at Muirfield was a close one, the British side having been buttressed by the new boy, John B. Beck, captain of the victorious 1938 Walker Cup side and raconteur and sherry connoisseur par excellence. After taking a $2\frac{1}{2}$ point lead in the sixsomes, the United States bowed in the singles and lost to the British by the slimmest of margins, $24\frac{1}{2}$ to $25\frac{1}{2}$ with the Canadians far behind at $4\frac{1}{2}$. That year also initiated the present schedule under which the Triangular is played biennially in odd years in rotation among Canada, Great Britain, and the United States.

Captain John Riddell driving off at Deauville, France.

In the 1958 Devonshire, the Cup was retained by the United States, but via a route opposite to that of the year before, the foursomes having been won and the singles halved. Among the winners were several freshmen, including Walter F. Pease, another Wall Street lawyer who was a regular for several years, and James D. Miller and James D. Ackerman, each of whom later became a USSGA captain and president. Another first timer in 1958 was H. H. Richardson, a Canadian by adoption who has distinguished himself through playing in twelve matches and service as president of the Canadian Seniors.

Admiral Cyril Benson, who joined the British Seniors' Society in 1939 and played in a number of Triangulars, went around Woking in the Senior medal in 1965 at the age of eighty-one in 77–16–61, had his handicap reduced from 18 to 17 at the age of eighty-six, and at the age of eighty-eight completed his last medal round at St. Andrews in 126 strokes buffeted by a gale gusting to 75 miles per hour.

In *Admiral Benson Sails the Links,* Henry Longhurst marveled over what he considered the Admiral's "finest hour," a gross 88 at the age of eighty-one for a round played on the Old Course at St. Andrews in punishing wind and cold. Speculating as to how it was done, Henry concluded that it was "simple golf," in which the Admiral just set a course and sailed on it, with a "battery" of only half a dozen elementary clubs, carried in a "patent contraption" manufactured in 1893. Turning in contrast to the absurdity of the "set" of 14 clubs carried in a "perambulator" or by a caddie, Henry scorned others who played that day:

The owners of some of this ironmongery and ancillary equipment took, many of them, 90 and 100 to get round. And the Admiral, carrying the whole damn lot in one hand at the '"trail arms position," got round in 88. If that does not make them think, nothing will. And I suppose the answer is just that. Nothing will.

In the sixteen-man lineup for the Devonshire Cup at the Kanawaki and Beaconsfield Golf Clubs in Montreal in 1960 were Richard S. ("Dick") Tufts and Ike Grainger, worthy contributors to golf through the USGA as well as the USSGA, H. C. ("Hank") Flower, perhaps the most zealous of all seniors, and Weller Noble, a very great player indeed. They and their colleagues squeaked through the foursomes $12\frac{1}{2}$ to $11\frac{1}{2}$ and won handsomely in the singles.

John Ellis Knowles

John Ellis Knowles of Apawamis was regarded by many in the know as "one of the greatest unknown golfers ever produced in American golf."

John Ellis Knowles built a successful business career in shipping and enjoyed to the very utmost a lifetime of dedication to golf. He held the club championship at his beloved Apawamis sixteen times and at Round Hill four times, won the prestigious Crump Cup at Pine Valley twice, the championships of the Westchester and Metropolitan Seniors twice each, and the USSGA title five times running from 1942 to 1946 and a sixth in 1954.

Over the twenty-five years from 1947 to 1972, Knowles played in thirteen Devonshire Cups and five Triangulars, and the points he contributed or was instrumental in contributing totaled 63 to 42 for the opponents. Equally significant were his countless off-the-course contributions to senior golf in this country and abroad over a period of thirty-five years. Ellis more than merited all the honors the USSGA bestowed, including the office of honorary president.

Ellis Knowles and his many trophies.

Born and raised in Pensacola, Florida, Knowles attended St. Paul's School in Garden City, and learned the fundamentals of the game, as well as its rules, customs, and traditions, at the famous Garden City links under the tutelage of Walter J. Travis, who had the youngster accompany him on the practice tee and on his rounds.

Knowles went to Yale, where he was an outstanding golfer, and won the Intercollegiate championship in 1907. He advanced to the semifinals of the US Amateur in 1906, where he lost to George S. Lyon of Canada.

Knowles went on to a career in the shipping business, as co-owner and vice-president of the Marine Transport Lines, which operated a large fleet of tankers and bulk cargo ships. Knowles played in the 1930 US Amateur at Merion, losing in the second round. Had he won, he would have faced Bobby Jones in a third round match — remember, the 1930 Amateur was the fourth leg of Jones' Grand Slam. Knowles' business career prevented him from ever playing in the Amateur again.

A governor and golf chairman for nine years at Apawamis, during which time an irrigation system was installed, Knowles at one time held the competitive 36-hole record at Apawamis with a 137, the last nine in 28, which was regarded at the time as a world record for a par-36 nine.

Ellis and son Jim Knowles were the first father and son to play on the same international team in 1970. Jim won ten club championships at Round Hill and five times at Ekwanok, and he was USSGA champion three times.

Jim Knowles has said that his father considered that his greatest contribution to the Seniors was in developing relationships between the American, the British, and the Canadian Seniors.

At his first US Seniors' Tournament, Ellis Knowles was greeted by fellow Senior Archie Reid, a former USGA president and the son of St. Andrew's John Reid, with the words, "So you've joined us old fossils at last. The Seniors get 'em all at the end,' eh Ellis? It's just a matter of patience." "What do you mean, old fossil?" Knowles retorted, "A man is only as old as he feels, and I feel pretty chipper. As a matter of fact, I'm hitting the ball farther, and scoring lower, at fifty-five years of age than I did as an eighteen year old soph at Yale." This from a former intercollegiate champion!

The Ekwanok course at the foot of the mountain.

Birth of the Invitational Tournaments 1962–1979

THE CONCEPT DATES BACK AT LEAST TO 1948, when the possibility of a match-play tournament was proposed and discussed at the Annual Meeting. Fred Riggin proposed the idea, submitting a detailed letter on the matter. After full discussion, the idea was referred to the Executive Committee. The general opinion at the meeting was that it would be wise to give very careful thought to such an endeavor. The Executive Committee at the time was preoccupied with the conversion of the annual tournament from four to two days at Apawamis and Blind Brook, and the matter disappeared for fourteen years.

The Championship Tournament at Apawamis had been in existence for fifty-seven years before the first Invitational Tournament came into being. It was June 1962 at Manchester, Vermont when forty-one US Seniors and their wives joined with nine Canadian Seniors to play in a tournament hosted by a group of senior members of the Ekwanok Country Club. The three-day event, which had been organized at the request of the USSGA Board of Governors, was an immediate success, and on the final day of play it was decided to schedule it again the following year.

> *The Invitational tournaments have become a very integral part of the United States Seniors, often the primary reason a new member joins the organization. The Invitationals are all conducted from essentially the same script, right down to the prizes, yet each one retains its own individual flavor.*
>
> *– Spoken at Blind Brook, 2004*

This decision paved the way for additional Invitationals that would serve to bring together US Seniors at various times of the year to renew friendships and to engage in competitions on golf courses of outstanding quality and reputation. The program has since expanded to thirteen tournaments coast to coast, and these competitions draw upwards of one thousand US Senior participants annually.

The events leading up to the Board of Governors' decision to encourage the formation of the first tournament are noteworthy, particularly since the idea came about as a result of a chance meeting of two members of the Association in California.

Weller Noble

Hank Flower

A MEETING AT CYPRESS POINT

It happened at the Cypress Point Club at Pebble Beach. It was late June 1961. The occasion was the annual Hook 'n' Eye Tournament held for Cypress Point members and their guests selected among other reasons for their congeniality, sportsmanship, and good humor.

The two Seniors, both invited guests who met on this occasion, had known each other from the time they played in the same foursome in the Championship Tournament at Apawamis in 1954. One was a Californian, a fine golfer who was beginning to shoot his age with some regularity, Weller Noble. The other, an Easterner, who had made his living on Madison Avenue and retired part-time to the hills of Vermont where he could enjoy his daily rounds of golf and reflect on his new responsibilities as vice-president of the United States Seniors' Golf Association, Henry Flower.

To put the mood of the Hook 'n' Eye in proper focus, it should be pointed out that this small but exclusive tournament was started during the days of Prohibition. As the members and guests completed their rounds it was observed that they would go into the Cypress Point Clubhouse and say, "Who can I get a drink from?" Apparently the same question was asked with such regularity that the Tournament took on the name "Hook 'n' Eye" and has retained this unique identification ever since.

Noble and Flower met on the first tee, and right away, Hank Flower was asked to explain how an Ivy Leaguer came to be invited to play in such a distinguished tournament as the Hook 'n' Eye. When their brief encounter was concluded Weller turned to Hank and said, "When we get back to the Clubhouse, I have some thoughts about the Apawamis Tournament that I'd like to share with you."

Later in the day they met in the Clubhouse and Weller volunteered some remarks about Eleanor's Teeth and slippery downhill putts that end up in bunkers below the green. Then, he added, "You easterners ask us to come all the way across the continent for two days of play and after that you send us back home again. Is that your idea of eastern hospitality and courtesy?"

Hank had to agree that it wasn't. Weller then asked, "Did it ever occur to you that some of us from the west coast might like to stay through the weekend and play some other eastern golf courses?"

Hank's reply came without hesitation. "Let's start to remedy that next June. After the Apawamis Tournament I'd like to take you to Manchester, Vermont, where we will spend the remainder of the week playing golf at Ekwanok, one of the most delightful golf courses in the east."

Weller accepted the invitation with his familiar broad smile and gentlemanly thanks. Hank offered to make all the arrangements and to provide some additional players for three or four rounds of congenial competitive golf.

During the summer Hank's imagination led him to a somewhat broader base for the proposed get-together in Vermont he had discussed with Weller. He brought the matter to the attention of the USSGA Executive Committee at their meeting in October and reported on his conversation with Weller and their plans for the following June. Everyone acknowledged that we had never given any thought to taking proper care of those members who might like to stay on for a few days after the Apawamis Tournament to play other golf courses.

The consensus was that we should lose no time in organizing a small Invitational Tournament in Vermont, provided that arrangements could be worked out with the Ekwanok club.

Hank contacted Jimmy Robbins, a US Senior and fellow member of Ekwanok, who immediately became enthusiastic and agreed to help. Next, there were talks with Ekwanok's outgoing president and president-elect, Charlie Sargent and Charlie Nichols, both of whom reacted favorably and said they would try to obtain Board approval. Within a week Hank was given the answer he had hoped for, the green light to proceed.

But it was now late October and before long Manchester would be covered with a blanket of snow, the clubhouse closed, and many Ekwanok members who could lend a helping hand to the planning and running of a tournament would soon be heading south for the winter. There were a number of decisions that had to be made: establish a format for the tournament, arrange for the printing of invitations and entry forms, determine the number and type of prizes, arrange for hotel space, and develop an entertainment program for the visiting players and wives.

A committee was formed with Hank Flower, chairman, assisted by Jimmy Robbins and Ekwanok seniors Allan Brown and John Byler. It was decided that Canadian Seniors participating in the International Matches would be invited along with US Seniors residing in the western states. It was further decided that US Seniors' officers would be encouraged to attend and that a number of Ekwanok seniors would be selected to serve as hosts to the visiting players with one assigned to each foursome.

The committee, acting on a suggestion from Ellis Knowles, agreed that a match play format would be unique in contrast to the stroke play of the Apawamis Tournament. Hence, they decided to set up the competition on the basis of individual match play against par, fifty-four holes over three days, and prizes awarded to win-

The Ekwanok clubhouse.

ners and runners-up, gross and net, for three days total as well as for each day's eighteen hole play.

The Club soon had a basis for proceeding with various details of the tournament. Club office secretary, Dorothy Marckres, moved into her "winter office," the living room of her home, where she was in regular contact by phone with Hank Flower reporting on the progress of each phase of the program. In the meantime, Hank worked with Weller Noble, Clay Bedford, and Jimmy Robbins and provided an invitation list of US and Canadian Seniors. The committee selected Ekwanok Seniors who were to serve as hosts and to complete the field planned for the tournament. Invitations were mailed March 1, 1962, and among the first to be returned along with the entry fee, a $25 check made out to The Ekwanok Seniors Tournament Fund, was an application signed by Weller Noble.

The selection of the Ekwanok Country Club turned out to be appropriate in many respects. Here was an 1899 golf course, designed from a basic plan laid out by Walter Travis, which, for the most part, had remained unchanged and unspoiled over the years. The course, interesting and challenging for a senior golfer, was not a back breaker. Nestled in a fertile valley surrounded by the Green Mountains to the east, Mount Equinox a half-mile to the west, and Mount Aeolus adjacent to the north, it would provide a magnificent, relaxed setting for the visiting guests.

The Village of Manchester had been a summer resort for 150 years, a place where a number of excellent small inns and restaurants as well as cultural points of interest could serve to supplement the hospitality to be provided by Ekwanok members in their homes. With the State of Vermont and Canada sharing a common border, it was appropriate that members of the Canadian Seniors' team would be welcomed and entertained along with their counterparts in the United States Seniors' Golf Association.

On the Thursday following the 1962 Apawamis Tournament, the guests began to arrive at the Ekwanok clubhouse. Some came early enough to play a practice round; others sat relaxed on the terrace enjoying the peaceful view of the mountains surrounding the clubhouse. That evening there was a welcoming cocktail party in the Club lounge and on the terrace. Thirty Ekwanok seniors and their wives, each wearing white carnations identifying them as host members, were there to greet the guests. It was the beginning of three glorious days of golf, dinner parties, sightseeing trips, antiquing, renewing friendships, and establishing new ones.

When it was all over any lingering feeling there may have been about "eastern hospitality and courtesy" certainly was not in evidence. Everyone, host and guest alike, had an enjoyable time, and before the last guest had departed it was decided to schedule the tournament again the following year.

One US Senior was particularly pleased with the outcome, partially because he knew he had played a part in fostering the idea of a new tournament, but for another reason too. He, Weller Noble, had won the top prize, low gross for 54 holes.

The first Invitational Tournament was a success because it had been carefully conceived and planned, but, in addition, there prevailed a spirit of friendliness and hospitality among the Ekwanok hosts and their wives, a spirit that reflected Hank Flower's charm and magnetic personality. Had it not been for his foresight and dedication to follow through on a new idea, the concept of the Invitational Tournament for the US Seniors may never have come into being.

In 1964 the tournament format was changed somewhat, again from a suggestion made by Ellis Knowles, when he said, "Golf as originally played in Scotland was a competition between individuals rather than individuals playing against the field. Why not have your match play tournament in flights and declare a winner for each flight?" Hence, the format subsequently used at virtually all of the Invitationals was established at Ekwanok in that year, a four-ball match in flights of sixteen (eight teams), all playing at scratch, except possibly the last flight if there is a wide differential in handicaps among those competing.

A Tradition

For more than 25 years, it has been a tradition at the Ekwanok Invitational to have the red coated Canadian Seniors lead the gathering in singing "O Canada," followed by Tournament Committee members leading a rendition of "God Bless America."

The demand to play in the Ekwanok Tournament increased as it continued to grow in popularity. In its third year, the field was enlarged to a maximum capacity of 128 players. At the same time, in order to accommodate additional US Seniors, the concept of having one Ekwanok host in each foursome was modified, and gradually over the years, the number of "Ekwanok Seniors" was reduced to about twelve.

In 1969 the Board decided to experiment with an Invitational on a "regional" basis, and a suggestion was made by William S. Terrell that a tournament be held on a new course in Pinehurst, the Country Club of North Carolina.

Terrell, along with Gordon Hill, who was then a recent past-president of the Association, had both become interested in developing the Invitational program to provide additional opportunities for our members to become better acquainted. Terrell had joined the Country Club of North Carolina and offered to work together with Hill in organizing such a tournament the second week in October, an offer which the Board readily approved.

Announcement of the new tournament was made to the membership and subsequently applications were received from sixty United States Seniors, about half of whom came from neighboring states. The balance were from Pennsylvania, New Jersey, New York, and a few from the New England area. The setting for such a tournament was ideal. Private homes and guest apartments surrounding the golf course made comfortable quarters for the visiting guests. A dining room serving three meals a day was set aside in the clubhouse for the contestants and their wives. All social activities, including nightly cocktail parties, a dinner dance, and an awards luncheon after the final day of play, were held in the spacious club rooms.

During several of the early years of the tournament the number of players participating did not permit a four-ball match play format, so the committee experimented with other methods of play, none of which seemed to be popular among the contestants.

Subsequently, club members in residence were recruited to complete the field required for a four-ball tournament, and this policy of filling in with local players was adopted and continued in future years here and later at other Invitationals.

Bill Terrell

Right: Gordon Hill

In June 1970 as the North Carolina Committee was planning its second tournament, the Ekwanok its ninth, the Board of Governors approved the formation of two more "regional" events, the first to be held in September in Narragansett, Rhode Island, at the Point Judith Country Club, and the second at the Mountain Lake Club in Lake Wales, Florida the following spring.

The Point Judith Tournament had been suggested by Royal Little, a Board member who offered to sponsor and organize a small tournament in the middle of September just three months away. Roy, a master at organizing anything, went to work immediately and by the time the twenty-seven Senior applicants and wives arrived on September 16 everything was in order.

The golf course, unknown to most of the guests, was built in the early 1900s as a short summer resort layout, but in 1964 it had been redesigned by Geoffrey Cornish and made into a championship course, interesting because of its setting near the seashore but lacking somewhat in reputation and perhaps challenge. Contestants were accommodated in comfortable apartments at the Dunes Club, a private club on the beach overlooking Rhode Island Sound. Roy Little's attention to detail and to the enjoyment of his guests was in evidence at every turn. Food and snacks had even been placed in each of the apartment refrigerators to welcome the guests on their arrival.

Royal Little

It was a successful tournament and those attending were treated to Roy's hospitality, which included boat rides for those interested in watching the Americas' Cup trials, inspection of Colonial homes in Narragansett and New Bedford, and a fascinating motion picture he had filmed on a recent wild animal safari in Kenya and Tanzania.

In September of 1971, the second Point Judith Tournament was held and forty US Seniors participated. On the final day of play a deluge of rain made a veritable lake out of 7 holes on the front side and play had to be rearranged in order to complete the full 18. Roy Little's disappointment in the weather was overshadowed by an unexpected announcement from the Dunes Club that it would not be possible for them to make the apartments available to our membership the following year. He discussed the problem with Chet Birch (who, with his partner Jim Murphy, was the tournament winner at Point Judith that year), and both reluctantly came to the conclusion that the tournament be discontinued since there were no nearby alternatives for the housing of guests.

Remembrance Value

William Beinecke recalls:

On one occasion when I played at Point Judith in the days before plates, my partner and I won our flight and each took home five dozen Titleists. Very nice, but not much remembrance value.

"Speaking though of remembrance value, who do you suppose hosted one of the Point Judith cocktail parties? Glenna Collett Vare. The only thing that could have impressed me more would have been to have had Bobby Jones walk in!

The Mountain Lake Clubhouse as painted by US Senior John Gerster for the cover of the 1992 yearbook.

MOUNTAIN LAKE

The first Mountain Lake Tournament was held seven months later in early April 1971. James H. Ackerman, who was president of the Association when the first Ekwanok Tournament was organized, had suggested a Mountain Lake Tournament at the Board meeting the previous June when the Point Judith Tournament was approved. Most of the Board members were familiar with Mountain Lake. They agreed it would be an ideal place for an Invitational and authorized Ackerman to proceed with the arrangements.

Founded in 1915 in central Florida, Mountain Lake had all the necessary ingredients for a successful tournament within the boundaries of its 3,500-acre property. It had a fine 18-hole golf course designed by Seth Raynor who had previously designed Fishers Island and Sleepy Hollow. There were ninety-two private homes distributed comfortably around the Lake and golf course on spacious rolling hills uncommon to most of Florida.

Guests who did not stay with members in private homes were accommodated in the Colony House centrally located near the first tee and complete with services of all kinds, including reading and card rooms, swimming pool, and two putting greens just a few paces away.

The first Mountain Lake Tournament had to be successful, and it was. While Jim Ackerman did a fine job as host and tournament chairman, all the residents of Mountain Lake, particularly the sixteen US Senior members in residence, joined with him in making the sixty-four Senior participants and their wives feel at home.

THE INVITATIONAL TOURNAMENTS COMMITTEE

There were now four Invitationals underway, and as the June 1971 Board meeting was approaching, it became apparent that any further expansion of the program would need guidance and coordination. Chester T. Birch, a Board member who had attended all four tournaments, including Ekwanok and North Carolina on several occasions, agreed to accept the chairmanship of the newly created Invitational Tournaments Committee.

Working with Hank Flower, Gordon Hill, and Jimmy Walker as his original committee, Chet had proposed that they drop the name "regional" as it might not apply to all tournaments. Instead, the Board agreed to adopt the name "Invitational," recognizing that local committees would determine the composition of the field of players.

Chet's Committee prepared some brief guidelines as an aid to host club chairmen and to promote uniformity in certain aspects of the tournaments. These guidelines were amended on a number of occasions, and today provide a comprehensive outline of virtually all subjects related to running an Invitational Tournament.

In addition, the committee took steps to evaluate alternatives that might alleviate the heavily subscribed Ekwanok Tournament and at the same time considered the possibility of additional sites that might have appeal to the nationwide membership.

KITTANSETT REPLACES POINT JUDITH

Following the decision to discontinue the Point Judith Invitational, it was decided to approach Dick Wakeman, a member of the Kittansett Club in nearby Marion, Massachusetts, to determine the possibility of having the September 1972 tournament at Kittansett as a replacement for Point Judith. On Wakeman's recommendation the Kittansett Board gave its enthusiastic approval, and in October this change in the schedule was reported to the Executive Committee.

At the same time a second tournament proposed by Roy Little was reported to the Executive Committee and approval was given to proceed with its planning and promotion. It was to be at the Lyford Cay Club in Nassau, Bahamas, the first week in December 1972.

The Kittansett course, with a reputation as an outstanding layout, had been chosen by the Walker Cup Committee as the site of the 1953 matches with Great Britain. Since there were only six bedrooms in the clubhouse, and no hotels in the area, the local committee arranged to accommodate the visiting players in members' homes

The Kittansett clubhouse.

adjacent to the club property. The plan worked well. The first year there were sixty-four participants, most of whom came from the New England area. Fifteen were members of Kittansett. In addition, six club members who were not US Seniors filled in to complete the field.

Those who had been to the Point Judith Tournament the year before could well remember the deluge of rain that came on the final day. Now they had something else to remember, for a violent northeaster hit the area the day before the Kittansett Tournament was to start, and it rained continuously during all three days of play. The entire golf course was flooded so that the use of carts was impossible. There were no caddies. The committee, after considering several alternatives, sent the contestants out on foot, each player carrying four clubs of his own choice. Nine-hole matches were held the first two days, but on the third day, as the rain subsided and the sunshine finally appeared, the full 18 holes were played.

In spite of the disappointment in the weather, everyone enjoyed the tournament. Carl Blanchard, a US Senior octogenarian from New Haven, Connecticut, brought his slide trombone and a sixteen-piece Dixieland jazz band composed of business executives from the New Haven area, and they provided music for a memorable dinner-dance the night before the final round. Carl's brother, Kin, accompanied him on the violin; both were World War I pilots. They entertained at Kittansett for several years, and also for a few years at Mountain Lake.

Undaunted by three days of rain, those who played in the first Kittansett Tournament declared it a success and even before their departure following the awarding of prizes, many were asking about "next year." In 1973 an enthusiastic field of sixty-four players returned to Kittansett and in the years that followed the number of players, in some years, pressed its capacity of ninety-six.

LYFORD CAY

Roy Little's initial tournament at the Lyford Cay Club in Nassau was the last of five Invitationals on the 1972 schedule. Thirty-six US Seniors and wives arrived at the Nassau airport in the Bahamas the first week in December, and after a ten-minute taxi ride, they arrived at the security gate of the famous Lyford Cay Club.

Lyford Cay, developed in the late 1950s by Edward P. Taylor, a prominent Canadian industrialist, had a worldwide reputation for excellence in every aspect of its operations. Its facilities included a first rate club-hotel, beach cottages, condominium apartments, one of the most beautiful swimming beaches in the Caribbean, Olympic size pool with comfortable cabanas, numerous tennis courts, yacht club and marina, and a fine golf course surrounded by the private homes of its members. Three distinctive dining venues add to the ambiance of the club. The elegant setting, mild climate of sunshine and gentle winds, together with the friendly atmosphere and genial hospitality of Roy Little made the tournament an immediate success.

The Lyford Cay clubhouse.

Over the next three years, however, the tournament drew only a small group of players as there was some objection to the timing of the tournament just two weeks before the Christmas holiday. In 1975 Roy discussed the problem with the Lyford Cay Board and they agreed to reserve space for the Seniors the last week in January, and it has been held around that time ever since. This proved to be a wise choice for the tournament has grown in popularity and in numbers, currently running at a capacity level of eighty contestants.

THE SENIOR PLATE

Chet Birch had established a custom of holding brief informal meetings at each Invitational to help chairmen solve their problems and to seek ideas for improvement. One of the subjects that frequently came up involved prizes and it was suggested that a standard prize be developed for all Invitationals. Syd Stokes, a new member of the committee, was asked to work on the idea with Roy Little and to come up with a recommendation. In due course a "Senior Plate" was approved, initially in pewter, but later it was made available in crystal and in Lenox china as optional choices for each Tournament Committee. The plate, first used in 1973, proved to be a useful and popular trophy. Virtually every Senior who has won them over the years still looks forward to winning additional plates to add to his collection.

SHINNECOCK HILLS SUPPLEMENTS EKWANOK

Ekwanok's twelfth tournament was being planned for June 1973 and the one problem facing the local committee was that of coping with the increased demand for the 128 available entries. The Invitational Tournaments Committee decided that the only solution was to schedule another tournament concurrent with the one at Ekwanok. Shinnecock Hills at Southampton on Long Island appeared to be a possibility. Less than a three-hour drive from Apawamis, and readily accessible to metropolitan area transportation facilities, it could offer an attractive site for visiting Seniors following the tournament at Rye. Roy Little, newly appointed chairman of the Invitational Committee, discussed the idea with Sanford Johnson, a US Senior who was a past president of the Shinnecock club. Sandy's reaction was favorable and shortly thereafter, with the concurrence of the Shinnecock Board, arrangements were completed for a tournament to be held in June 1973.

The response to the announcement of the tournament was enthusiastic, particularly among those who were familiar with Shinnecock Hills' reputation. Incorporated in 1891 at the very beginning of organized golf in America, it was one of the five clubs that formed an association in 1894 which became the USGA the following year. It hosted the second annual United States Amateur and Open Championships in 1896 and numerous other national and international tournaments over a period of many

The Shinnecock Hills course in the valley behind the clubhouse.

years. Outstanding players who come to Shinnecock Hills from all over the world have an admiration and respect for the challenge of golf offered by this fine course.

The original clubhouse, the first to be designed by Stanford White, can still be recognized amid various modest alterations that have been added from time to time.

A perfect place for a Seniors' tournament! But the one drawback was insufficient housing. No one club or hotel (except a new one then under construction) was large enough to accommodate the number of people ultimately planned. However, it was well worth a try, on a limited basis, for the first year.

There were seventeen US Seniors and fifteen Shinnecock Hills members filling in to complete a field of sixteen teams that competed in a three-day medal-play event. The weather was excellent, the course in magnificent condition, and all had a good time. The committee met at the conclusion of this first year experiment and decided to establish the tournament as a regular event. Further, since construction of the new hotel was making satisfactory progress, it was agreed that the field could be expanded in 1974.

In two years' time the tournament grew to sixty-four players and later it expanded to eighty before reverting back to sixty-four. In its second year the committee

The Shinnecock Hills clubhouse as seen from the ninth tee.

arranged for play on the nearby National Golf Links and the Maidstone course in East Hampton, a field of seventy-two players, twenty-four on each course each day. Although at one time the use of both National and Maidstone was discontinued, all three clubs today host the Invitational.

While the housing of guests in the new hotel was not up to the standards established at other Invitationals, there were several other factors that contributed materially to the success of the Shinnecock Hills Tournament. The quality and reputation of the golf course was certainly a major factor. Also, the three committee members, Sandy Johnson, Bob Carney, and Chuck Stevenson, who opened up their homes each year, and along with their wives entertained the entire field of visiting guests, contributed to the early success of the tournament. In addition, the Shinnecock Hills clubhouse, in its charm and simplicity serving as a reminder of golf in the past century, also provided excellent headquarters for all of the tournament activities and particularly the Saturday night dinner-dance complete with the most danceable music of Lester Lanin and his orchestra. In more recent years, the dinner has been held at Maidstone.

The National clubhouse.

The Maidstone clubhouse.

THE MONTEREY PENINSULA INVITATIONAL

In 1973 Roy Little expanded his committee to include the chairmen of each of
the Invitationals, so now it had six members all experienced in the running of these
events. He held a committee meeting on Monday afternoon during the Apawamis
Tournament and invited the officers of the Association to join in the discussion. The
possibility of a tournament on the Pacific Coast had been discussed at earlier meetings but no one could come up with the right person to put the tournament together. All agreed that they should try to organize such a tournament in 1974 and it was
suggested that Roy approach Thomas R. Dwyer who had just been appointed Western
Section representative on the Membership Committee and would become a Board
member at the annual meeting on Wednesday.

Dwyer was receptive to the idea. He said he would try to arrange an Invitational
on the Monterey Peninsula the latter part of April, at a time that would not conflict
with the tournament at Mountain Lake. The first thing to be done was to check on
hotel accommodations at the Del Monte Lodge. If they were available he knew that
play could be arranged automatically on the Pebble Beach and Spyglass courses and
the tournament would have a basis for getting underway. Fortunately, a sufficient
number of rooms were available from April 21 to 25, a perfect time for the tournament, and the contract was signed on the spot.

The local committee decided to select a third golf course from among the several outstanding layouts in that area. While Cypress Point was the one they had in
mind, they knew it would be difficult to get the approval of the Cypress Board, and
if approval came at all, it might take more time than the committee was willing to
risk. So, in order to put the tournament package together, they accepted a generous
offer that had been made by Monterey Peninsula, a private club which had two fine
eighteens of interesting design located next to Cypress Point. Now, with arrangements

completed to have the tournament on three golf courses of outstanding character and reputation, and located conveniently adjacent to each other, the committee was ready to make its announcement to the membership.

Considering the fact that there were only fifty US Seniors in the entire state of California, the tournament did well in its first year to attract forty-seven members, about half of whom were from the West Coast and the balance from the Midwest and East. Tournament format initially was stroke play, better ball of partners, gross and net, fifty-four holes over three days. A number of the visiting guests played a practice round at Cypress Point, a welcome privilege for those who were able to make such arrangements in advance.

The following year Dwyer was successful in his negotiations with Cypress Point and each year thereafter the relationship with the club was strengthened by the growing number of US Senior members of Cypress taking a more active interest in the tournament. In due course, the number of players increased to its maximum of sixty-four, and after five years of experimenting with various combinations of golf courses that included Cypress Point, Pebble Beach, Spyglass Hill, Carmel Valley, and Monterey Peninsula, the 1979 tournament was played only at Cypress Point. So now another tournament had been declared a success and the Cypress Point Club, where the chance meeting of Weller Noble and Hank Flower brought about the first Invitational at Ekwanok, became further involved as host of the original West Coast Tournament.

RESTRAINT AND UNIFORMITY

In June 1976, two months after the first West Coast Tournament, Roy Little, who had done so much to develop the invitational program, retired from the Board, and Syd Stokes was appointed to take his place and to become chairman of the Invitational Committee. By that time seven tournaments were in operation on eleven golf courses. In twelve years the number of annual entries increased from forty-one to over four hundred. There had been only one casualty, Point Judith, and even that tournament might have continued if hotel accommodations had been available. All tournaments were feeling the increase in demand each year and additional flights were added to keep up with the growing number of entries. While Ekwanok was the only one that had reached its expansion limit in 1976, it would not be long before the others would begin to feel the pressures of popularity.

Anticipating the problems of continued growth, Syd Stokes and his Committee went to work to expand the Invitational Tournament Guidelines to include priorities for inviting players, rotating players in over-subscribed tournaments, and a multitude of suggestions and ideas that had been tried and found to be successful. But the basic principles contained in the guidelines stressed the importance of safeguarding the prestige of the Association by maintaining "a quality of excellence, a high regard for the rules of golf, and by promoting the spirit of courtesy and sportsmanship expected in all aspects of the game."

Syd Stokes

The expansion of the Invitational program had met with a certain amount of caution on the part of some members. There were a few who felt that these events could detract from the Annual Championship at Apawamis, and in the long run, even change the character of the Association.

Reacting to this attitude, isolated as it was, the Board was somewhat guarded in reporting to the membership on the first "Regional" held at North Carolina and in announcing plans for the tournament at Point Judith the following year. The 1969 Yearbook referred to these tournaments as being "experimental" and that they would not "transcend the Annual Championship at Apawamis."

While the matter never became an issue, any expansion of the program was considered by the Board with a certain amount of restraint. Those on the Invitational Tournaments Committee, however, having had firsthand experience observing membership reaction to the program, firmly believed that these events would benefit the organization and even enhance the importance of the Apawamis Tournament.

During the summer of 1974 Stokes and his committee made a study of attendance at the various Invitationals and found that those who were supporting them were the same members who were playing at Apawamis, and on a more regular basis than the balance of the membership. At the same time, the committee noted that the growth in attendance at the Apawamis Tournament coincided with the expansion of the Invitational program.

When these facts were reported to the Board, the Invitational Committee and the Board both felt reassured that the expansion of these tournaments had taken place in an orderly fashion and that any further broadening of the program could be appropriately controlled within the specifications detailed in the Guidelines.

SEMINOLE

Some of the data included in the guidelines were simply "guidelines," others were rules that had been approved either by the Invitational Tournaments Committee or by the Board. One of the rules stated that no new tournament would be approved by the Board until after a "trial run" had been made by members of the Committee to check on accommodations, the golf course, and other facilities. Syd Stokes had discussed with Hank Flower the possibility of a November tournament at Seminole and Jupiter Island where Hank enjoyed membership in both clubs. They decided it was worth investigating and subsequently arrangements were made for a "trial run" in November 1974, the week before Thanksgiving.

Several members of the committee and members of Seminole were invited, along with their wives, to participate in the appraisal. From the very beginning it was evident that both clubs would be fully cooperative and welcome a tournament in the middle of November. The committee concluded that the combination of these facilities could only end up in a successful tournament and it was decided that a recommendation be made to the Executive Committee for a November 1975 tournament with William C. Ridgway, Jr. as chairman.

Soon after the Executive Committee gave its approval to proceed, Bill Ridgway sent a return postcard to the entire membership to determine the extent of interest in the tournament. Previously, his committee had decided that they would like to have a field of eighty players, a number that could be handled comfortably by both clubs. But, when the postcards were returned, 190 indicated they would be interested in the 1975 tournament and another 250 said they would like to play the following year.

Ridgway and his Committee were now confronted with the problem of expanding the field. But by how much? Facilities at Jupiter Island could easily accommodate additional guests, but in order to provide afternoon golf for Seminole members not playing in the 1975 tournament, it was determined that the field could not exceed ninety-six players, six flights of sixteen. They decided to

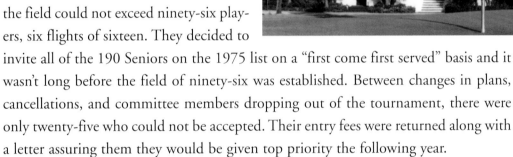

The Seminole clubhouse.

invite all of the 190 Seniors on the 1975 list on a "first come first served" basis and it wasn't long before the field of ninety-six was established. Between changes in plans, cancellations, and committee members dropping out of the tournament, there were only twenty-five who could not be accepted. Their entry fees were returned along with a letter assuring them they would be given top priority the following year.

As predicted, the tournament was a huge success. The Seminole Invitational today includes seven flights.

Seminole, a Donald Ross masterpiece, considered by some to be one of the finest courses ever created, was in top condition, and everyone, particularly Allan Ryan, Seminole's president, made the visitors feel welcome and at home. Likewise, Jupiter Island, an elegant club with an atmosphere of simplicity and informality, was an excellent choice for the Seniors and their wives. It provided a good golf course where the ladies could play each day and a Beach Club with spacious facilities and a variety of services. The Golf House Terrace was the scene of the welcoming cocktail party and the Beach Club provided an appropriate setting for the dinner-dance the night following the final round of the tournament. On that occasion prizes were awarded to tournament winners and it was obvious that everyone enjoyed themselves thoroughly.

As promised by Ridgway's committee, Seniors who could not attend the first year were invited to the 1976 tournament, and subsequently, a system of rotation was established for those who were anxious to attend on a regular basis. The rotation plan, which Seniors would refer to by telling others they had received one of "Ridgway's Dear John letters," gave applicants an opportunity to play at least once and the assurance they would be invited back again after they had been deferred for one year.

THE SENIORS' COLORS

A new US Seniors' flag, with the Association crest superimposed on the familiar colors worn in the necktie, was flown for the first time at the Seminole Tournament. It was the Invitational Tournaments Committee that requested the Board to develop such a flag, one that could be displayed at all tournaments. Board members Syd Stokes and John Wilbur were appointed to work on the project. It took several months to create a design, select colors and materials, and to have a prototype produced. When the finished flag was delivered a few days before the tournament it was raised for the first time on the tall staff adjacent to the Seminole clubhouse.

It was interesting to note that in the course of Stokes' investigation of the senior colors, it was revealed that they were originally developed by the Senior Golfers' Society, our sister organization in Great Britain, presumably in the early 1930s. In their history, *The Story of Senior Golf,* they refer to the colors "port and the sere and yellow leaf" as being distinctive and appropriate, and pointed out that they were worn by members of senior golf societies and associations in all parts of the English-speaking world and by the French, Dutch, and Belgians as well.

THE MIDWEST INVITATIONAL

At the June 1976 meeting of the Invitational Tournaments Committee at Apawamis, it was noted that seven of the eight Invitationals were in the east, the one exception Cypress Point on the West Coast. Syd Stokes had previously explored the possibility of a Chicago Tournament with John Ames, Morrison Waud, and Joseph Rich and he reported at the meeting that their reaction had been favorable. Bill Terrell, president of the Association, suggested that Syd Stokes and Bob Shaw, chairman of the Mountain Lake Tournament, attend the International Matches with Canada to be held the following month at the Old Elm Club in Highland Park for the purpose of investigating such a tournament with other Seniors in attendance.

They did get together at Old Elm with Ames, Waud, Rich, and several other Seniors who lived in the Chicago area, and this resulted in a decision to have a tournament the last week in July 1977 at Lake Forest, some twenty miles north of Chicago, and that play be arranged on three golf courses: Onwentsia, Shoreacres, and Old Elm. Joe Rich, chairman of membership for the Midwest section, agreed to serve as tournament chairman. He invited seven other Seniors representing each of the three clubs to serve with him on the local committee. At the outset they decided to call the tournament "The Mid-West Invitational" to suggest regional sponsorship and to encourage participation by Seniors living in the Midwest.

The three courses, all different in character, gave variety to the three days of play. Onwentsia, the oldest of the three, was located in Lake Forest on the Henry Cobb farm along Green Bay Road. The club had been organized in 1893 with a 7-hole course located on a bluff overlooking Lake Michigan. At the time the new course was built the Indian word "Onwentsia" was chosen as the name of the club, signifying a "meeting place for sporting braves and their squaws." Mr. Cobb's residence served as the clubhouse until 1919 when a new clubhouse was built, a magnificent English Tudor building equipped with spacious facilities that provides excellent headquarters for the Midwest tournament.

Shoreacres in Lake Bluff was founded in 1916 by a group of Chicago people that included such illustrious names as Field, Armour, McCormick, Insull, Ryerson, and Stevenson among the original incorporators. Construction of the Seth Raynor–designed course was delayed because of World War I and was not completed until 1921. The Shoreacres clubhouse overlooking the lake provides a gracious setting for a festive dinner-dance planned for the second night.

The Shoreacres clubhouse.

Old Elm, located in Highland Park just south of Lake Forest, was organized in 1913 by a group of Onwentsia members. It was for men only with golf as its sole feature. At the time, Onwentsia had a rule against Sunday golf, and, as most men worked six days a week in those days, Old Elm offered a satisfactory solution. The clubhouse, patterned after a Mexican hacienda, was designed by a well known Chicago architect, Benjamin Marshall, who served as house chairman for many years. The scene of US Seniors' 1976 International Matches with Canada, Old Elm provided an excellent third course and related facilities for the Midwest Invitational.

In its first year the tournament attracted the anticipated field of eighty players which included a half dozen local club members filling in as a result of last minute cancellations. Its success was declared by all who attended, thereby giving reassurance to an enthusiastic committee that the Midwest Invitational would become established as an annual event.

The Midwest Tournament brought the total number of Invitationals to nine by 1979. Each one, an annual event, was supported by a constantly changing nucleus of US Seniors who looked forward to returning to those tournaments they enjoyed year after year. From the small beginning of forty-one Seniors attending the first tournament in 1962, the number of participants in 1978 reached a high of 740, a number easily exceeding those playing in the Apawamis Tournament at that time.

The original purpose, to provide additional rounds of golf for those attending the Annual Championship, had gradually taken on the added dimension of bringing the membership closer together. At the same time the US Seniors were given the opportunity to play on a number of outstanding golf courses of recognized quality and reputation coast to coast. Whatever the outcome, the Invitational Tournaments program served to strengthen friendships within the Association and made each member aware of how privileged he was to be a US Senior. It will never be known whether or not Weller Noble had all this in mind.

A group of former presidents: seated (left to right) are Warren Ingersoll, Ellis Knowles, and Ike Grainger; standing (left to right) are James H. Ackerman, Gordon M. Hill, Henry C. Flower, James D. Miller, and William Ward Foshay.

New Foundations: 1962–1979

DURING THIS PERIOD, as described in the previous chapter, much attention focused on the new Invitational Tournaments which gave the
members additional opportunities to play together as a group, and at
some of the most desirable courses in the United States. Meanwhile, certain issues regarding the Annual Tournament and the International
Matches needed to be resolved.

Membership continued to be strong during these years, and a quota
system was used mandating that members play often enough to maintain
their membership and priority on the invitation lists of the various
Invitational Tournaments.

THE ANNUAL TOURNAMENTS

In an effort to contribute to the game of golf, the Executive
Committee in 1967 worked out the "Suggested Procedure For Faster
Play." Written by member Richard S. Tufts, the "Rules For Courtesy"
booklet was distributed to the members before the annual tournament
and helped improve the pace of play to an average of four hours per
round. Many clubs and organizations adopted these rules, and by 1970,
24,275 of the 25,000 copies printed had been sold, netting the USSGA a
profit of $713.87. In 1971 the USSGA decided to print 25,000 more
"fast play" booklets, including revisions made by Hank Flower and
Warner Shelly.

Richard S. Tufts of Pinehurst.

Richard S. Tufts

Richard S. Tufts, who passed away in 1980, was one of the founders of the Carolina Golf Association. Active with the Southern Golf Association, he served a term as president of the USGA (1956–1957). But he is best remembered for bringing Pinehurst worldwide prominence as a golf resort. Tufts published a book called "Rules of Golf," and was the non-playing captain of the 1963 United States Walker Cup team. A former director of the Western Seniors Golf Association, he served on the Board of the USSGA and the American Seniors Golf Association. He was honored in 1950 by the Golf Writers of America with the William Richardson Award for service to golf, and by the USGA in 1967 with the Bob Jones Award for his distinguished sportsmanship.

Beginning in 1966 the USSGA was able to have a doctor on call at each course during the entire annual tournament, at a cost of $60 per day. Also, United Hospital in Port Chester was made aware that a possible emergency could arise at the tournament. This, and other expenses, including $500 to both Apawamis and Westchester Country Club, mandated that the cost of playing in the annual tournament be increased from $20 to $25, and the cost of the dinner from $12.50 to $15.

In 1967, to speed play, the Board decided to reduce the entry to four hundred (rather than four hundred twenty), and to reduce the overall membership to nine hundred fifty. That, or use three courses and increase the membership to twelve hundred. It was also recommended that three station wagons be obtained to drive players to the tenth tee at Westchester; that was unnecessary at Apawamis due to the shorter distance.

Also in 1967 the annual tournament was moved from the last week of June to the first week to avoid the hotter weather.

In 1968 it was once again proposed that a third course, in addition to Apawamis and Westchester, be used for the annual tournament either for the championship flight or by the older players. Stanwich and Blind Brook were suggested for the two roles, respectively.

Another possible format suggested was a three-day tournament, with the members divided into three groups, two playing each day, with the group including the most senior players idle the middle day; provisions for outside play would be made available on the day off. Both proposals were sent back to the committee for further study; neither ever was used.

In 1970 Round Hill Club offered its facilities for the 1971 annual tournament, replacing Westchester Country Club which, because of the conflict with the Westchester Classic, had become unavailable. Lodging would still be available at Westchester Country Club, and a small bus or station wagon would be provided to transport members between Apawamis, Round Hill, and Westchester. During the early 1970s, many members used the Westchester Country Club for accommodations. The Stanwich Club nearby in Greenwich extended the use of its golf course to those members who remained in the area after the annual tournament.

Curiously, the Association's minutes in this period constantly referred to Westchester Country Club by its original name, the Westchester Biltmore, which the club had not used since 1929.

In 1972, 420 members played in the annual tournament at Apawamis and Round Hill. To speed up play, it was recommended that groups hit up on par 3s, that a ranger roam the course, and for a few years, that one member of each foursome be designated the official scorer, responsible for the pace of his group.

In 1972 a third course was once again proposed, and by October, an arrangement had been made with Blind Brook for the older seniors. Blind Brook agreed to host the A and AA classes for both their rounds in 1973, making possible an increase in the number of participants in the annual tournament at

Long-serving USSGA Secretary Everett Fisher and Prescott S. Bush, Jr.

Apawamis and Round Hill. A field of sixty-one competed at Blind Brook in 1973.

These changes notwithstanding, the putting contests, long a popular adjunct to the annual tournament, continued at Apawamis, with a separate winner named on both Tuesday and Wednesday.

Prescott S. Bush died in 1972, and later in the year James W. Walker announced a trophy, which was donated by him and his three brothers and the four sons of Prescott Bush. And so the Prescott S. Bush Memorial Trophy was established in 1973, to be awarded to the member achieving the low gross over 36 holes in those classes competing at Blind Brook. Jim Ackerman's became the first name on the Bush Trophy.

The annual dinner remained at Apawamis, preceded by cocktails on the terrace, with the traditional music of the bag-pipes before and Ben Cutler's Trio during the banquet. The Cutler orchestra played until Ben Cutler was in his nineties.

In 1976 the Membership Committee selected 65 new members from 476 applicants, and began considering whether membership should be by invitation rather than by application. The "Membership by Invitation" process was adopted in 1978, when 72 men were invited to become members, bringing the total membership to 944. As a result of the new methodology, a long waiting list was reduced sharply. To facilitate its mission of developing a truly national membership, the Membership Committee was reorganized in 1976 to include sectional chairs.

The British Senior Open Amateur Championship

The Royal and Ancient initiated its equivalent to the US Senior Amateur in 1969 when the first British Senior Open Amateur Championship was played at Formby. Three members of the USSGA have won the 54-hole stroke-play tournament. The first was J. C. "Johnny" Owens in 1984, and he was followed in 1985 by Dale Morey. More recently, Bill Shean won in 1999.

James D. Miller.

In 1979 prizes at the annual tournament were awarded to the overall champion and runner-up, as well as the winner and runner-up, gross and net, in each age category, with ties in these categories decided by the toss of a coin. Previously, there had also been awards for third low gross and net only. Today duplicate prizes are awarded in case of ties in all categories except for the overall champion, a practice that began in 2003.

THE INTERNATIONAL MATCHES

In connection with the International Matches, the practice of including veterans over sixty-five, which had been introduced informally a few years before, was given official status in the Devonshire Cup in 1962. Each team had eight players selected "at large" and four chosen from both of the age groups sixty-five to sixty-nine and seventy and over. This enhanced a long-standing practice of having sixteen players per side in the Devonshire Cup Matches, one dating back at least to 1933. Led by newcomer Joseph Morrill, Jr., the 1961 USSGA champion, the United States retained the Cup, and Old Elm received a Steuben bowl from the USSGA as a token of thanks for permitting its facilities to be used.

Fred Brand, Jr.

Fred Brand, Jr.

Fred Brand, Jr., of Oakmont won the Annual Tournament in 1965, his first year as a Senior.

The Pittsburgh-based insurance man won the West Pennsylvania Junior and Amateur Championships twice each and thereafter devoted his life to golf. He served as president of the Western Pennsylvania and Pennsylvania Golf Associations, served on the PGA National Advisory Board for almost four decades, and officiated at thirty US Opens and thrity-seven Masters. A member of the USSGA Executive Committee from 1959 to 1969, he was honored with the Bob Jones Award in 1997.

The Triangular and the Devonshire were again combined at Montreal in 1963. With three twelve-man teams competing for the Derby Cup and two sixteen-man teams for the Devonshire, matters became so confused as to cause Captain Jim Miller to remark in the Bulletin:

The scoring was somewhat complicated because of the fact that the Duke of Devonshire Cup was also competed for by the Canadian and U. S. teams – and the dual competition was played with 16-man teams, whereas the Triangular competition was played with 12-man teams. Sixsomes were played on the first day, August 29th, and singles matches on the final day, August 30th. Point scoring was not on a Nassau basis – just one point for each match.

The Triangular became a contest between Canada and the United States that year, and along with the Devonshire qualified among the most closely contested ever, to that time. With a side composed mainly of veterans, the United States in the end prevailed over such experienced Canadians as Somerville and Richardson and recent additions such as N. C. Barnabe, George Hevenor, and W. D. ("Bill") Taylor, who after seeing service in many intervening matches, took office in 1978 as the Canadian captain. The final scores for the Devonshire were 25½ to 22½, and for the Triangular 22½ to 19½ to 12 for the overmatched British team. On behalf of the United States team, USSGA President Gordon Hill presented a Steuben bowl to Royal Montreal.

The two International Matches were forever separated after 1963. Beginning in 1964 at Shinnecock Hills, the Devonshire was converted to a biennial event to be played in even number years and the Triangular to be in the odd years. That year there appeared in the United States lineup for the first time William S. Terrell, who later played in numerous International Matches (fourteen in fifteen years), and saw service as USSGA captain and president as well. Aided by the 2½ points Terrell and Joe Morrill scored in the foursomes and the ½ point Terrell pried from Sandy Somerville, the United States took the Cup 45½ to 36½.

In 1974 members of the USSGA were asked for voluntary contributions to a "Foreign Visitors Expense Fund" for the International Matches. For many years, the USSGA underwrote the expenses of the British and Canadian players for five days when they were in this country for the matches. It had always been a reciprocal arrangement, but did not cover the US Seniors in this country. The Fund was short-lived, and today all US Seniors competing in International Matches pay their own personal expenses away from the host club.

The Triangular Matches continued with twelve-man teams, although for many years the teams also included eight men over sixty-five brought along to continue friendships and compete informally. But while the formal team competed for the Derby Cup, the older men were left without competition. In 1973 it was decided to have a separate formal team of eight men over sixty-five, including four over seventy, compete at match play for a trophy to be put up by the Americans and Canadians. And so in 1975 the Knowles-Somerville Cup was introduced as a prize for this competition. The Derby Cup format continued to consist of six three-ball sixsomes on the first day, then twelve three-ball singles the second day, while the Knowles-Somerville play consisted of four six-ball foursomes and eight singles matches.

On the day before the match-play competition, the formal teams competed at stroke play for the Founders Cup, as they had done since 1934, while the supplementary group continued to compete for the Aitken-Salver, which was presented in 1969 by the widow of A. R. Aitken, who won the Founders Cup in 1936.

In 1976 a further change in format was agreed upon to take effect during the 1978 Devonshire Cup Matches. The competition would include three days of play at match play, in four-ball, foursomes, and singles play. The individual stroke play competition would be decided during the practice round.

The Knowles-Somerville Cup.

C. Ross "Sandy" Somerville

Charles Ross "Sandy" Somerville was born in London, Ontario, in 1903, and became an athlete of renown in football, ice hockey, and cricket, and also Canada's finest amateur golfer. In addition to other titles, be won the Canadian Amateur championship six times, and in 1932 he became the United States Amateur Champion, the second foreigner in history to do so.

Bobby Jones once wrote that his final victory in the Grand Slam of 1930 was made possible by a break in his first-round match in the United States Amateur which was against Somerville. Jones holed for a birdie from eight feet on the seventh hole to go one up, and he felt that had he not managed to do so, Somerville would have made his seven-footer and won the hole and the tide of play might have gone the other way. Sandy played the first 9 holes at even par, and found himself 4 down to Jones, then rallied to make the match very close.

Sandy won the Canadian Seniors four times, played in nine Devonshire Cup and six Triangular Matches, and served as Canada's team captain and president.

At the time of his death, Sandy Somerville was the USSGA's honorary Canadian member. He is a member of the Canadian Golf Hall of Fame.

Sandy Somerville (left) and Jim Knowles.

Team Play

Four USSGA officers were invited to play in an international team tournament marking Royal Montreal's one hundredth anniversary in 1973. William Ward Foshay, John Ellis Knowles, Warren Ingersoll, and Henry A. Wilmerding represented the USSGA for the celebration.

By 1976 Jim Ackerman had taken part in almost all the matches played in the preceding twenty years, not having missed one in the ten years through 1966 and only four in the next ten. Actually he played in eleven Devonshires, four Derby Cups and one Knowles-Somerville, and contributed 46 to his opponents' 45 points.

During the 1972 Devonshire Cup match at the Country Club of North Carolina, a caddie is quoted as saying, "well the card say 196, but it plays like 200."

In 1978 "Rab" Isham impressed everyone when he used a four-iron to ace the fourteenth hole at the Toronto Golf Club in the Devonshire Cup Matches. Rab called his home club, Old Elm, and asked the steward to set up drinks on him. Two senior members sleeping at the bar enjoyed his generosity. The club treasurer heard what had happened, and made up a bill for Rab that included three bartenders, an orchestra, champagne, hors d'oeuvres, and additional stuff . . .

International team captains Jim Knowles, Canada's Bill Taylor, and David Blair of Great Britain.

Ellis Knowles Remembered

After the death of Ellis Knowles on March 18, 1977, at age ninety-one, The Apawamis Club presented the USSGA with the John Ellis Knowles Key at the annual meeting on June 8.

In 1979 the USSGA presented to the R&A the John Ellis Knowles Trophy, a Steuben glass pyramidion, to be presented annually to the golfer aged fifty-five or over with the lowest combined aggregate net score for the spring and autumn medal meetings of the R&A.

Despite advancing age, Ellis Knowles continued to shoot his age or better, including four times in the Seniors' annual tournaments: 73 and 72 at age seventy-three, and 82 and 80 at age eighty-three.

Ellis Knowles spoke briefly and eloquently at the annual dinner in 1968 on behalf of changing the name of the organization to "The Senior Golfers' Society of the United States." His idea was referred to the Executive Committee, and ultimately not adopted. Meanwhile, Knowles was unanimously elected honorary president of the Seniors.

James B. "Jimmy" Knowles won the USSGA annual championship in 1971 and 1974, establishing the Knowles as the first father-son winners. In 1963 Robert W. Smith and son Robert Jr. played together for the fifth consecutive year.

In 1974 Gordon Hill was elected USSGA historian for life.

Bill Terrell was called SOB — sweet old Bill.

As a collegian, Joseph Morrill, Jr., was the goalie for Harvard's ice hockey team, and also played on the golf team.

David "Spec" Goldman, so-named because his face was speckled with freckles, won 165 tournaments on two continents in seven decades of competition. He was runner-up to Lawson Little in the 1934 US Amateur. He won the Texas Amateur and the World Seniors Championship (twice), and reached the finals of the Western Amateur, French Amateur, and the Trans-Mississippi, and the US Senior Amateur (twice). He served with the USGA Junior committee for more than twenty years. He won the annual tournament twice, in 1970 and 1972.

Curtis Person would often say, "My one rule is: never let business interfere with golf." Owner of a car dealership in Tennessee, Person won the Mississippi Amateur and Tennessee Open twice each as a young man, but attained his greatest success in golf once he became a senior. He won more than seventy-five senior championships, including the US Seniors, the US Senior Amateur, Eastern Seniors, Southern Seniors, North and South Seniors, International Seniors, and World Senior Four-Ball. Person was a co-founder and six-year chairman of the Danny Thomas Memphis Classic.

David "Spec" Goldman and Curtis Person.

Joseph C. Dey dedicated his life to service to golf. He served as executive director of the USGA from 1935 to 1968, then as commissioner of the PGA Tour from 1969 to 1974. He was named captain of the Royal and Ancient in 1975, and was honored with the prestigious Bob Jones Award in 1977.

Dale Morey had an outstanding competitive career, winning at least 261 tournaments, including the Southern Amateur and US Senior Amateur twice each, and was runner-up in the US Amateur (to Gene Littler) in 1953. Overall, he qualified for the US Amateur twenty-seven times. He played on three Walker and two World Cup teams. Morey once carded a 59 on a 6,500-yard, par-72 course! Administratively, he served as a director or officer of the Southern Golf Association from 1963 through 1990, including one term as president.

Dr. Edgar Rice "Ed" Updegraff of Boone, Iowa, was one of five brothers, all of whom followed their father into the medical profession, Ed as a urologist. He was the Iowa high school golf champion in 1939, and runner-up in the Iowa Amateur at age eighteen. He went on to win two Western and four Southwestern Amateur titles, reach the semi-finals of the 1963 British Amateur, qualify for the US Amateur seventeen times, play in the Masters six times, and win the US Senior Amateur in 1981, as well as two US Seniors' titles. He played on three victorious Walker Cup teams, and captained another. Curiously, Ed played cross-handed, reasoning that was the only way he could get the ball airborne. Never a long driver, he became a very skilled iron player. Ed received the Bob Jones Award in 1999.

Left: At Shinnecock Hills are Dale Morey and John Landen.

Dee Forte and Billy Joe Patton.

William J. "Billy Joe" Patton attained golfing immortality in 1954 when he nearly became the first (and only) amateur to win the Masters. The long-hitting Patton won the driving contest before the tournament, then put a charge into the final day's play when he aced the fifth hole. Patton lost the tournament when his second shot at the par-5 thirteenth found the creek, resulting in a double-bogie 7. Patton turned to his silenced gallery and said, "This is no funeral. Let's smile again." Ultimately, Patton finished one shot behind Sam Snead.

Patton's ace brought USGA executive director (and future US Senior) Joe Dey into play as the official with Patton's group. Patton's ball was wedged between the flagstick and the side of the cup, still in view as the players walked up. Dey advised Billy Joe to move the stick so that the ball would fall down into the hole, rather than just picking it out of the hole.

During his playing career, Billy Joe Patton won the North and South Amateur three times and the Southern Amateur twice. He was low amateur in the Masters and US Open twice each. He played on five Walker Cup teams, and was non-playing captain on another. He also played on four America's Cup and two World Cup teams. Billy Joe Patton won the Bob Jones Award for distinguished sportsmanship in 1982.

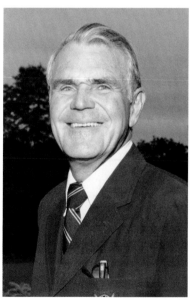

Jim Hand

James R. Hand has been a golfer all of his life, four decades of which he spent in service to the game, at first with the Westchester Golf Association, then with the Metropolitan Golf Association, and finally with the USGA, which he served as president from 1984 to 1986. Jim was chairman of the Championship Committee from 1978 through 1983, and was responsible for setting up US Open courses to be tough, but fair. Jim served the USSGA as treasurer from 1977 to 1983 and was team captain in 1989–1990. When asked, "Can you shoot your age?" Jim Hand once responded. "Yes, on a bad day."

The Competitions

The winner in 1962 was Congressman Jack Westland of Everett, Washington, playing from Burning Tree. He won a playoff over John A. Bartlett, 73 to 86. Westland was the 1952 US Amateur champion, runner-up to Francis Ouimet in 1931, and a three-time Walker Cup player. Although the advance entry was a new high, Black Monday, May 28, 1962, caused many last minute withdrawals; no scoring records were broken, and certainly some of the participants appeared in a state of shock after the market's sharp drop. A heavy rain fell on the first day, and a soggy course hampered the early players the second day.

The annual tournament in 1964 overlapped the Thunderbird Classic, also at Westchester Country Club, which gave the Seniors exclusive use of the South Course, 110 rooms, and a private room for dinner and lunch. The weather that year was fine until Wednesday noon, when dark clouds and heavy rain came and temperatures dropped. The rain continued for the remainder of the day, which was "not fit for man nor beast." Nonetheless, many of the Seniors continued to play. On the other hand, the Pro-Am on the West Course was held up at 2:00 P.M. and called off at 4:00 P.M.

In 1972 the average score on Round Hill's par-3 eleventh hole was 4.59. One foursome of Harvard classmates totaled 33 strokes on Apawamis' long par-5 ninth hole.

Right: Jack Westland

At the Invitationals

An important aspect of the Invitationals is that provision is always made for the wives attending. Golf is available, if not at the host club, then at a nearby club. Where possible, beach clubs are also made available.

At Ekwanok, the ladies have played a tournament at the Manchester Country Club and the new Dorset Field Club course, and likewise at the Jupiter Island Club during the Seminole Invitational.

William C. "Bill" Campbell

Few US Seniors have been more accomplished in golf than William C. "Bill" Campbell. A World War II vet and Princeton graduate, Campbell has been a lifelong resident of Huntington, West Virginia.

As a golfer, Campbell won the US Amateur in 1964, and qualified for the championship thirty-seven times, including thirty-three consecutively. He also played in fifteen US Opens and eighteen Masters, was runner-up in the 1954 British Amateur, and was a four-time winner of the prestigious North and South Amateur. He won the US Senior Amateur in 1979, and repeated in 1980. And finally, he played on eight US Walker Cup teams, one year (1955) as captain, and was undefeated in singles play, winning seven times and halving the other match. Bill once won a long-driving contest at the Masters, with Sam Snead second, using a driver Snead had given him a few years earlier.

Like many US Seniors, Campbell has given back to golf as much as he has taken from the game. He served on the USGA Executive Committee twice, first from 1962 to 1965, then a second term between 1977 and 1984, his final two years as president of the Association. In 1987 he was named captain of the Royal and Ancient Golf Club, becoming the first person ever to have headed both golf bodies.

Campbell was honored by the USGA in 1956 with the Bob Jones Award honoring distinguished sportsmanship, and has in more recent times been honored by a variety of other golfing organizations.

In the inaugural US Senior Open at Winged Foot East in 1980, Bill Campbell was runner-up to Roberto deVicenzo. In fact, the USSGA swept the first four amateur positions: Ed Tutwiler, Lew Oehmig, and John Kline were the second, third, and fourth low amateurs in the event. Campbell and Oehmig were the only amateur team ever to compete in the Legends of Golf.

Bill tells the story of flying to England with his wife so that he might attend a special dinner at Buckingham Palace with Prince Andrew and all the other living captains of the Royal and Ancient. At the end of the evening, after he had returned to his wife in the hotel, both reflected on what had transpired, and were amazed that such a thing could happen to an insurance salesman from a small town in West Virginia.

Bill Campbell and Joe Dey, two former captains of the R&A.

At the R&A's 250th Anniversary celebration in 2004 are Bill Campbell; Everett Fisher; and Prince Andrew, the Duke of York and R&A captain, with the Steuben glass bowl presented by the USSGA.

CHAPTER 12

The Modern Era: 1980–2004

WITH MEMBERSHIP BY INVITATION A REALITY IN 1978, the quality of the membership seemed assured. Yet the membership was large and active, and other problems had to be resolved. At the time, the USSGA membership was becoming more national, which was a stated goal of the Membership Committee. Another emphasis was on new members who were young, strong players to bolster the international teams. The membership was at 926 in 1982, and 440 of them played in the annual tournament. A couple of new membership rules were established in 1991: first, no member may propose two candidates the same year (now revised to "same time"), and second, no Board member may propose any candidate at all.

Notwithstanding the "slow play" booklets of 1967, slow play continued to be a concern, not only at the annual tournament, but now also at the Invitationals, in part because it could create host club member resentment. A small step was taken when a shotgun start was used for the Tuesday round at Blind Brook in 1981, then for both rounds there in 1982 when eighty-one "super seniors" played. A decade later, the same concern was raised once again. Not everyone playing in the annual tournament finished his round in four hours or less. The problem of slow play still exists, and remains a major concern of the Board.

> *The essence of our Association is the quality of its membership*
>
> — Samuel R. Callaway, president, 1984
>
> *It is said that there are no friends like old friends, and this may or may not be true. But at this stage in life, to make a new friend who becomes a good friend is very special.*
>
> — Spoken at Blind Brook, 2004

The use of the first and tenth tees at the annual tournament simply didn't solve the problem, and was discontinued in 2001. Of course, the stroke-play format of the tournament, in which every shot is counted, makes fast play difficult.

Although the membership was active, a good portion of them no longer were able to play golf, yet their presence on the roster prevented desirable younger men from attaining membership. In 1987 the Membership Committee pondered establishing an "Associate" class for those no longer able to play golf, but wishing to maintain their association with the USSGA and attend social events and the annual dinner without feeling that they should resign. This class was established in 1988, and twenty-five members immediately moved into the new category (allowing the election of an equal number of regular members). Associate membership carries with it reduced dues, but the member is no longer eligible to play in USSGA tournaments.

Long-serving Treasurer Peter Philip (right) and Tournament Committee Chairman Walter Robbins (left).

To pursue the objective of making the Association a truly national organization, great emphasis was placed by the committee on candidates from outside the Northeast. In 1982 the Western section was divided in two, one made up of the Great Plains and Mountain states and the other made up of the West Coast plus Alaska and Hawaii.

As the millennium approached, the annual tournament witnessed record turnouts. Three classes, A, AA, and AAA continued to play at Blind Brook each year, and a slight rearrangement was made in the ages defining classes D and E at Apawamis and Round Hill. At the beginning of 1996 there were 982 regular and 263 emeritus members. The annual tournament set another record in 2001, attracting 550 entries, 519 of whom played, both all-time highs. Starting in 2002 the Tournament Committee established a target of 470 players as the maximum number to compete in the annual tournament, and with this in mind they cut off acceptances at 520 players. This has worked quite well, and the number of players at each of the three courses has been balanced. However, the slow play problem, particularly on days with blistering heat as encountered in 2004, has not been totally solved.

Ouimet and Lowery Remembered

On September 20, 1988, three USSGA members at The Country Club, Ted Emerson, Bob Watts, and Bob Jenney, presented to the USSGA a large bronze plaque honoring Francis Ouimet's victory in the 1913 US Open there, seventy-five years earlier, and also honoring his caddie, Edward Lowery, also a USSGA member. The picture on the plaque is the same as the image on the US postage stamp issued commemorating the anniversary.

Right: Francis Ouimet, winner of the 1913 US Open.

The Metropolitan Golf Association

From 1930 to 1951 the USSGA maintained an administrative office of its own on Lexington Avenue. Then when "Golf House" was established by the United States Golf Association in 1951 at 40 East Thirty-eighth Street, space was rented there by the Seniors. It was in 1955 that the Seniors made arrangements with the Metropolitan Golf Association (MGA) to take over much of its day to day administrative work, including important administrative aspects of the annual championship.

In 1966 the MGA had to evacuate their quarters at Golf House, and obtained a larger area on the thirteenth floor at 60 East Forty-second Street, where the Seniors had their own room, with a conference room available for meetings. That arrangement prevailed when the MGA moved its offices to Mamaroneck (1981–1994) and then to Golf Central in Elmsford (1994–present).

Handling the USSGA's affairs over the years have been MGA staff members Betsy Hoagg, Kathleen Connick, Mary Cabriele, Mary McKay, Peggy Wise (1990–1999), and since 1999, Bernadette Bleichert, who is assisted by Lynn Turnesa. Among Bernadette's responsibilities today are administrative assistance with the tournaments, finances, preparation of yearbooks, maintenance of records of the association, and a host of miscellaneous matters in support of the officers. Every officer and committee chairman relies on her assistance.

Peggy Wise with James P. Gorter.

The USGA's Golf House in New York City.

Bernadette Bleichert with (left to right) Walt Robbins, Patton Kline, and George "Mickey" Poole.

Pictured at Round Hill Club in June 2004 are six of the seven living presidents: from left to right, Willard S. Heminway, Jr.; Edward C. Steele; M. Cabell Woodward, Jr.; John W. Eden; William F. Souders, and James P. Gorter. William T. Bacon was absent.

Walker Cup Team Members

Over the years, a significant number of USSGA members have been Walker Cup players. The list includes Bill Campbell, Johnny Dawson, W. C. Fownes, Bob Gardner, Vinny Giles, Watts Gunn, Bill Hyndman, Fred Kammer, Robert

Edgar R. Updegraff

W. Knowles, Max Marsten, Roland McKenzie, Dale Morey, Francis Ouimet, Billy Joe Patton, George Rotan, Jess Sweetser, Willie Turnesa, Ed Tutwiler, Dr. Edgar Updegraff, and Jack Westland.

Five future US Seniors have served as playing captains of Walker Cup teams, while seven have served as non-playing captains. They are William C. Fownes, Robert Gardner, Francis Ouimet, Willie Turnesa, and Bill Campbell as playing captains; Vinny Giles, Lew Oehmig, Francis Ouimet, Jess Sweetser, Richard Tufts, Jack Westland, and John Winters as non-playing captains.

THE INTERNATIONAL MATCHES

In 1990 it was decided that future Devonshire Cup teams would include four players seventy-five years of age or older.

By 1995 the format for the Triangular Matches had changed slightly. The friendly four-ball matches on the first day were scored using the Stableford system. The three days of competition consisted of individual stroke play, three-ball sixsomes matches, and singles matches. Each team included twenty players and two officials.

The Weller Noble Trophy, presented in 1980 by a group of USSGA members from California's Claremont Club, was awarded at the Triangular Matches to the low net score by a team member or an "officer delegate." Weller Noble was distinguished for having shot his age at least six hundred times.

A recent addition is the T^3, a tournament team trophy donated by the British team, open to all players in the individual stroke play competition. The trophy goes to the Association having the lowest combined scratch scores using four cards only. Included are two cards from players sixty-five years of age and over, one of whom is to be seventy or over. The first "T^3" competition took place at Muirfield in 1989.

Since 2002, the non-team member officials have competed at the International Matches each year in a 36 hole, medal play net competition for the Heminway Trophy, donated by then USSGA President Spike Heminway. John Powell, secretary of the Canadian Seniors, was victorious in each of the first two years with Heminway himself winning at Pine Valley in 2004.

All of the international team trophies are on exhibit in the USSGA alcove at Apawamis, except at the time of the International Matches, when they move to the host site.

In 1979 the USSGA started a program to offer standardized prizes at the Invitational Tournaments – Lenox China plates bearing the USSGA logo against a cream background with gold and burgundy surrounds. The winners of each flight, always in pairs, would receive an eleven-inch plate, while all other prize winners would get nine-inch plates. The only exception is Ekwanok, which continues to award a distinctive plate.

Dick Remsen's study is decorated with thirteen "winner's" plates from the Invitationals. Although the back of the plates say "not to be used with food," it is known that both Sam Reeves and Bill Bacon have served dinner and salad on these plates to large groups of Seniors and their wives.

Several new Invitational Tournaments have been added in recent years, starting with Sea Island in 1981, then Cape Cod in 1986, Indian River in 1992, and Palm Desert, California, in 1997. The Country Club, Somerset Hills, Castle Pines, and Garden of the Gods were each played for a few years before being discontinued for a variety of reasons, including concerns of conflicts with member play.

At the Invitationals

Ogden Risley made two holes-in-one at Mountain Lake in 1983.

In the first round of the first flight of the 2003 Desert Invitational at The Hideway, Chuck Rolles and Steve Clarkson played two pending USSGA candidates who were playing as substitutes. The match was tied at the completion of 18 holes, and still tied after 5 sudden death holes when darkness arrived. Jack Mettler, who was running the tournament, directed both teams to appear at 8:00 A.M., an hour and a half early the next morning, so that the match could be completed before the second round began. After seven more holes, the match remained deadlocked, and Mettler ordered a chip-off from 30 yards, which Clarkson won. Clarkson and Rolles went on to win their next two matches and the First Flight plates. The contestants mentioned afterwards how much fun their first-round match had been, how they joked about keeping it alive until sundown, and how the two members joshed with the two candidates about how impolite it would be for them to win.

One year at Seminole, playing from the blue tees, Paul Wise and Dick Thigpen were 3-down to Lee Ford and Jim Hoeffer after 12 holes. Six birdies followed as everyone played well: Dick at the thirteenth, Paul at the fourteenth and fifteenth to tie the match, Lee at the seventeenth to regain the lead, Dick at the eighteenth to force extra holes, then finally Paul at the twentieth hole to win the match.

Remember the night at Mountain Lake when Monte Bee sat at the piano singing "The Tadpole Boogie"?

Chuck Stevenson once fainted on the green at Seminole, right behind his ball, perfectly lined up. Since he was away, his partners waited, until one of them said, "God, Chuck is really taking this seriously!"

One year at the Mountain Lake Invitational, Ted Krug aced the tenth hole, his shot hitting the pin quite hard. Jack Mettler, one of his opponents, beat him to the green, tossed a ball into a greenside bunker, and informed Krug of his "fate." Just as Krug was about to play his bunker shot, his partner, Buzz Taylor, who was in on the prank, announced, "Hold on, looks like there's a ball in the hole!"

Lew Oehmig once holed a long putt out of a dry hazard at Seminole using one of the early long putters.

In the finals of the 2004 Sea Island Tournament, former US Amateur champion Vinny Giles and his partner, John Fogarty, won over reigning US Seniors champion Peter Roby and his partner, Holcombe Green. Despite their age, both Giles and Roby played to 0.3 handicap indices!

The original Cloisters at Sea Island

SEA ISLAND

The Sea Island Invitational started in March of 1981 under the leadership of chairman Carson Lyman, and has continued to the present with the one exception noted below. Among the barrier islands along the southeastern coast of Georgia, Sea Island was purchased in 1926 by Howard Coffin, who already owned two thousand acres of the Retreat Plantation on adjoining St. Simon's Island that would become the Sea Island Golf Club.

Coffin planned to develop a world-class golf resort at Sea Island, and in 1926 engaged Walter Travis as his golf architect. Travis died after completing just the Plantation 9, and the English firm Colt and Alison was hired to complete the Seaside 9. At the same time, Coffin and his cousin, Bill Jones, began building the Addison Mizner designed Cloister Hotel, which opened in October 1928. The property has been operated through the years by the Sea Island Company under the leadership of the Jones family, with Bill Jones III now serving as its chairman. Two other 9s, the Retreat and Marshside, were added in 1959 and 1973, respectively. The Retreat 9 was designed by Dick Wilson, Marshside by Joe Lee.

Four chairmen of the Sea Island Invitational, from left to right: Bill Frederick, George Walker, Cartan Clarke, and Michael Joyce, the current chairman.

THE COUNTRY CLUB/SOMERSET HILLS

The annual report of 1983 noted the plan for another satellite at The Country Club in Brookline, Massachusetts, in 1984, and also noted that the USSGA was looking for a third site for an event immediately after the annual tournament. Somerset Hills played that role for four years, starting in 1985. Both satellite tournaments were soon discontinued, however, because of conflicting demands for member play.

CAPE COD

The Cape Cod Invitational started in 1986 as a replacement for the two-year early-June Invitational at The Country Club. Robert Watts had chaired that event, but found irreconcilable conflicts with the Board of Governors over the early-June dates. When it became clear that The Country Club would not be available in 1986, George Rowland, a member of both The Country Club and Wianno, suggested to Norman

The Wianno clubhouse.

Boucher, a Senior who was chairman of the Wianno Golf Committee, that he put together a group to take on the job of initiating and running an early-June tournament. Norm Boucher, aided by his wife Phyllis, and a number of other US Seniors in the Osterville area, did an excellent job of getting this event on the calendar and off to a good start.

The Cape Cod Invitational was played at three clubs – Wianno, Hyannisport, and Oyster Harbors – in both 1986 and 1987, and again at all three clubs every year since 1997, giving visitors to Cape Cod three very different and challenging courses. In all but one of the years 1989 to 1996, Wianno was joined by one of the other two clubs as tournament host. The Willow Bend Golf Club was co-host in 1989.

Wianno has been the host site from the beginning because of its large hotel facility on Nantucket Sound. The club can accommodate large gatherings in its dining room and ballroom. In addition, a number of attractive guest rooms make the Wianno Club an excellent headquarters.

COLORADO

The Castle Pines Invitational started in September 1987, and had great significance geographically. It lasted through 1992, when the Castle Pines membership decided that the club could no longer give up so many dates at the end of the season – the club also hosted the PGA Tour's stableford event in late August.

In 1994 a short-lived Invitational was established at Garden of the Gods in Colorado Springs chaired initially by Bob Boucher. Early in the twentieth century, Katharine Lee Bates was so impressed by the beauty of the area that she was inspired to write "America the Beautiful." Each year at the tournament dinner, the Seniors were entertained by a group of Air Force Academy cadets who were part of a "song and dance club" at the academy. At the end of their revue they stood straight and tall and sang "America the Beautiful," and then invited the seniors to stand and sing with them. Any senior who was there will tell you it was an inspiring and "spine-tingling" experience, one they will never forget. The demise of the Garden of the Gods Invitational can be attributed to the fact that there were relatively few USSGA members in the general area and fewer still on site to manage the tournament.

INDIAN RIVER

In the late 1980s many USSGA members who resided in or visited Florida believed that a third USSGA Invitational Tournament in Florida was desirable, and could be successful. Initially there was some reluctance on the part of members of the Executive Committee, some of whom felt there already were a sufficient number of Invitationals. The green light was finally given in 1991, however, with the Riomar Country Club in Vero Beach designated as headquarters for the Indian River Invitational, which would commence the following year (1992). The large number of Seniors, as well as excellent golf courses and private clubs, in the area made the location a natural for the new tournament. The tournament was scheduled for the last week of April, when the heavy seasonal play on the area's courses would have abated somewhat as the South Florida snowbirds were starting to head north.

The Riomar clubhouse.

Riomar has continued to be the host club for thirteen years. Until recently it also was the site for the final matches, but a few years ago some members of the tournament committee felt that a stronger challenge was needed for the last day. The practice round and mixed couples tournaments have continued at Riomar, with the ensuing Seniors' matches at Hawk's Nest (a participant since the first year) and John's Island West (to be succeeded by RedStick in 2005), then the final matches at Bent Pine. The Indian River and Windsor courses were used in the Invitational's early years.

The tournament's social activities are varied, starting with a welcoming barbecue on Monday night at Riomar. Various USSGA members host "heavy hors d'oeuvre" parties on Tuesday. A dinner-dance the evening before the finals was hosted for many years by the now defunct Riomar Bay Yacht Club, then more recently at John's Island and then Bent Pine. An awards luncheon follows the completion of match and consolation play.

With approximately one hundred USSGA members residing in the Vero Beach area, the tournament could be very locally oriented. The committee chairman, however, encourages maximum "out of area" participation, and attempts to limit the percentage of local residents. The tournament was chaired by Ralph King for the first five years. The Invitational's thriving traditions will continue in spite of the fact that the region was slammed by Hurricanes Frances and Jeanne in a three-week period in 2004.

The Palm Desert

The idea of having another Invitational Tournament in California was proposed by Ray Knowles to Norm Boucher initially in 1995. After much discussion, the tournament was approved and scheduled for December 1997 at The Vintage Club in Indian Wells with the helpful assistance of Ralph King, the Invitationals chairman at the time. The first tournament was oversubscribed by twenty-nine, and the sixty-four who did attend came from thirty-four different states. Everyone had a great time, including the wives who also played at The Vintage Club.

The 1998 tournament was canceled when The Vintage Club became unavailable. The Palm Desert Invitational was then played on three different courses in 1999, the Citrus Course at La Quinta, Rancho La Quinta, and Eldorado Country Club. Eldorado was replaced by the new Pate Course at Rancho La Quinta, but a date later in December limited attendance. Eldorado returned as host in 2001, when the new Reserve Club was added, and Tuesday night dinners in members' homes advanced the event to a new social level. The Pate Course replaced The Reserve Club in 2002, and then in 2003 the Thunderbird Country Club and The Hideway joined with Rancho La Quinta as venues. The golf course at Eldorado, the event's perennial host club, was completely torn up in 2003, and replaced by a new Tom Fazio design. It hosted the 2004 tournament along with The Reserve, Rancho LaQuinta, and Bermuda Dunes.

THE WEATHERMAN IS NOT A SENIOR

The weather has often played havoc with the Invitationals schedule. In 1982, for example, Seminole was canceled after downpours, then thunderstorms, on the first day prevented the use of carts on the second day. In 1991 Kittansett was severely damaged by Hurricane Bob. The Invitational was canceled, and a donation made to the club by the USSGA to assist in repairs.

In 1996 Ekwanok was very wet, and Kittansett was washed out. And in 1998 Cypress Point was inundated, and therefore canceled. In 1999 the Cypress Point and Indian River Invitationals were disturbed by bad weather, and Hurricane Floyd wiped out the second day at Kittansett.

Sea Island and the Country Club of North Carolina both were under construction in 1999, and the tournaments were moved to the Hampton Club in South Carolina and to three courses in the Pinehurst area, with everyone finishing up at Pinehurst No. 2. The Kittansett Invitational was canceled in 2001, scheduled as it was one week after September 11. A contribution was made to the club in recognition of its preparations for the Invitational. In 2003 at Seminole heavy rains washed out much of the second and all of the third day.

Jonathan Clark (left) with Roy Plum, chairman of the Seminole Invitational. Clark, in the absence of his partner, had just lost a three-hole putt-off for the first flight plate at the rainy 2003 tournament.

OTHER HAPPENINGS

In 2000, a special two-day invitational tournament with its own format was scheduled in Santa Barbara, California. Played at the Valley Club and Birnam Wood, this tournament continued into 2004, and was contested either just before or following the Cypress Point Invitational. This tournament has now been discontinued. In recent years, USSGA members have also played in a number of informal events. These include a one-day tournament at San Francisco Golf Club immediately following the Cypress Point Invitational and informal gatherings frequently held among Seniors on Nantucket Island or Cape Cod, and in Florida.

In 1988 the USSGA presented a plate to the Country Club of North Carolina recognizing more than fifteen years of Invitational Tournaments there, expressing the Seniors' gratitude. Similar plates were presented to Ekwanok, Lyford Cay, Mountain Lake, Cypress Point, Shinnecock Hills, and Kittansett for fifteen-plus years in 1989.

All Invitationals are conducted at scratch, with eight teams per flight, arranged by the tournament committees. They have become the backbone of the organization. The players either stay at the host club, local hotels, or in the homes of USSGA members. The first day of the event is reserved for a practice round or a mixed tournament. The actual tournament takes place on the final three days, with a "beaten" competition for those losing on the second day that has been played in a variety of formats.

Note that at the Invitationals, there is no such thing as a championship flight; rather, a first flight including the sixteen low handicap participants, and then typically an additional four or five flights. The same prizes are awarded to all flights, and half the contestants win a prize. And rumor has it that Albert B. Crutcher may have won as many plates as Richie Remsen, although not all in the first flight. While all of the Invitationals share the same golf format, they each enjoy their own special flavor.

As one member put it, the annual tournament is the one place where a member must suffer alone on his own ball; nonetheless, they usually come back to see everybody, year after year. The nametags everyone wears facilitate the renewal of old friendships. The Invitationals, on the other hand, are designed as anything but lonely competitions. Through the participation of spouses and the wonderful social events, together with the match-play team format where one often plays with a new partner, the acquaintance chain is generally lengthened substantially for the membership and their spouses.

Visitors From Across the Sea

Following the lead of the British Seniors and the Canadian Seniors in making international competitions available to members who probably would not be on the Triangular or Devonshire Cup teams, twelve British Seniors, most of them with wives, were guests of the US Seniors in 1986 and played matches with them at The Country Club, Round Hill, Somerset Hills, Gulph Mills, and Merion.

This trip was so successful for both sides that it was repeated in 1990 when twelve US Seniors, nine with wives, played matches in the London area, in East Anglia, in Lancashire, and finally at Prestwick against ten different teams of British Seniors. Most of the matches were foursomes (alternate shots) and generally the guests stayed in the private homes of the hosts.

In September of 1997 twelve British Seniors visited Lake Forest, Illinois, and also went to the Twin Cities in Minnesota, playing as many as ten matches with US Seniors. And in 2000 a group of thirteen US Seniors, most accompanied by golfing wives, made the trip to England to play ten courses, including many lesser known ones, and they were followed in 2003 by a group of British Seniors who visited Florida during the month of February. Their journey started in Orlando, moved to Florida's west coast, then proceeded across "Alligator Alley" to Seminole and Jupiter Island, and concluded in Vero Beach.

The Memorial Fund

Following up on a suggestion by Bill Bacon, in 1995 the Association established a Memorial Fund with its own tax exempt status and independent trustees, initially George Hauptfuhrer, Bill Bacon, and Everett Fisher. Peter Philip has recently been added to the list of trustees. Charitable donations were encouraged to be made to the Fund in memory of particular USSGA members or in general support of the Fund itself. The Fund in turn makes contributions to other I.R.S. approved charities. Contributions were to be directed to golfing activities such as junior golf, environmental and horticultural organizations, and scholarships.

The Memorial Fund climbed over $100,000 in 2000. In recent years it has made contributions to the Foundations of the Metropolitan and Connecticut State Golf Associations (the latter's major iniative is the First Tee), and to the scholarship funds of host clubs of the invitational tournaments.

The Competitions

Since 1971 all but one champion of the annual tournament has taken less than 150 strokes for 36 holes. The three lowest remain Tommy Robbins' 140 in 1951, and 141s by Johnny Dawson in 1960 and Ed Tutwiler in 1978.

The bagpipers who play at Apawamis for the annual tournament each year.

The annual championship had not lost a day to the weather until 1980, when heavy rains and two electric storms wiped out Tuesday's play. The weather interfered again for the second time in five years in 1985, when the second day was canceled.

For the first time ever in 1988, there were co-champions at the annual tournament, Team Captain Dr. Ed Updegraff and Jim Vickers, who tied at 147. Heavy rains on Thursday canceled their 18-hole playoff, and resulted in a new rule for playoffs: sudden death, weather permitting, starting at the first hole.

Dr. Updegraff won the annual tournament again in 1992 in his third decade as a Senior (he also won in 1979).

Playoffs are not uncommon, and often correlate with wet weather. The annual championship in 1993 went into sudden death at Apawamis. Jack Hesler of Scioto, a former winner of the Indiana and Ohio Amateurs, finished early with a pair of 74s for 148, then had to wait out a two-hour rain delay from 3:00 P.M. to 5:00 P.M. When play resumed, David Zenker of Morristown, New Jersey, birdied his last two holes (the eighth and ninth at Apawamis) as dusk fell to card his second 74 and tie Hesler. Both hit the first green in regulation after teeing off at 8:00 P.M., and Hesler got down in 2 putts to win the title.

There was a three-way playoff in 1999 between two former champs, Jack Hesler and Harcourt Kemp, and Larry Bell of Saucon Valley. Some fifty to sixty Seniors in blue blazers followed them down the first fairway at Apawamis as the playoff commenced. Kemp's approach bounced over the green, leading to a bogey that ended his chances as Hesler had a regulation par, while Bell holed a 15-footer to stay alive.

On the second hole (Apawamis' eighteenth) Bell hit his drive up against a tree. It was no typical Apawamis tree, however. It had been planted shortly before the tournament "to harbor fear in the minds of those who would play down the left side to avoid the out-of-bounds on the right." As Larry approached his ball, he found a gallery of Seniors assessing his predicament, which included a tree branch in his face as he addressed the ball. "With every Senior present awaiting my decision, I chose the hero's approach rather than a wimp out with a chip shot to the adjacent fairway. I put my best "eyes closed" swing on it, and the ball came muffling out about twenty yards closer to the green." Larry took a bogie, and lost the championship to Hesler's routine par.

The championship was shortened in 2000 because of wet weather — four and one half inches of rain fell on Tuesday, completely canceling both days at Blind Brook. Wednesday's leaders at Round Hill (Vinny Giles) and Apawamis (William Ploeger) won the right to compete in a sudden death play-off. After both narrowly missed birdies on the first hole, and after Ploeger narrowly missed on the eighteenth, Giles holed his birdie putt to win.

In a similar situation in 2003, heavy rains drenched the courses on Wednesday morning, canceling regular play. James W. "Billy" Key had shot 70 at Apawamis in his Tuesday round, while Peter B. Roby and J. Phillip Patterson had shot 74s at Round Hill, and the three of them had to play-off to decide the championship. Their window of opportunity came early Wednesday afternoon when the rains let up, and the playoff course consisted of the fifteenth and sixteenth holes high on the ridge, which were relatively dry. Key bowed out on the first playoff hole, but Roby and Patterson continued for five additional holes (with bogie being their best score) before Roby holed a twelve-foot putt for par and the victory.

Harcourt Kemp, three-time USSGA champion and current vice-president, shot a 68 at Apawamis in 1998 after playing the first 11 holes 7 under par.

When Cab Woodward was chairman of the annual tournament committee, he unselfishly refrained from playing in order to patrol the courses so as to lend assistance wherever needed, a protocol followed by each succeeding chairman. At one point at the ninth green at Apawamis, he was informed that one contestant had confronted a problem in the form of a sticky mass of bubblegum just off the green, to which his ball had become thoroughly stuck. Upon request, Cab ruled that the player in question was correct in having taken relief by dropping another ball within one club length not nearer the hole. One of the other contestants had disagreed, so the player involved had to play two balls, one with relief and one without.

Later on, back in the Clubhouse, a telephone call was placed to Golf House at Far Hills and the problem was presented to Tom Meeks, the USSGA Rules guru. The response came back to the member who was opposed to the granting of relief "I am sorry, Mr. Bloch, but Mr. Woodward is quite correct and we will consider including this situation in the next Rules of Golf decision book published by the USGA." When Cab Woodward realized that he had questioned the then president of the USGA, he confessed that he would not have been so adamant if he had been aware of Stuart Bloch's identity. "If I had known who I was dealing with, you would have had a completely different ruling," Woodward joked.

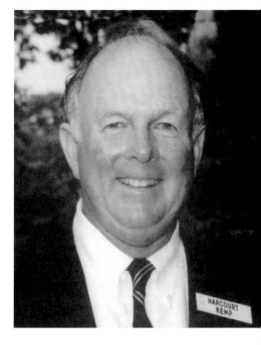

Harcourt Kemp

The short eleventh hole at Round Hill, the par 3 across the pond, has often spelled "disaster" for unfortunate Seniors. None other than Billy Joe Patton once shot a 12 there (it was his second hole of the day). And one day a foursome took a total of 43 strokes there, including one par. In 2003 two members were heard commenting that they hadn't slept well for three months anticipating playing the feared eleventh hole — only to have their round at Round Hill canceled by rain.

In his first annual tournament, Fred Yarrington shot an 11 on the eleventh hole at Apawamis, then another 11 on the eleventh at Round Hill. His golf improved, thankfully, and a couple of years later, he finished 3-4-2 at Apawamis, and says he was most proud of the 3 on the tough par-3 sixteenth hole.

One golfer hit his caddie on the head at Apawamis' eleventh hole, and the ball caromed out of bounds, giving the perpetrator two different two-stroke penalties, and a second chance off the tee.

Bill Souders

At Apawamis during the annual tournament, USSGA members often park their cars alongside the eighteenth fairway. Many have sliced in that direction, but one member with very precise radar sliced a dent into his own car!

About five years ago I was paired with John Sienkiewicz, Bill Walker, and Dick Woolworth. We had just finished playing the 14th hole and had started up the hill to the 15th tee when Sienkiewicz hollered, "I'm going to get a coke. Go ahead and hit. I'll be right there." He caught up, hit away, and we proceeded down the fairway to find our tee shots.

We quickly found Bill and Dick in the left rough, and I was certain the ball in the fairway was mine, but it turned out to be John's. Where was my ball? Dick suggested it must have kicked to the right towards the trees. I was sure I'd hit it down the middle, and Bill Walker, lending vehement support, said "I know it was down the middle, I saw it. It has to be just in the edge of the rough."

While the search continued, something told me to search my pockets, and much to my embarrassment, there it was. I'd found my ball. The bottom line: I had forgotten to tee off.

— Sam Fleming

They Came To Play

Three USSGA members, Joe Dey, Francis Ouimet and Bill Campbell, have been the only American Captains of the Royal and Ancient Golf Club.

Former USGA President Isaac B. Grainger was a USSGA member starting in 1951 (and president from 1959 to 1961), and his son, Ike, Jr., has been a member since 1975. Thomas M. Bloch became a member in 1965, and son Stuart Bloch has been a member since 1989, and served as USGA president 1992–1993.

Lew Oehmig and Maury Hanson.

Two former Met Amateur champions from the distant past, Gardiner White (1921) and T. Suffern "Tommy" Tailor, Jr. (1932, 1934) were USSGA members.

USSGA members Prescott S. Bush (1950–1971) and Marvin Pierce (1948–1966) were the fathers of George and Barbara Bush.

Lewis Oehmig of Lookout Mountain, Tennessee, won the Tennessee Amateur eight times spanning five decades from 1937 to 1970. He won the US Senior Amateur three times, and was three times the runner-up. He served as captain of the 1977 US Walker Cup team at Shinnecock Hills, and was USSGA team captain from 1981 to 1983. He also won the Bob Jones Award.

Howard Clark received the Herb Graffis award for his many contributions to golf.

Downing Gray was the non-playing captain of the US Walker Cup team at Quaker Ridge in 1997.

In 2002 Everett Fisher retired after serving twenty-one years as USSGA secretary and was replaced by Jonathan M. Clark. While the job of overseeing the annual preparation of the yearbooks was originally the responsibilty of the vice president, this demanding task was assigned to the secretary beginning in 1982. As a result, Everett was responsible for the yearbooks from 1982 to 2002.

It has been said that Everett Fisher possesses the Association's memory. Everett was inducted into the Connecticut Golf Hall of Fame in 2001, for his years of service as a director and secretary to the Connecticut State Golf Association. He has also been named an honorary member of the British Senior Golfers' Society, and has served for many years as a special intermediary in the United States for the Royal and Ancient Golf Club. Among his other accomplishments, he was president of Round Hill Club from 1967 to 1970.

Thomas G. Cousins is a major real estate developer in the Atlanta region, known for rebuilding depressed neighborhoods. Recently, he rebuilt the East Lake Club, its golf course and surrounding neighborhood. East Lake is where Bobby Jones learned the game.

Bill Souders served as USSGA president from 1991 to 1993 and as team secretary 2001–2004, and has been a great player for many years. In fact, with different partners, he won both the Lyford Cay and Seminole Invitationals in 2004.

There have been enough Yale Wiffenpoofs in the USSGA to provide entertainment at the annual dinner for a number of years. Prominent among them were the quartet of John Griswold, Stowe Phelps, and Bob and Crawford Johnson. Current President John Eden was also a "Whiff."

Winchester Hotchkiss, a great-grandson of Horace Hotchkiss, has been a US Senior for twenty years, and is the first descendant of the founder to become a member. His brother, Horace Hotchkiss IV, is a tennis player and has never touched a golf club. Horace Hotchkiss II played golf, but not as a US Senior, and Horace Hotchkiss III died before age fifty-five.

As a golfer, Maurice Smith shot his age nearly every Fourth of July, which was his birthday. He was a balloonist during World War I, spotting American artillery for a young colonel named Douglas MacArthur. He was shot down into a river near Bastogne, but survived to become an active member of the USSGA.

Burton Hawerg is noted as a "one-man army," who showed tremendous valor in hand-to-hand combat against the Japanese in World War II. A Maryland tennis champion and Harvard baseball captain, he won the Navy Cross on Saipan. He later became managing partner at Alex Brown, the oldest investment bank in the United States, one that had helped finance the War of 1812.

William "Buck" Kernan, a relatively-new member from Pinehurst, is a retired four-star general who, during an illustrious career in the United States Army, was a Ranger, commanded the 18th Airborne Corps, and served in Vietnam and Panama. He served recently as an advisor in Iraq.

In 1994 *Sports Illustrated* named US Senior Roone Arledge the third most influential person in American sports in the last four decades (behind Mohammed Ali and Michael Jordan). In 1990 a *Life Magazine* poll included Arledge among the "100 Most Important Americans of the 20th Century." President of ABC Sports from 1968 to 1986 (and the president of ABC News), Arledge brought Americans NFL Monday Night Football, 20/20, and World News Tonight among numerous other television innovations.

Marvin M. "Vinny" Giles is one of the most accomplished of the US Seniors, having won both the US Amateur (1972) and British Amateur (1975). He is a seven-time Virginia Amateur champ, has been low amateur in the Masters, US Open, and US Senior Open, has played on four Walker Cup teams, and was Walker Cup team captain in 1993. Since 1973 he has been president of Octagon Golf, a firm that provides management services to professional golfers. He was USSGA champion in 2000 and 2001.

Rees Jones, one of the leading golf course architects of the day, is an active member of the US Seniors. A son of Robert Trent Jones, Rees has become as noted for his work preparing courses (such as Bethpage Black, The Country Club, Congressional, Baltusrol, and Medinah) for the US Open as for his own creative work, courses like Atlantic and The Bridge on the east end of Long Island, Nantucket, Haig Point off Hilton Head, Ocean Forest at Sea Island, and RedStick at Vero Beach.

Vinny Giles

Triangular captains are, from left to right, David Blair, Ed Ervasti, and Howard Clark.

In 1997 Canadian team secretary Bill Maize shot a 71 on his seventy-first birthday to help the Canadians win the Knowles-Somerville Cup by one point at the Toronto Golf Club.

When shown the list of USSGA team members for the Devonshire Cup matches in 1982, a sterling group of golfers, USSGA President William V. Platt commented to Team Captain Lew Oehmig, "They obviously have been selected for their lively sociability, their propensity for booze, and their enduring love for the opposite sex." Needless to say, they were victorious.

When Rick Runkle suffered a back injury in July of 1986, and had to withdraw from the Devonshire Cup team, Captain Bill Campbell called Lincoln "Link" Kinnicutt, who happened to be fishing in some icy, rushing river in Iceland. When Campbell's message reached him, Link rushed "directly" to the airport and headed for Royal Ottawa, where he helped win 8 of a possible 9 points. Ray Getliffe, a former Canadian hockey star, won the George S. Lyon Cup with a net of 70.

The Honors Course used for the Devonshire Cup matches of 1992 had a slope rating (151 from the championship tees) second only to Pine Valley at the time. Nonetheless, in one foursome, Don Hewson of Canada took 26 putts, while the USSGA's Bill Black took 24, and had five birdies.

At the 1993 Triangular Match held at Pinehurst, Donald Ross, Captain of the British Senior Golfers' Society, was often seen posing next to the Donald Ross statue, emulating the swing of the statue's honoree. There were two aces on the No. 2 course in the practice round, by Eli Tullis of USSGA and Glen Seely of Canada. The match between Ed Updegraff and Michael Lunt reenacted the semifinals of the 1963 British Amateur (which Lunt won) and a match in the 1965 Walker Cup – their 1993 match ended even. Canadian Senior Ed Ervasti, age seventy-nine, had a gross 74 in the opening day medal play on Pinehurst No. 6.

Team captains and association presidents at Capilano in 1985. Seated (left to right) are Howard L. Clark, Justice G. R. W. Owen, and Sir John Carmichael; standing are David Stirk, Ray Getliffe, and William J. Patton.

The weather for the 1999 Triangular Matches at Castle Pines went from beautiful for the practice round, to cold and windy on the first day (scores were in the 90s instead of in the 70s), snow on the second day, postponing play, and beautiful again on the final two days.

Eight men who had played in ten or more International Matches were honored at the 2002 match in Canada. They were: Jack Hesler, Bill Souders, Bill Black, Billy Key, Jim Frost, Chuck Van Linge, John Owens, and Richie Remsen. The latter two have played in an amazing nineteen and twenty-five matches, respectively.

In 2000 Harcourt Kemp underwent surgery on the day after the annual tournament. A few weeks later, at the International matches at the Honors Course, one US player dropped out, and Kemp substituted, playing very well while "swinging easily."

One year Eli Tullis and Bill Campbell were playing alternate shot against the Canadians. Campbell hit his ball inside a steep ditch with water at the bottom; on their next shot, Eli then used a club to support himself and prevent himself from falling into the water. He incurred a penalty, but after the tournament complained to the USGA and got the rule changed.

Billy Key recalls the cost of making a hole-in-one at the Devonshire Cup matches in 2002, which were held at the Riverside Country Club in Saskatoon, Canada. It happened during the practice round, when he was playing with a Canadian and a member of the British team. He asked them to "keep it a deep, dark secret," but that was not to be. Soon Key found himself hosting a "very long" cocktail party for sixty-five in the club bar. When Billy had the bartender announce "last call," he was nearly trampled by the sudden rush to the bar. When settlement time came, Billy found the silver lining in an otherwise bleak situation — he was able to pay using Canadian dollars!

During the 1987 Triangular at Shinnecock Hills, one sixsome including several Rules experts faced a difficult problem — one player teed off on two consecutive holes. "Oh God, what do we do?" they wondered, as panic set in.

The wind blew so fiercely during the medal round of the Triangular Matches at Hoylake in 2001 that Sir Michael Bonallack, former captain and secretary of the R&A, said that "under these condittions, the British Open could not have been played because the balls would have blown off the greens." Nonetheless, half the field finished, and two players broke 90.

Team captains, secretaries, and association presidents at 1991 Derby Cup Match in Calgary. From left to right are: Donald Ross, Bruce Forbes, Bill Souders, Jim Hand, Ray Getliffe, Robert Walker, I. H. F. Findlay, William Maize, and Fran Roberts.

The victorious 2003 USSGA Triangular Team: (standing, left to right) Michael J. Timbers; Arthur M. Rogers, Jr.; Richard Remsen, Jr.; O. Gordon Brewer, Jr.; Jonathan M. Clark; Charles L. Van Linge; William C. Coleman; Michael Sanger; William F. Shean, Jr.; James L. Frost; Stanton E. Shuler; Jack Hesler; Peter B. Roby; John Owens; A. Harcourt Kemp; Jack R. Lamey; and Willard Heminway. In front, Paul Spengler, President John W. Eden, Team Captain Clark F. MacKenzie, Team Secretary William Souders, and James Key.

"A Seniors' Event"

In the late 1990s, US Senior Sam Fleming wrote a poem entitled "A Seniors' Event," which was read by USSGA President Cab Woodward at the Annual Dinner. Thereafter, it was adapted to song — to the music of "Jamaica Farewell" — by Charlie Arnold and John Eden. Sometimes sung at Invitationals, it goes as follows:

Verse 1 (and Chorus)

A Seniors' Event is quite a scene
From club to club, from tee to green
Most are gray in blazers of blue
It's hard to tell just who is who.

Verse 2

When the sun comes up, it's all white hats
With the Seniors' logos from shirts to spats
Khaki trousers and spikeless shoes
It's hard to tell just whose is whose.
(Chorus)

Verse 3

In the evening the ladies come to dance
In colorful skirts and satin pants
Bosoms appear, bedecked with tags
Yielding names for aging wags.
(Chorus)

Verse 4

Every day the game is on
Driving short and skulling long
Obsessed with the need for playing fast
Yet a gimme putt's a thing of the past.
(Chorus)

Verse 5

And when they've finished crossing swords
The time has come to receive awards
Hopes are high for a Seniors' plate
Small is good and big is great!
(Chorus)

Fran Roberts

Fran Roberts (left) with John Landen.

Brigadier General Francis J. "Fran" Roberts of Pinehurst retired in 2000 as International Team secretary after fifteen years, and was replaced by Bill Souders. Fran was asked by USSGA President Sam Calloway in 1983 to accompany the International team as a playing alternate, a position he would hold for three years. In 1986, Fran was asked to perform a service of more lasting nature, to serve as the team secretary, a newly-created position on the part of the USSGA, but one of long-standing with the British and Canadian seniors.

In his new role, Fran brought order to the files, helped with reports, prepared a Blue Book of Procedures and Statistics, and corresponded with the British and Canadian Associations, everything it took to make the international matches run smoothly. In 2003, in connection with the Triangular Matches at Essex, Ontario, he was made an honorary member of the Canadian Seniors.

Fran Roberts hails from Pittsfield, Massachusetts, and was a West Point graduate of 1942. He caddied as a child, and played golf while at West Point, although not on the team. Roberts fought in World War II under General George S. Patton at the Ziegfried Line, Battle of the Bulge, and Bastogne, and later served as brigadier general in Korea and Vietnam. Following the Korean war he taught at West Point, and was director of athletics there from 1956 to 1959.

In the early 1960s he worked in the Department of Defense, and was in the Pentagon as an advisor for eleven straight days during the Cuban Missile Crisis. He served on the Board of the Olympic Committee (for the Tokyo Olympics).

Richard S. Remsen, Jr.

Richie Remsen and Carl Timpson.

No story about the US Seniors would be complete without mention of a member whose game seems to improve with the years, namely, Richard S. "Richie" Remsen, Jr. His list of accomplishments is long. Perhaps his most unique achievement took place in the 1989 Pacific Coast Tournament at Cypress Point. Three days in a row he scored a 2 on the intimidating sixteenth hole, and to top it off, when he and his partner, Dick Giddings, were 2 down with three holes to play, he birdied the seventeenth and eighteenth as well to win the first flight.

Remsen was recently called "the best 83-year-old golfer in the world." He had a 4 handicap at the time. Winner of the 1981 North and South Senior, Remsen once finished with three birdies at Apawamis to win the annual tournament. He won the Bush Memorial for the fifth consecutive year in 2001.

Remsen has played in the International Matches for twenty-five years. He also played in the Crosby Pro-Am for twenty-two consecutive years, and won the prestigious Anderson Memorial at Winged Foot with fellow US Senior Carl Timpson in 1965.

When asked about shooting his age, Remsen recently replied, "Haven't shot that high in years."

The Seventy-fifth Anniversary Year

The US Seniors celebrated its Diamond Jubilee Seventy-fifth Anniversary in 1980. Bill Platt was the chairman of the festivities, and a number of British and Canadian seniors were guests at the Annual Tournament and participated in a special competition.

Present at Apawamis were Jack Nash, president of the Canadian Seniors Golf Association; Ed Ervasti, Canadian captain; Sandy Somerville, past president and honorary USSGA member; and Gordon Taylor, past president of the Canadian Seniors. Also Alec Hill, president of the British Senior Golfers' Society, and a former Walker Cupper, Ken Thomas, the Society's captain, and Stewart Lawson, captain of the Royal and Ancient.

The British presented the USSGA with a magnificent reproduction of a nineteenth-century guildhall chair, to be used as the president's chair, and the Canadians hoped to present a work of Canadian art that unfortunately was stolen from a car at the Rye Hilton the night before. A second work was presented at the Devonshire Cup Matches in July, and now resides in the Apawamis trophy case.

The seventy-fifth anniversary history, known as the "Red Book," was published for the occasion.

The 1994 Devonshire Cup officers:
Fran Roberts, US secretary;
Bob Everson, Canadian captain;
Bill Bacon, US president;
Gerry Fitzpatrick, Canadian president;
Billy Key, US captain; and
Bill Maize, Canadian secretary.

The recently renovated twelfth hole at Apawamis.
Photograph by Marilyn Gerrish

The Clubs:
Apawamis, Round Hill, and Blind Brook

THE APAWAMIS CLUB

APAWAMIS HAS BEEN THE HOME CLUB OF THE US SENIORS for a full century. It has hosted both the annual meeting (typically on the second day) and the annual dinner and awards ceremony on the third day. The club traces its roots to 1890, when Rye was a small community with a population of about 1,000. The countryside was used for farming, as it had been a century before when food supplies from Rye helped feed elements of both armies during the Revolutionary War. The Apawamis Club was formed at the Union Chapel on July 22, 1890, to "further the intercourse of its members, and promote the welfare of the neighborhood." The club's name is a contraction of the Mohegan "Appoqua Mis," meaning "the covering tree," and is part of the local lexicon dating back to the seventeenth century.

When Apawamis was incorporated on January 1, 1891, it became the first men's social club to be chartered by the state of New York. The club had fifty-five members at the time, and its first "clubhouse" consisted of two parlor rooms leased from a local boardinghouse.

Through its early years, Apawamis members did take a strong interest in the civic and cultural development of Rye. The social aspect of the club consisted of family activities during the day and an occasional "literary meeting" in the evening. Ultimately, even the social activities took a back seat to golf.

The recently renovated Apawamis clubhouse as seen from the eighteenth green.

On February 2, 1891, Apawamis found its first more or less permanent home, a four-acre estate known as "Kirklawn" on the Boston Post Road, now the site of the Church of the Resurrection. In 1896 Apawamis leased the nearby Anderson farm, a few blocks from the clubhouse and not far from the Sound, and hired a man from Slazingers for $10 to "stake out" a 9-hole golf course. This primitive course with dirt greens was all the club could afford at the time.

In March of 1897 the club was on the move again, this time leasing the Jib farm east of the Boston Post Road, just south of the railroad crossing. The property consisted of 30 acres and included a dwelling which became the second Apawamis clubhouse. With the addition of an adjacent 15-acre farm, there was room for a 9-hole course, which featured such unusual hazards as a swamp, apple orchards, trolley tracks, railroad tracks, and a railroad signal tower.

Another move was inevitable, however. With a steadily increasing membership, a larger plot of land capable of housing a full 18-hole golf course was becoming a necessity. In 1898 Apawamis was permitted to select 120 acres from the estate of Charles Park, a tract deemed most suitable for the construction of a golf course. The purchase price was $50,000. Formerly farmland and woodland, just two miles from the club's original site, the property contained thousands of yards of ledge rock and stone fence, the removal of which proved to be an ongoing problem for several years. The new 18-hole golf course was designed by the club's green chairman, Maturin Ballou, who was assisted by the noted Scottish professional/architect Willie Dunn, and was ready for play by June of 1899.

Much of Apawamis' clubhouse was destroyed by a fire which occurred during a blizzard on February 4, 1907. Only the forward portion of the house was saved. The new clubhouse was finished by August of 1908. That clubhouse, unpretentious but comfortable, served the club until the recent renovations completed in 2002.

Tennis also proved popular at Apawamis, and six courts were in place by 1910. Additional tennis, squash, and paddle tennis courts have been added since.

The Depression did not treat Apawamis kindly. The membership count dwindled – there were seventy vacancies rather than the long waiting list of the previous decade. In 1934 the club made a bold move, acquiring the property for its Beach Club, which formally opened on August 7, 1934. It was a brilliant stroke, one that made the club more attractive, and helped rebuild the membership. By April of 1935 Apawamis had a long waiting list once again. No other club in the area recovered as quickly.

Apawamis' swimming pool was built during the 1950s, coinciding with the sale of the club's facilities at the beach. This move immediately transformed Apawamis from a golf oriented club to a country club. In fact, a terrace and dance floor soon replaced the former first tee in front of the clubhouse, taking 30 yards off the starting hole.

Apawamis has hosted a number of national and regional golf championships over the years, including the 1978 Curtis Cup and the 1911 US Amateur. The latter was a landmark event, pitting the finest American amateurs against the storied British champion, Harold Hilton. Hilton won his way to the finals rather easily, but found his rival, young Fred Herreshoff of Garden City Golf and Ekwanok, a difficult foe. Herreshoff rallied over the final 9 holes to force the match into extra holes, only to watch Hilton bank a mishit shot off a large boulder to the right of the first green onto the green to set up a championship-winning par. It was the shot heard round the world, and thereafter that boulder was known as Hilton's Rock.

The recently revised Eleanor's Teeth at the fourth green. Photograph by Marilyn Gerrish

The event that eventually grew up to become the Westchester Classic had its genesis at Apawamis in the 1950s as a one-day pro-amateur conducted for the benefit of United Hospital in Port Chester. The driving force was William Jennings, former president of the New York Rangers. The inspiration came from Mrs. Jennings, her mother, and her grandmother, the latter founder of United Hospital.

Apawamis has provided the US Seniors with ten presidents – Frank Presbrey,

Frederick S. Wheeler, James G. Harbord, Findlay Douglas, Livingston Platt, Ellis Knowles, Jerome V. Roscoe, William V. Platt, William H. Todd, and W. Cabell "Cab" Woodward, Jr. – and two team captains for the international matches – Frank Presbrey and Ellis Knowles. Three Apawamis members – James D. Foot, Findlay Douglas, and Ellis Knowles – have been USSGA champions, Knowles (six times) and Foot (five times), the most prolific in US Seniors' history.

ROUND HILL CLUB

The Round Hill Club's involvement with the US Seniors dates back to 1971, when its course and clubhouse were first made available for the Annual Championship, sharing the event with Apawamis and Blind Brook (in 1973). It has been the regular host for the Board of Governors (and other committee) meetings and the President's Dinner for the Board and Committee members which are held on the Monday before the annual meeting.

The club traces its origins to 1922, a time when there were two sporting clubs in Greenwich – the Field Club, which offered its members tennis and squash facilities, and the Greenwich Country Club, which was not family-oriented at the time and whose golf course was very congested. Clearly, there was a need for a new social center in Greenwich, one that catered to a broad range of athletic activities, including golf.

And so the Round Hill Club was organized in July 1922 as a year-round facility for the entire family, children included. In August of 1922 the new club purchased 217 acres, located on the Willson Meadows in the "Round Hill" section of Greenwich's "back country," so-called because of the roundish hill north of the Merritt Parkway.

The site was chosen after consultation with Walter Travis, who designed the golf course. It featured exciting topographical properties, to this day a most memorable feature of the course. Construction was watched over by Emilio "Mollie" Strazza, the club's grounds superintendent from 1922 until 1964. At one time a sculptor, Strazza contributed his artistic flair, particularly his deployment of trees and mounds, to make each hole a pleasant vista. Round Hill opened officially on July 19, 1924.

Another prominent Round Hill "employee" was golf professional Billie Burke, winner of the 1931 US Open after two 36-hole playoffs, winning on the 144th hole!

The course today resembles the original quite closely, although a number of tees have been or are in the process of being added, which lengthens the course substantially from the championship tees. One major change came in 1965 when Robert Trent Jones built the present eleventh hole and the pond at the eleventh and twelfth. Interestingly, Jones' hole followed Travis' original blueprint. In addition, while the original course had many more bunkers than exist today – they apparently were filled in during the Depression – trees now protect many areas once guarded by bunkers. Much of the recent work has been done by Ken Dye, the noted golf course architect from Houston.

An early candidate for the club's name was "Monarch Oak," after the majestic oak that once stood between the fifth and eighth fairways. The tree on the club's logo is the elm that once watched over the left side of the eighteenth fairway. It died in 1978, approximately 140 years old at the time. A sugar maple has recently been planted in the same location, in honor of deceased Senior Bill Breed.

The Round Hill clubhouse as renovated in 2003.

The watery eleventh hole at Round Hill.

Round Hill's English-style stone clubhouse was originally designed by William Delano of New York. Situated on a high knoll overlooking the golf course, it was enlarged in 1959–1960, the main focus of the project being the dining room, bar, and men's locker room.

Under the guiding hand of architect Jim Rogers, the clubhouse in 2002–2003 underwent a further renovation that encompassed the men's locker room and library, the kitchen, main dining room, and bar. One byproduct of the renovation is the club's first grill room for informal dining. In addition, a new state of the art golf course maintenance facility also was completed in 2003. A future renovation of the indoor racquets facility will include a full-scale fitness center.

In addition to the golf course, the members also enjoy outdoor tennis and paddle tennis courts, an indoor racquets facility with two tennis courts, singles and doubles squash courts, skeet and trap shooting in the winter, and a swimming pool and adjacent well-equipped play area for children.

Round Hill has been the site of many important golfing events, including its role as co-host with the Stanwich Club of the 2002 US Mid-Amateur Championship. In that event, Round Hill's course was used with Stanwich for on-site qualifying rounds.

Round Hill has provided the US Seniors with four presidents – Hank Flower, Ward Foshay, John Gates, and Willard "Spike" Heminway – and two team captains for the international matches – Ward Foshay and Jim Knowles. Also, the last two USSGA secretaries have been Round Hill members – Everett Fisher for an astonishing twenty-two years (1981–2002), followed by Jonathan M. Clark. Everett was and Jonathan currently is president of Round Hill Club. Round Hill has contributed two USSGA champions, John Chapman in 1931 and Jim Knowles in 1971 and 1974. Ellis Knowles, Jim's father, a former Round Hill member and four times Round Hill champion, later became president and then honorary president of the USSGA, and was six times its champion.

Prescott S. Bush was the son-in-law of George Herbert Walker, donor of the Walker Cup. Two sons of the donor, G. H. Walker, Jr. and Dr. John M. Walker, were active golfing members of Round Hill, as are grandsons William H. T. and Prescott S. Bush. Jr., both US Seniors.

The view of the clubhouse from the ninth tee as painted by US Senior and Round Hill member John Gerster for the cover of the 1995–1996 yearbook.

The Blind Brook clubhouse with the golf course in the background.

BLIND BROOK CLUB

Blind Brook has been associated with the annual tournament on and off since 1949, and has hosted the most senior members of the association on a regular basis since 1973.

The club's origins trace to the summer of 1915, when William Hamlin Childs, a New York-based restaurateur, visited the Old Elm Club near Chicago. Old Elm was an exclusive, all-male retreat where restfulness and tranquillity were the rule of the day, with seldom a wait at the first tee. The concept appealed to Childs. The possibility of recreating it in Westchester County captured his imagination.

Upon returning to New York, Childs enlisted the aid of Edmund C. Converse and Frederick S. Wheeler. Within two weeks, the trio had put together a group of 150 men, each willing to contribute $3,000 to cover the acquisition of land and construction costs for a clubhouse and golf course. By late fall of 1915 the Blind Brook Club was born. Childs served as the club's first president, until his death in 1928. His portrait hangs over the fireplace in the men's lounge.

The 200-acre site was chosen in part because of its gentle contours, which promised to eliminate the need for excessive hill climbing. The name chosen for the club was borrowed from a stream with origins near Bedford that flows through Westchester County before emptying into Long Island Sound near Milton Point. Blind Brook, in fact, acts as a western border of the club's property.

To design their golf course, Blind Brook's founders turned to Charles Blair Macdonald, and presented him with an unusual request. They were not interested in a championship course of staggering length. Rather, they wanted a course they could enjoy, a challenging layout of moderate length and tempered hazards. This concept has made it an easy walking course for the USSGA's most senior members.

After presenting his ideas as to the routing of the course, Macdonald turned the project over to his right-hand man, Seth Raynor. What resulted was a design bearing some of the trademarks of a Macdonald-Raynor course – excellent copies of famous European holes and large, undulating, multi-tiered greens.

The approach to the sixteenth green.

Uphill to the thirteenth green.

The Golf Committee then secured the services of William Rusack from the Old Course at St. Andrews in Scotland. Rusack purchased a pony to ride the course from hole to hole supervising the construction, insuring that the Macdonald-Raynor vision was properly carried out. He became Blind Brook's first professional and greenskeeper when the course opened.

Blind Brook's clubhouse was designed by Frank Ashburton Moore. It was built in the Italian style, of terra cotta blocks stuccoed in gray, with broad verandahs overlooking the golf course. There are no tennis courts, and no swimming pool – Blind Brook is strictly a golf club.

Blind Brook has been called, and rightfully so, " a center for distinguished gentlemen who have mellowed in golf." Former President Dwight Eisenhower, at one time an honorary member of the USSGA, was a dues-paying member at Blind Brook, before becoming an honorary at that club as well. It is said that he considered Augusta National and Blind Brook his favorite courses. The president's portrait hangs in the sitting room.

Blind Brook has provided the US Seniors with six presidents – Frederick S. Wheeler, Frederick H. Ecker, Findlay Douglas, James D. Miller, Howard L. Clark, and William M. Rees – and two team captains for the international matches – James D. Miller and Howard L. Clark. To date, Findlay Douglas is the only Blind Brook member to have won the USSGA championship.

Within the Birch Grove,
painted by Luigi Lucioni in 1957
looking across the sixth hole of
Ekwanok. The original is part of
the permanent collection of the
Southern Vermont Arts Center,
Manchester, Vermont.

172

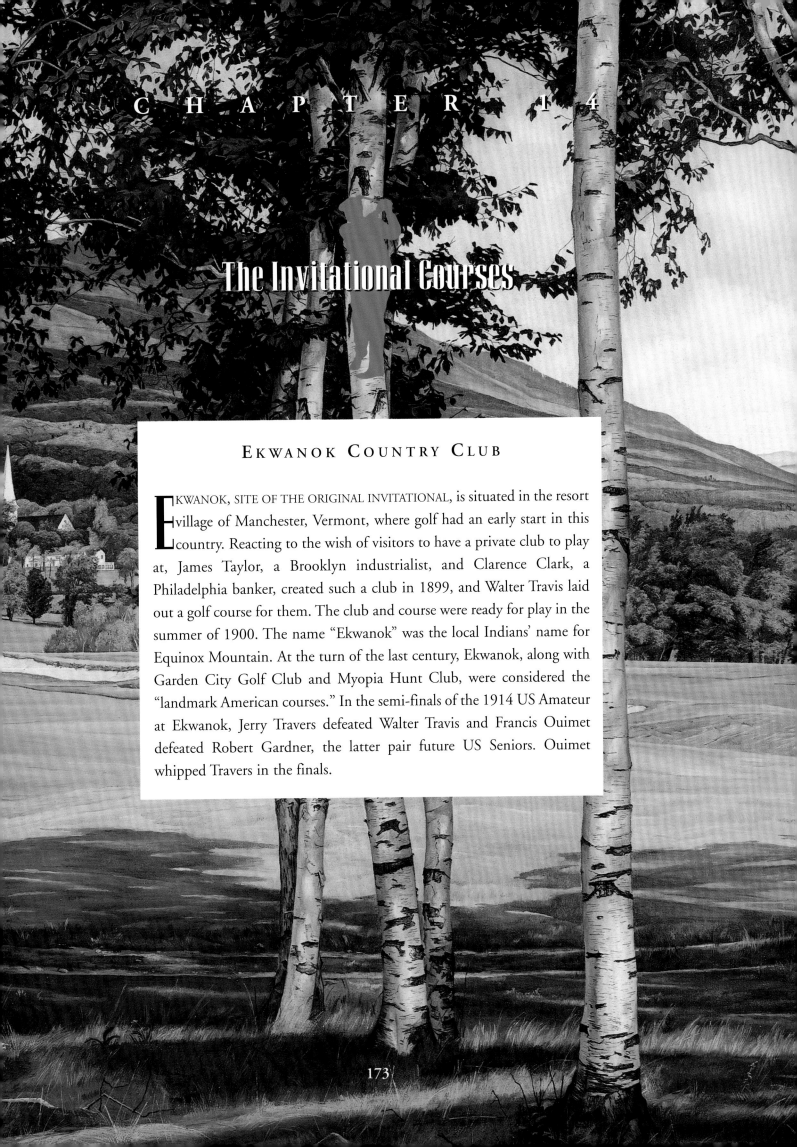

CHAPTER 14

The Invitational Courses

EKWANOK COUNTRY CLUB

EKWANOK, SITE OF THE ORIGINAL INVITATIONAL, is situated in the resort village of Manchester, Vermont, where golf had an early start in this country. Reacting to the wish of visitors to have a private club to play at, James Taylor, a Brooklyn industrialist, and Clarence Clark, a Philadelphia banker, created such a club in 1899, and Walter Travis laid out a golf course for them. The club and course were ready for play in the summer of 1900. The name "Ekwanok" was the local Indians' name for Equinox Mountain. At the turn of the last century, Ekwanok, along with Garden City Golf Club and Myopia Hunt Club, were considered the "landmark American courses." In the semi-finals of the 1914 US Amateur at Ekwanok, Jerry Travers defeated Walter Travis and Francis Ouimet defeated Robert Gardner, the latter pair future US Seniors. Ouimet whipped Travers in the finals.

The fourth hole on the Dogwood 9.

COUNTRY CLUB OF NORTH CAROLINA

The Country Club of North Carolina became host of the second invitational in 1970. Designed as a championship layout by Ellis Maples and William Byrd, the course at the Country Club of North Carolina was first opened in 1963, and a third 9 was added in 1969. It was immediately recognized as a real test of golf and rated among the top courses in the United States. The Country Club of North Carolina hosted the 1980 US Amateur, which was won by future PGA Tour professional Hal Sutton.

The huge bunker fronting the eleventh green.

MOUNTAIN LAKE CLUB

The Mountain Lake Invitational started in 1971. Founded in 1915 in central Florida, Mountain Lake has within the boundaries of its 3,500-acre property a fine 18-hole golf course designed by Seth Raynor, and approximately one hundred private homes distributed comfortably around the lake and golf course on spacious rolling hills uncommon to most of Florida. The entire area had been beautifully landscaped by Frederick Law Olmstead who became famous as the designer of New York's Central Park and Chicago's Jackson and Garfield Parks. An added feature is the Bok Tower, the highest point in Central Florida, with its magnificent carillon.

The par-3 third hole.

THE KITTANSETT CLUB

Kittansett has been a popular, albeit wet, invitational host since 1972. The course was designed in 1922 by Frederick H. Hood and built on a point of land that projects into Buzzards Bay. The name "Kittansett" had been taken from the Indian word meaning "near the sea." A true seaside course with interesting trees, shrubs, and bunkers, it was further endowed with vistas of the bay from the clubhouse and from several of the holes where changes in wind direction and velocity could make drastic changes in the play of the course. Kittansett hosted the 1953 Walker Cup Matches.

LYFORD CAY CLUB

The left-dogleg sixteenth hole.

In 1972 Lyford Cay became the host club for the only "international" invitational on the USSGA calendar. The golf course was designed, with great difficulty and some initial reluctance, by Dick Wilson on what previously had been an enormous natural swamp. Wilson was one of eight architects to have rejected the possibility of ever building a course on the site. Construction started in 1958, with crews working day and night. The resort opened in 1959. The golf course is one of the very best in the Caribbean Islands.

The par-3 seventeenth hole.

SHINNECOCK HILLS GOLF CLUB

One of three host clubs for the Long Island Invitational, held since 1975, Shinnecock Hills was incorporated in 1891 at the very beginning of organized golf in America. It was one of the five clubs that formed an association in 1894 which became the USGA the following year. Shinnecock hosted the second annual United States Amateur and Open championships in 1896, a Walker Cup Match (1977), and three recent US Opens (1986, 1995, and 2004). Outstanding players come to Shinnecock from all over the world and leave with an admiration and respect for the challenge of golf offered by this fine course.

The present Shinnecock Hills golf course, designed by Toomey and Flynn, opened in 1931. It replaced a course originally designed by Willie Davis, then altered by Willie Dunn and Charles Blair Macdonald. The original clubhouse, the first to be designed by Stanford White, can still be recognized amid various modest alterations that have been added from time to time.

NATIONAL GOLF LINKS OF AMERICA

The fifteenth green, with the sixteenth hole and windmill in background.

The National Golf Links in Southampton, adjacent to Shinnecock Hills, represents Charles Blair Macdonald's turn-of-the-century experiment in uplifting American golf course architecture. Macdonald, already familiar with the British links, traveled throughout the British Isles, taking detailed notes on holes or features of holes he particularly liked. By the magic of transatlantic translation, he incorporated them in his highly acclaimed design at the National. And so we find at National the first American Redan, Alps, Eden, Road, and Bottle holes, as well as many intriguing originals. The National Golf Links hosted the inaugural Walker Cup Matches in 1922. It has been a host club for the Long Island Invitational off and on for almost three decades.

The par-3 fourteenth hole, hard by the ocean.

THE MAIDSTONE CLUB

The third of three host clubs for the Long Island Invitational, The Maidstone Club in East Hampton is one of America's oldest, dating back to 1891. It wasn't until 1922, however, when Willie Park redesigned the original course, indeed expanded it to 36 holes, that Maidstone gained notoriety as a golf club. Among Park's new holes were several outstanding ones in the dunes between the ocean and Hook Pond, a few of which are considered among the finest in the world. When the wind howls, which it does frequently, Maidstone is often thought by many Seniors to play the hardest of the three great Long Island Invitational courses.

A special view of the sixteenth green, with the seventeenth tee and Monterey Bay in the background.

CYPRESS POINT CLUB

A West Coast Invitational was first held at the Cypress Point Club in 1975. The club was organized for the specific purpose of building a great golf course in the most unique and beautiful setting imaginable, one in which the course seems the work of nature and not of man. So spoke Samuel Morse, the visionary who developed the entire Monterey Peninsula. At Cypress Point, Morse had two notable partners. One was Marion Hollins, former US Women's Amateur champion, who actually conceived the club and chose the property. The other was Dr. Alister MacKenzie, who designed the final version of the course that has consistently ranked as one of the very best in the United States. Construction of the course began in 1927, and the first round was played in 1928. Cypress Point has hosted a number of important events, including the 1981 Walker Cup matches.

The very difficult par-3 fifth hole.

SEMINOLE GOLF CLUB

When a group of Palm Beach socialites, headed by E. F. Hutton, sought to build a links-style golf course equal to the best in the world, they looked well to the north of Palm Beach and found a 100-acre site that included two parallel strips of windswept, treeless dunesland, one on the ocean, that were separated by swampland. They engaged Donald Ross to build their golf course because he knew how to drain the swampland and therefore join the two strips of dunesland. They also brought on Marion Wyeth, designer of many of Palm Beach's mansions, to build the clubhouse. Their Seminole Golf Club, which was dedicated strictly to golf, opened in 1929, and their Ross masterpiece is considered by some to be one of the finest courses ever created. Since 1975 Seminole has been the site for the Invitational Tournament held in early November each year.

The watery second hole at Onwentsia.
Photo by AirShots

ONWENTSIA CLUB

Part of the Midwest Invitational held each year in July since 1977, Onwentsia was laid out by the brothers James and Robert Foulis of St. Andrews, 9 holes in 1896, the second 9 in 1898. James Foulis was the first professional at the Chicago Golf Club, and winner of the 1896 US Open. Among the early tournaments held at Onwentsia were the US Amateur Championship in 1899 and the US Open in 1906, the latter won by Alex Smith. Onwentsia is recognized as one of the first one hundred clubs in the United States.

The ninth (left) and eighteenth holes at Shoreacres heading towards the clubhouse and Lake Michigan.
Photo by AirShots

SHOREACRES

Also co-host of the Midwest Invitational, Shoreacres was designed by Seth Raynor on rolling bluffs along the shore of Lake Michigan. On many holes the golfer is confronted with ravines, gorges, and boundaries that are beautiful to behold but treacherous to play. The course clearly bears the imprint of Charles Blair Macdonald and his protégé, Seth Raynor, with copies of great British holes, boldly-contoured greens, and deep bunkers with grassy faces.

OLD ELM

Old Elm's golf course is a fine Donald Ross/H. S. Colt collaboration. The course is short and relatively flat, and the greens make it a great course. Some are crowned in the Ross style, all are very fast, placing vital import on staying below the hole. Old Elm has been a popular host for the Devonshire Cup Matches, a role the club has played five times since 1962, as well as the Midwest Invitational.

The fourth hole at Old Elm, with Lake Michigan in the distant background. Photo by AirShots

The fourth hole on the Seaside 9.

SEA ISLAND GOLF CLUB

The Sea Island Invitational was inaugurated in 1981. Since then, the resort has undergone some significant change. Today, the US Seniors play the redesigned Plantation (by Rees Jones), Seaside (by Tom Fazio), and Retreat (by Davis Love) nines, and also have the opportunity to play the new Ocean Forest Golf Club, designed by Rees Jones, which hosted the Walker Cup in 2001.

The facilities at Sea Island have recently been upgraded. The Lodge at the Sea Island Golf Club opened in 2001. The original Cloisters Hotel has been demolished, and a new hotel is being constructed, scheduled to be opened by the spring of 2006. The ongoing construction has had no impact on the housing or comfort of the Seniors attending the annual tournament at Sea Island.

The ninth at Wianno.

CAPE COD

Host club for the Cape Cod Invitational since 1986, Wianno opened in 1916 with a 9-hole course designed by Leonard Biles. Donald Ross was hired in 1919 to redesign the original 9 and add additional holes on land that had been assembled by the club.

Hyannisport Club, located four miles east of Osterville, sits high on a hill above Nantucket Sound. Spectacular water views and variable wind conditions make this course, laid out originally by Alex Findlay and redesigned by Donald Ross, one of the best golfing challenges on Cape Cod.

Oyster Harbors is on an island enclave just west of Osterville, accessible by drawbridge and guarded by a gated windmill. Designed by Donald Ross in 1927, Oyster Harbors offers large greens, many manicured bunkers, and tree-lined fairways, with the surrounding waterways visible from just one hole.

The fifteenth at Hyannisport.

Below: An aerial view of Oyster Harbors.

United States Seniors' Golf Association

The par-3 eleventh hole at Hawk's Nest.

INDIAN RIVER – RIOMAR

The Indian River Invitational has been played since its inception in 1992 over a variety of courses. Riomar is the oldest of these, its Herbert Strong course opened in 1919 and later revised by Joe Lee. Bent Pine, designed by Joe Lee; Hawk's Nest, a Jim Fazio layout; and John's Island West, a Tom Fazio layout, have been used for several years, and this year the new Rees Jones course at RedStick will join the rota.

The par-3 seventh hole at RedStick.

The thirteenth hole at Riomar.

United States Seniors' Golf Association

The dramatic par-5 eighteenth hole at Rancho La Quinta.

PALM DESERT

Over its relatively short existence begun in 1997, the Desert Invitational has been played over several courses, typically three each year. The Eldorado Country Club, which is considered the host club, was the venue for the Walker Cup in 1959, and has hosted the PGA Tour's Desert Classic, as has the Bermuda Dunes Country Club.

Rancho La Quinta, which was designed in 1988 by Robert Trent Jones, Jr., is majestically framed by the Santa Rosa Mountains, and features water in play on several holes, indeed fronting the green on the 561-yard eighteenth hole.

The Reserve, built by Tom Weiskopf and Jay Moorish in 1998, is located in the hills offering panoramic views of the Palm Springs area.

USSGA 100th Anniversary

Gather U.S. Seniors
We've reached our hundredth year.
Hats off to Horace Hotchkiss
We wish that he was here.
And to those in every decade
Who led us on the way,
Through war and peace, rain or shine,
Class E to Triple A.

Seniors well remember,
When turning back the clock,
Those greens at Apawamis
And the hills of Shinnecock.
Thanks for the memories
Of satellites far and wide,
From Cypress Point to Seminole
We've had a privileged ride.

Hold on to all those medals
And stacks of Senior plates
And plan to take them with you
Through the pearly gates
Let's not forget the Founders Cup,
Symbol of the bond,
With Canadians to the north,
And Brits across the pond.

With a passion for the game,
We'll carry on the tradition
Of ferocity and friendship
Found in every competition.
So, brush off your wrinkled blazers,
Polish up the brass.
To Senior golfers, here and gone,
We tip a shaky glass.

— Samuel W. Fleming, June 2004

HAS HORACE HOTCHKISS' VISION of more than a century ago been fulfilled? Some might suggest well beyond expectations. The original goal of assembling a group of "seniors" for an annual golfing competition at Apawamis in Rye, New York, has, over its first one hundred years, been transformed into the reality of a vibrant organization with a membership selected from across the country, engaged in year-round events at many of the greatest golfing venues in the United States.

And there is a global aspect, too, with the first "satellite" tournament conducted each year outside the United States, along with the long-standing annual international team matches that are played at such storied venues as Royal Montreal, Muirfield, Royal Liverpool, Pine Valley, Sunningdale, and Royal County Down. In short, the USSGA has become a dynamic association deeply involved with the very best aspects of the amateur game and, in the process, has substantiated beyond doubt that golf is the game of a lifetime.

Few, if any, of the greatest advocates of Horace Hotchkiss' undertaking, back in 1905, could have foreseen the important role the USSGA would have in encouraging the active participation of men fifty-five years and older in the world of golf. Reaping the benefits of advanced technologies and physical fitness, USSGA members today play extremely high quality golf often into, and occasionally through, their ninth decade. The growth and success of the organization substantiates the belief in "long life through golf." In a challenged society and world, golf at all levels, and especially at the senior level, helps give life balance and perspective.

Furthermore, our association has spawned the Canadian Seniors, the British Seniors, and numerous other organizations devoted to senior golf throughout the world. Here in the United States, the USSGA has been the model for dozens of seniors' golfing associations around the country. The annual championship of the USSGA led the USGA in 1955 and the Royal and Ancient in 1969 to add Senior Amateurs to their list of annual golf competitions. Not just a few of these championships, at home and in the United Kingdom, have been won by USSGA members.

A rigorous membership process leads to organizational continuity, and even more importantly, to new and lasting friendships. Indeed, the quality of the membership is the core strength of the USSGA. Also playing a critical role, now more than ever, are the wives of USSGA members who add enormously to the Invitational Tournaments, both on and off the course. In fact, it has become an important membership consideration whether a prospective senior's wife, active golfer or not, enjoys the game and will participate in the satellite events with her husband.

The USSGA will celebrate its centennial in 2005. The USSGA's own William C. "Bill" Campbell, legendary contributor to amateur golf in so many ways, both on and off the course, will be the principal speaker at the annual dinner, at which time a new award will be announced in his honor. The William C. Campbell Award will be presented to a US Senior for his outstanding contributions to the game of golf through the US Seniors and otherwise. It is further anticipated that the award will be presented to a deserving senior, either one who is with us, or posthumously, at future USSGA annual meetings.

As part of the Centennial celebration, an experiment will be conducted in 2005 at Bedford Golf and Tennis Club, which will be used to supplement Apawamis, Round Hill, and Blind Brook. A Stableford system will be used at Bedford, and hopefully will result in members playing faster while still enjoying a competitive event.

In addition, through an amendment to the By-Laws, the Honorary Membership category has been reinstated in 2005 after a long absence. It is anticipated that two new honorary members will be announced in June 2005 at the Centennial dinner celebration, and will be "inducted" at the Triangular Matches in December 2005 at Seminole. On the Sunday before the Triangular competition commences, past USSGA international team members will assemble at the Jupiter Island Club in Hobe Sound, Florida, to play in a competition with the present international team members. They will all dine together that evening, with special recognition accorded to all former team captains who are present.

What are the challenges going forward? While complacency must be avoided, it is difficult to believe that the game of golf will not remain enormously popular, both at home and around the globe. Undoubtedly changes will occur, most likely relating primarily to procedures rather than objectives. The USSGA needs to both persevere and change, yet change should be measured and well thought out. In particular, it will be essential to continue to foster relationships with the satellite host clubs so that USSGA members may continue to enjoy the privilege of golfing at these very special venues.

In sum, the USSGA appears as well positioned as ever to play the role, as expressed in its By-Laws, of encouraging friendly competition in golf among seniors, while continuing to promote the best interests and traditional spirit of the game of golf. Maintaining the values and integrity of the game will continue to be an essential challenge, and the USSGA remains committed to playing its important role.

USSGA Trophies
Top row, left to right: US Seniors' Cup, Derby Cup, and Devonshire Cup.
Bottom row, left to right: Founders Cup, Boston Bowl, Lyon Trohpy.

USSGA Officers

HONORARY PRESIDENTS

1917–1929	Horace L. Hotchkiss
1945–1946	Frederick Snare
1955–1957	John G. Jackson
1957–1977	John Ellis Knowles
1960–1977	John Arthur Brown
1961–1968	Livingston Platt
1971–1980	Richard S. Tufts

PRESIDENTS

1917–1919	Darwin P. Kingsley	Sleepy Hollow
1919–1922	Frank Presbrey	Apawamis
1922–1924	Frederick Snare	Garden City Golf Club
1924–1926	Robert W. Lesley	Merion
1926–1929	Frederick S. Wheeler	Blind Brook
1929–1931	Frank L. Woodward	Denver
1931–1933	Frederick H. Ecker	Blind Brook
1933–1937	James G. Harbord	Apawamis
1937–1941	Findlay Douglas	National/Blind Brook
1941–1945	John G. Jackson	National/Deepdale
1945–1947	William H. Standley	(San Diego)
1947–1950	John Arthur Brown	Pine Valley
1950–1952	Livingston Platt	Apawamis
1952–1954	John Ellis Knowles	Apawamis
1954–1955	Charles W. Littlefield	Montclair
1955–1956	Charles V. Benton	Fishers Island
1956–1957	Joseph M. Wells	East Liverpool
1957–1959	John Arthur Brown	Pine Valley
1959–1961	Isaac B. Grainger	Montclair
1961–1963	James H. Ackerman	Springdale/Mountain Lake
1963–1965	Gordon M. Hill	Garden City Golf Club
1965–1967	Henry C. Flower, Jr.	Round Hill
1967–1969	James D. Miller	Blind Brook
1969–1971	John D. Ames	Old Elm
1971–1973	William Ward Foshay	Round Hill
1973–1975	Warren Ingersoll	Gulph Mills
1975–1977	William S. Terrell	Charlotte
1977–1979	Jerome V. Roscoe	Apawamis
1979–1981	John B. Gates	Round Hill
1981–1983	William V. Platt	Apawamis/Jupiter
1983–1985	Samuel R. Callaway	Piping Rock
1985–1987	Howard L. Clark	Blind Brook/Seminole
1987–1989	William H. Todd	Apawamis
1989–1991	William M. Rees	Blind Brook
1991–1993	William F. Souders	Wee Burn
1993–1995	William T. Bacon, Jr.	Old Elm
1995–1997	Edward C. Steele	Seminole
1997–1999	M. Cabell Woodward, Jr.	Apawamis
1999–2001	James P. Gorter	Seminole
2001–2003	Willard S. Heminway, Jr.	Round Hill
2003–	John W. Eden	Mountain Lake

VICE PRESIDENTS

1917–1919	Justice Mahlon Pitney	1954–1956	Joseph M. Wells
	Morgan J. O'Brien	1955–1956	Francis D. Ouimet
1919–1922	William O. Henderson	1956–1957	James D. Standish, Jr.
	Robert W. Lesley	1956–1957	Isaac B. Grainger
1922–1923	Alexander H. Revell	1957–1959	Francis Ouimet
	Thad C. Bell	1957–1959	Gardiner W. White
1923–1924	Morgan J. O'Brien	1959–1961	James H. Ackerman
	Winthrop Sargeant	1959–1961	Franklin G. Clement
1924–1926	Frederick S. Wheeler	1961–1963	Gordon M. Hill
	Hugh Halsell	1961–1965	Henry C. Flower, Jr.
1926–1928	Hugh Halsell	1963–1966	Franklin G. Clement
	Frank L. Woodward	1965–1967	James D. Miller
1929–1931	Frederick H. Ecker	1966–1967	James M. Robbins
1931–1933	Gen. J. Ernest Smith	1967–1969	John D. Ames
1931–1936	Findlay S. Douglas	1967–1969	William Ward Foshay
1933–1937	Martin J. Condon	1969–1971	Warner S. Shelly
1936–1938	Jerome A. Peck	1969–1971	Phillips R. Turnbull
1937–1939	William D. Mitchell	1971–1973	Warren Ingersoll
1938–1940	Silas H. Strawn	1973–1975	William S. Terrell
1939–1941	John G. Jackson	1974–1977	Jerome V. Roscoe
1940–1942	Gen J. Ernest Smith	1977–1979	John B. Gates
1941–1942	Walter R. Tuckerman	1979–1981	William V. Platt
1942–1943	Archibald M. Reid	1981–1983	Samuel R. Callaway
1943–1946	Hon. James A. Foley	1983–1985	Howard L. Clark
1944–1946	Morton G. Bogue	1985–1987	William H. Todd
1946–1947	Grantland Rice	1987–1989	William M. Rees
1946–1948	Dr. Marvin M. Cullom	1989–1993	William T. Bacon, Jr.
1947–1948	Charles B. Brophy	1991–1993	George R. Harding
1948–1950	Livingston Platt	1993–1995	Edward C. Steele
1948–1949	Walter R. Tuckerman	1995–1997	M. Cabell Woodward, Jr.
1949–1952	Frederick H. Haggerson	1997–1999	James P. Gorter
1950–1952	John Ellis Knowles	1999–2001	Willard S. Heminway, Jr.
1952–1954	Charles W. Littlefield	2001–2003	John W. Eden
1952–1954	Robert H. Gardner	2003–	A. Harcourt Kemp
1954–1955	Charles V. Benton		

TREASURER

1917–1919	Walter Brown
1919–1935	Joseph A. Flynn
1935–1947	William H. Conroy
1947–1956	John T. Harrison
1956	George A. Dixon
1956–1961	James D. Miller
1961–1966	Walter F. Pease
1966–1968	J. Edmund Bradley
1968–1974	William E. Hutton
1974–1977	Hoyt Ammidon
1977–1983	James R. Hand
1983–1987	Ellmore C. Patterson
1987–1992	Frank L. Mansell
1992–2002	Peter V. N. Phillip
2002–	Stephen M. McPherson

SECRETARY

1917–1918	Walter Brown
1918–1922	W. H. Hale
1922–1923	William Bliss
1923–1924	Charles Warren Hunt
1924–1930	Harry S. Hamilton
1930–1938	S. Clifton Mabon
1938–1947	George A. Nicol, Jr.
1947–1952	Sherrill Sherman
1952–1954	Gardiner W. White
1954–1957	Edmund H. Driggs
1957–1964	Mason B. Starring, Jr.
1964–1965	J. Lester Van Name
1965–1966	James M. Robbins
1966–1968	Lewis B. Cuyler
1968–1974	Henry A. Wilmerding
1974–1979	John R. Webster
1979–1981	Joseph C. Dey
1981–2002	Everett Fisher
2002–	Jonathan M. Clark

COMMITTEE CHAIRMEN

EXECUTIVE COMMITTEE

1924–1927	William Fellowes Morgan	1964–1965	James D. Miller	1987–1989	Howad L. Clark
1927–1945	Frederick Snare	1965–1967	Gordon M. Hill	1989–1991	William H. Todd
1945–1946	John G. Jackson	1967–1972	Henry C. Flower, Jr.	1991–1993	William M. Rees
1946–1947	William A. Irvin	1972–1973	John D. Ames	1993–1995	William F. Souders
1947–1950	John Ellis Knowles	1973–1975	William Ward Foshay	1995–1997	William T. Bacon, Jr.
1950–1952	Charles W. Littlefield	1975–1977	Warren Ingersoll	1997–1999	Edward C. Steele
1952–1956	Livingston Platt	1977–1979	William S. Terrell	1999–2001	M. Cabell Woodward, Jr.
1956–1957	C. V. Benton	1979–1981	Jerome V. Roscoe	2001–2003	James P. Gorter
1957–1961	Livingston Platt	1981–1983	Joseph C. Dey	2003–	Willard S. Heminway, Jr.
1961–1963	Isaac B. Grainger	1983–1985	William V. Platt		
1963–1964	James H. Ackerman	1985–1987	Samuel R. Callaway		

MEMBERSHIP COMMITTEE

1917–1927	Elias M. Johnson	1948–1951	William J. Priestley	1977–1981	Samuel R. Callaway
1927–1932	George C. Austin	1951–1952	Stanley A. Sweet	1981–1985	Joseph E. Rich
1932–1933	David L. Luke	1952–1956	Charles F. Robbins	1985–1986	F. Stanton Deland
1933–1934	B. L. Winchell	1956–1957	Earl A. Ross	1986–1993	John S. Griswold
1934–1937	David N. Tallman	1957–1967	James E. Shields	1993–1999	Willard S. Heminway, Jr.
1937–1941	Edgar S. Bowling	1967–1970	Phillips R. Turnbull	1999–2004	John A. Scully
1941–1946	S. Clifton Mabon	1970–1973	Warren Ingersoll	2004–	Donald B. Davidson
1946–1948	Dr. Orrin S. Wightman	1973–1977	John B. Gates		

TOURNAMENT COMMITTEE

1917–1918	Frank Presbrey	1957–1960	John W. Hubbell	1983–1986	William H. Todd
1918–1921	Frederick J. Wessels	1960–1961	Gordon M. Hill	1986–1987	William M. Rees
1921–1923	Dwight L. Elmendorf	1961–1963	James D. Miller	1987–1989	Frederick D. Remsen
1923–1937	Jerome A. Peck	1963–1967	Vincent C. Ross	1989–1993	H. Lawrence Parker
1937–1948	Charles B. Brophy	1967–1968	Renwick B. Dimond	1993–1995	M. Cabell Woodward, Jr.
1948–1952	Henry A. Goode	1968–1971	William A. Morgan	1995–1999	Walter S. Robbins
1952–1954	Charles V. Benton	1971–1975	Jerome V. Roscoe	1999–2002	Samuel McC. Yonce
1954–1957	Romeyn B. Scribner	1975–1979	William V. Platt	2002–	Langdon P. Cook
		1979–1983	Edwin H. Crandell		

INVITATIONAL TOURNAMENTS COMMITTEE

1971–1973	Chester T. Birch	1992–1997	Norman Boucher, Chairman
1973–1975	Royal Little	1992–1993	Edward C. Steele, Vice–Chairman
1975–1977	Sydney N. Stokes	1993–1997	Ralph T. King, Vice–Chairman
1977–1981	Robert J. Shaw	1997–2001	Ralph T. King, Chairman
1981–1984	John S. Wilbur		L. Patton Kline, Vice–Chairman
1984–1987	Benjamin Grosscup, Chairman	2001–2004	L. Patton Kline, Chairman
	Dr. Thomas Royster, Vice-Chairman		J. Gilbride McManus, Vice Chairman
1987–1989	Dr. Thomas Royster, Chairman	2004–	J. Gilbride McManus, Chairman
	William T. Bacon, Jr., Vice-Chairman		Lance R. Odden, Vice Chairman
1989–1992	William T. Bacon, Jr., Chairman		
	Norman Boucher, Vice-Chairman		

TEAM OFFICIALS

TEAM CAPTAINS

1917–1918	Frank Presbrey	Apawamis
1919	William Clark	Misquamicut
1920–1921	Frederick Snare	Garden City Golf Club
1922–1923	Francis M. Bacon	unavailable
1924–1944	Frederick Snare	Garden City Golf Club
1945–1949	John G. Jackson	National/Deepdale
1950–1951	John Arthur Brown	Pine Valley
1952–1956	John F. Riddell, Jr.	Garden City Golf Club
1957	Thomas M. Belshe	Burning Tree
1958	Franklin G. Clement	Old Elm
1959	John Ellis Knowles	Apawamis
1960	James H. Ackerman	Springdale/Mountain Lake
1961–1962	Franklin G. Clement	Old Elm
1963	James D. Miller	Blind Brook
1964–1965	Weller Noble	Claremont
1966–1968	John D. Ames	Old Elm
1969–1970	Robert W. Goldwater	Phoenix
1971–1972	William S. Terrell	Charlotte
1973–1974	Warner S. Shelly	Pine Valley
1975–1976	William Ward Foshay	Round Hill
1977–1978	James B. Knowles	Round Hill/Ekwanok
1979–1980	Howard L. Clark	Blind Brook/Seminole
1981–1982	Lewis W. Oehmig	Lookout Mountain
1983–1984	William J. Patton	Mimosa Hills
1985–1986	William C. Campbell	Guyan
1987–1988	Edgar R. Updegraff	Hartford
1989–1990	James R. Hand	SleepyHollow/Ekwanok
1991–1992	John C. Owens	Idle Hour
1993–1994	James W. Key	Green Island
1995–1996	William F. Souders	Wee Burn
1997–1998	William H. Black	National
1999–2000	A. Harcourt Kemp	Louisville
2001–2004	Clark F. MacKenzie	Green Spring Valley

TEAM SECRETARIES

1985–2000	Brig. Gen. Francis J. Roberts	
2001–	William F. Souders	

B.

The Annual Tournament
Champions

Year	Winner and Club	Score	Year	Winner and Club	Score
1905	James D. Foot, Apawamis	179	1956	Franklin G. Clement, Old Elm	144
1906	James D. Foot, Apawamis	184	1957	Franklin G. Clement, Old Elm	146
1907	Dr. Carl E. Martin, Greenwich	177	1958	John W. Dawson, Eldorado	143
1908	James D. Foot, Apawamis	166	1959	John W. Dawson, Eldorado	143
1909	James D. Foot, Apawamis	169	1960	John W. Dawson, Eldorado	141
1910	Frank A. Wright, Baltusrol	162	1961	Joseph Morrill, Jr., Wyantenuck	142
1911	James D. Foot, Apawamis	160	1962	George Dawson, Glen Oak	143
1912	James A. Tyng, Baltusrol	166	1963	Jack Westland, Burning Tree	146
1913	Walter Fairbanks, Denver	166	1964	J. Wolcott Brown, Manasquan River	147
1914	Frank A. Wright, Baltusrol	167	1965	Fred Brand, Jr., Oakmont	148
1915	James A. Tyng, Baltusrol	166	1966	George Haggarty, Detroit	145
1916	C. G. Waldo, Brooklawn	167	1967	Robert B. Kiersky, Bob O'Link	142
1917	W.E. Truesdell, Garden City Golf Club	172	1968	Curtis Person, Colonial	143
1918	W.E. Truesdell, Garden City Golf Club	172	1969	William P. Scott, Jr., Cypress Point	143
1919	William Clark, Misquanicut	169	1970	David "Spec" Goldman. Brookhaven	144
1920	Hugh Halsell, Dallas	162	1971	James B. Knowles, Round Hill	150
1921	Martin J. Condon, Memphis	161	1972	David "Spec" Goldman. Brookhaven	146
1922	Frederick Snare, Garden City Golf Club	162	1973	Robert B. Kiersky, Pine Tree	147
1923	Hugh Halsell, Dallas	156	1974	James B. Knowles, Ekwanok	143
1924	Claude M. Hart, Brae Burn	161	1975	Dale Morey, Willow Creek	144
1925	Frederick Snare, Garden City Golf Club	156	1976	Dale Morey, Willow Creek	147
1926	Frank H. Hoyt, Engineers	152	1977	Dale Morey, Willow Creek	144
1927	Hugh Halsell, Dallas	158	1978	Ed Tutwiler, Crooked Stick	141
1928	Dr. Charles H. Walter, Sequoyah	158	1979	Dr. Edgar R. Updegraff, Tucson	143
1929	Dr. George T. Gregg, Oakmont	156	1980	Wm. H. Zimmerman, Green Island	73
1930	Dr. George T. Gregg. Oakmont	155	1981	Wm. Hyndman, III, Huntingdon Valley	143
1931	John D. Chapman, Greenwich	159	1982	L. W. Oehmig, Lookout Mountain	145
1932	Findlay S. Douglas, Apawamis	148	1983	Maj. Gen. John Kline, Champions	149
1933	Raleigh W. Lee, Scioto	156	1984	Wm. Hyndman, III, Huntingdon Valley	143
1934	Charles H. Jennings, Roaring Gap	158	1985	Robert J. K. Hart, Rockaway Hunt	77
1935	Christopher W. Deibel, Youngstown	153	1986	Ed Tutwiler, Crooked Stick	144
1936	Richard H. Doughty, Detroit	148	1987	Richard Remsen, Seminole	147
1937	Raleigh W. Lee, Scioto	154	1988	Dr. Edgar R. Updegraff, Tucson	147
1938	Raleigh W. Lee, Scioto	158		James W. Vickers, Castle Pines	147
1939	Charles H. Jennings, Roaring Gap	148	1989	Charles Van Linge, Sharon Heights	148
1940	Charles H. Jennings, Roaring Gap	149	1990	James L. Frost, Broadmoor	146
1941	Alvah H. Pierce, Brae Burn	157	1991	John C. Owens, Idle Hour	148
1942	John Ellis Knowles, Apawamis	143	1992	Dr. Edgar R. Updegraff, Tucson	145
1943	John Ellis Knowles, Apawamis	147	1993	Jack Hesler, Scioto	148
1944	John Ellis Knowles, Apawamis	145	1994	James L. Frost, Broadmoor	146
1945	John Ellis Knowles, Apawamis	149	1995	Jack Hesler, Scioto	143
1946	John Ellis Knowles, Apawamis	155	1996	Harcourt Kemp, Louisville	144
1947	Col. M. S. Lindgrove, Baltusrol	146	1997	O. Gordon Brewer, Pine Valley	147
1948	John F. Riddell, Garden City Golf Club	149	1998	Harcourt Kemp, Louisville	145
1949	Joseph M. Wells, East Liverpool	145	1999	Jack Hesler, Muirfield Village	152
1950	Alfred C. Ulmer, Timuquana	146	2000	Marvin M. Giles, III,C.C. of Virginia	71
1951	Thomas C. Robbins, Winged Foot	140	2001	Marvin M. Giles, III, Kinloch	148
1952	Thomas C. Robbins, Winged Foot	147	2002	Harcourt Kemp, Louisville	146
1953	Frank D. Ross, Wampanoag	142	2003	Peter B. Roby, C. C. of Rochester	74
1954	John Ellis Knowles, Apawamis	148	2004	Thomas M. Graham, C. C. of Fairfield	149
1955	John W. Roberts, Scioto	148			

PRESCOTT BUSH MEMORIAL TROPHY WINNERS
Low Gross at Blind Brook

Year	Winner	Scores	Total	Year	Winner	Scores	Total
1973	James H. Ackerman	79–76	155	1989	Harold E. Foreman	82–79	161
1974	James H. Ackerman	81–77	158	1990	William H. Dyer	80–82	162
	John W. Roberts	76–82	158	1991	George W. Pottle	80–78	158
1975	Anderson Borthwick	74–77	151	1992	John F. Pottle	83–76	159
1976	Anderson Borthwick	73–76	149	1993	George L. Cornell	81	81
1977	Anderson Borthwick	76–80	156	1994	C. Theodore Krug	85–79	164
1978	Anderson Borthwick	83–77	160	1995	Arthur C. Williams	80–78	158
1979	Charles M. Mackall	82–76	158	1996	Richard Remsen	75–76	151
1980	Anderson Borthwick	81	81	1997	Richard Remsen	83–74	157
1981	Anderson Borthwick	82–81	163	1998	Richard Remsen	78–82	160
1982	William S. Terrell	76–76	152	1999	Richard Remsen	79–81	160
1983	Willis de la Cour	83–82	165	2000	play canceled – not awarded		
1984	Raymond F. Evans	82–79	161	2001	Richard Remsen	70–79	149
1985	Robert B. Kiersky	78	78	2002	William H. Black	76–75	151
1986	Curtis Person, Sr.	76–77	153	2003	Jack Hesler	74	74
1987	Raymond F. Evans	77–83	160	2004	James L. Garard, Jr	80–75	155
1988	Capt. Pliny G. Holt	79–81	160				

BOSTON BOWL WINNERS
Low Net
Apawamis, Round Hill, and Blind Brook Members

Year	Winner	Year	Winner	Year	Winner
1913	Andrew Shiland	1945	Prior Sinclair	1977	Frank R. Lyon, Jr.
1914	Horace L. Hotchkiss	1946	Lyman C. Judson	1978	Samuel R. Watkins
1915	Martin Garey	1947	Lyman C. Judson	1979	Stanley T. Crossland
1916	Horace L. Hotchkiss	1948	Joseph A. Lee	1980	Stanley T. Crossland
1917	Wesley M. Oler	1949	Five man tie	1981	William H. Todd
1918	Thomas E. Kirby	1950	Livingston Platt	1982	Stanley T. Crossland
1919	Thomas E. Kirby	1951	William M. Young	1983	William M. Rees
1920	William Lester	1952	Dr. N. Vern Peterson	1984	Everett Fisher
1921	Joseph J. O'Donohue, Jr.	1953	Stewart S. Hathaway	1985	George P. Bent, III
1922	Horace L. Hotchkiss	1954	Parker Newhall	1986	Theodore I. Dunn, Jr.
1923	Horace L. Hotchkiss	1955	Romeyn B. Scribner	1987	Francis C. Rooney, Jr.
1924	John Bister	1956	John Ellis Knowles	1988	James D. Farley
1925	William C. Lester	1957	Francis B. Upham, Jr.	1989	Emil Mosbacher, Jr.
1926	William C. Lester	1958	John Ellis Knowles	1990	Thomas S. Murphy
1927	James Clarke	1959	John M. Fisher	1991	William M. Rees
1928	Frederick S. Wheeler	1960	George T. Martin	1992	James D. Farley
1929	Robert W. Martin	1961	Bayard W. Read	1993	Robert A. Powers
1930	Edward W. Harris	1962	William L. Culbert	1994	Reginald H. Jones
1931	John W. Hornor	1963	Lanphear Buck	1995	Andrew C. Sigler
1932	Edward A. Choate	1964	Dr. Edward P. Scully	1996	Francis C. Rooney, Jr.
1933	John W. Hornor	1965	Foster Nichols	1997	Edmund R. Swanberg
1934	J. Howard Ardrey	1966	Harry C. Mills	1998	Louis T. Hagopian
1935	T. Ashley Dent	1967	John Ellis Knowles	1999	John McGillicuddy
1936	Col. James A. Coates	1968	Edward A.M. Cobden		Frederick S. Wonham
1937	Seth M. Milliken	1969	John Ellis Knowles	2000	Stephen T. Vehslage
1938	C. Reginald Lea	1970	John Ellis Knowles	2001	Leland B. Paton
1939	Ralph H. Hubbard	1971	Edward A.M. Cobden	2002	Francis C. Rooney, Jr.
1940	Ralph H. Hubbard	1972	John Ellis Knowles	2003	Jonathan M. Clark
1941	William A.P. Phipps	1973	John Ellis Knowles		John F. McGillicuddy
1942	William H. Conroy	1974	Stanley T. Crossland	2004	Frederick D. Remsen
1943	Seth M. Milliken	1975	Edwin H. Crandell		
1944	Redmond McCosker	1976	Samuel R. Watkins		

C.

INTERNATIONAL TEAM MATCHES
UNITED STATES – CANADA
For The Duke of Devonshire Cup

Year		Pts		Pts	Course	Year		Pts		Pts	Course
1918	Canada	20	USA	16	Royal Montreal	1958	USA	40½	Canada	31½	RoyalOttawa,
1919	USA	21	Canada	7	Apawamis						Rivermead
1920	USA	17	Canada	12	Royal Ottawa	1959	USA	19½	Canada	4½	Pine Valley
1921	USA	26	Canada	2	Apawamis	1960	USA	42½	Canada	29½	Beaconsfield,
1922	USA	24½	Canada	20½	Scarboro						Kanawaki
1923	Canada	18	USA	13	Royal Montreal	1961	USA	16	Canada	2	Woking
1924	USA	24	Canada	8	Apawamis	1962	USA	53½	Canada	18½	Old Elm
1925	USA	25½	Canada	16½	St. Andrews, N.B.	1963	USA	25½	Canada	22½	Royal Montreal
1926	USA	18	Canada	8	Apawamis	1964	USA	45½	Canada	26½	Shinnecock Hills
1927	USA	19	Canada	12	Royal Montreal	1965	USA	13	Canada	5	Royal St. George's
1928	USA	17	Canada	6	Lambton	1966	USA	44½	Canada	27½	Mississauga,
1929	USA	19	Canada	16	Royal Ottawa						Toronto
1930	USA	24½	Canada	10½	Toronto	1968	Canada	37	USA	35	Royal Ottawa,
1931	USA	26½	Canada	18½	Apawamis						Rivermead
1932	USA	29½	Canada	15½	Apawamis	1970	USA	43	Canada	29	Old Elm
1933	USA	20	Canada	11	Seigniory	1972	USA	38½	Canada	33½	C. C. of North
1934	USA	22½	Canada	22½	Royal Montreal						Carolina
1935	USA	30	Canada	8	Apawamis	1974	Canada	40½	USA	31½	Scarboro
1936	USA	26	Canada	13	National Golf Links	1976	USA	42½	Canada	29½	Old Elm
1937	USA	25½	Canada	19½	Lambton	1978	Canada	48½	USA	47½	Toronto
1938	USA	31	Canada	14	Toronto	1980	USA	51½	Canada	44½	The Country Club
1939	USA	29	Canada	16	Blind Brook	1982	USA	53	Canada	43	London Hunt
1940–1945 – War Years						1984	USA	70½	Canada	20½	Old Elm
1946	USA	30½	Canada	5½	Apawamis	1986	USA	69	Canada	27	Royal Ottawa
1947	USA	26	Canada	19	Rosedale	1988	USA	56	Canada	40	Castle Pines
1948	USA	36½	Canada	8½	National Golf Links	1990	Canada	54	USA	42	Scarboro
1949	USA	27	Canada	18	Toronto	1992	USA	77	Canada	43	The Honors Course
1950	USA	38	Canada	7	National Golf Links	1994	USA	75½	Canada	44½	Mt. Bruno
1951	USA	33½	Canada	14½	Lambton	1996	USA	84	Canada	36	Old Elm
1952	USA	36½	Canada	8½	Pine Valley	1998	USA	72	Canada	48	Redtail
1953	USA	43½	Canada	10½	Toronto	2000	USA	34½	Canada	25½	The Honors Course
1955	USA	56	Canada	12½	National Golf Links	2002	USA	67	Canada	53	Riverside
1956	USA	39	Canada	9	Mississauga	2004	USA	59½	Canada	60½	Pine Valley
1957	USA	38½	Canada	30	Garden City Golf Club						

UNITED STATES SENIORS' TROPHY
Individual Champion, Medal Round

Year	Winner	Gross Score	Course
1923	G. S. Lyon (Can.)	80	Royal Montreal
1927	C. P. Wilson (Can.)	81	Royal Montreal
1928	H. Halsell (US)	79	Lambton
1929	Dr. G. T. Gregg (US)	78	Royal Ottawa
1930	G. S. Lyon (Can.)	75	Toronto
1931	G. S. Lyon (Can.)	78	Apawamis
1932	G. S. Lyon (Can.)	74	Apawamis
1933	R. W. Lee (US)	80	Seigniory
1934	R. W. Smith (US)	78	Royal Montreal
1935	R. W. Lee (US)	76	Apawamis
1936	F. S. Douglas (US)	81	National Golf Links
1937	R. W. Lee (US)		
	R. M. Gray (Can)	79	Lambton
1938	R. M. Gray (Can.)	77	Toronto
1939	W. A. Ryan (US)	73	Blind Brook
1946	J. E. Knowles (US)	70	Apawamis
1947	D. L. Tower (US)	75	Rosedale
1948	J. M. Wells (US)	76	National Golf Links
1949	Dr. G. F. Laing (Can.)	74	Toronto
1950	J. M. Wells (US)	75	National Golf Links
1951	Col. M. S. Lindgrove (US)	73	Lambton
1952	T. C. Robbins (US)	75	Pine Valley
1953	F. D. Ross (US)		
	P. C. Jarboe (US)	73	Toronto
1955	M. R. Smith (US)	76	National Golf Links
1956	T. C. Robbins (US)	73	Mississauga, Toronto
1957	Dr. G. F. Laing (Can.)		
	L. Haldeman (US)		
	M. R. Smith (US)	78	Garden City Golf Club
1958	H. H. Richardson (Can.)	72	Royal Ottawa
1960	V. V. Roby (US)	70	Beaconsfield, Kanawaki
1962	N/A		Old Elm
1964	C. R. Somerville (Can.)	74	Shinnecock Hills
1966	C. R. Somerville (Can.)		
	R. B. Kiersky (US)	75	Mississauga, Toronto
1968	G. Taylor (Can.)	72	Rivermead, Royal Ottawa
1970	C. Person (US)	74	Old Elm
1972	D. Goldman (US)		
	E. Meister(US)	73	C. C. of North Carolina
1974	J. Hand (US)		
	M. Noyes (Can.)	72	Scarboro, Toronto
1976	H. Welch (US)	72	Old Elm
1978	T. Woodall (Can.)	70	Toronto
1980	E. Bentley (Can.)	73	The Country Club
1982	Ed Tutwiler (US)	72	London Hunt
1984	Ed Tutwiler (US)	71	Old Elm
1986	R. Giddings (US)	71	Royal Ottawa
1988	J. M. Key (US)	78	Castle Pines
1990	G. Seely (Can.)	68	Scarboro
1992	J. M. Key (US)	74	The Honors Course
1994	G. H. Bostwick Jr. (US)	70	Mt. Bruno
1996	Jack Hesler (US)	71	Old Elm
1998	Jack Hesler (US)		
	R. Fugere (Can.)	73	Redtail
2000	Bruce Brewer (Can.)	73	The Honors Course
2002	N. Goldman (Can.)	69	Riverside
2004	Robert Fugere (Can.)	71	Pine Valley

GEORGE S. LYON MEMORIAL TROPHY
Low Net, Medal Round

Year	Winner	Net Score	Course
1938	Robert M. Gray (Can.)	72	Toronto
1939	Robert M. Gray (Can.)		
	W. A. Ryan (US)	69	Blind Brook
1946	Dr. E.J. Kempf (US)		
	Fred L. Riggin (US)	70	Apawamis
1947	Dr. W. C. Givens (Can.)	66	Rosedale
1948	J. F. Riddell (US)		
	J. M. Wells (US)	72	National Golf Links
1949	Dr. G. F. Laing (Can.)	68	Toronto
1950	D. L. Tower (US)	71	National Golf Links
1951	A. B. McEwen (Can.)	68	Lambton
1952	D. D. MacLachlan (Can.)	69	Pine Valley
1953	A. L. Code (Can.)	66	Toronto
1955	Paul Dunkel (US)	NA	National Golf Links
1956	Dr. H. L. Esterberg (US)	68	Toronto
1957	Dr. G. F. Laing (Can.)	71	Garden City Golf Club
1958	H. H. Richardson (Can.)	65	Royal Ottawa
1960	I. B. Grainger (US)	66	Beaconsfield
1962	L. H. T. Clegg (Can.)	72	Old Elm
1963	N. C. Barnabe (Can.)	70	Royal Montreal
1964	Ben Merwin (Can.)	70	Shinnecock Hills
1966	H. G. Love (Can.)	70	Mississauga, Toronto
1968	G. B. Taylor (Can.)	66	Rivermead, Royal Ottawa
1970	W. Terrell (US)	70	Old Elm
1972	G. B. Taylor (Can.)	69	C. C. of North Carolina
1974	H. Ammidon (US)		
	W. S. Terrell (US)	68	Scarboro
1976	H. Ammidon (US)	68	Old Elm
1978	R. Penney (Can.)		
	T. Woodall (Can.)	67	Toronto
1980	W. S. Terrell (US)	69	The Country Club
1982	Ed Tutwiler (US)		
	Ed Ervasti (Can.)	70	London Hunt
1984	Ray Evans (US)		
	Ed Ervasti (Can.)	72	Old Elm
1986	Ray Getliffe (Can.)	70	Royal Ottawa
1988	W. H. Todd (US)	75	Castle Pines
1990	Glen Seely (Can.)	67	Scarboro
1992	R. Remsen (US)	72	The Honors Course
1994	J. R. Hand (US)		
	R. D Harvey (Can.)	70	Mt. Bruno
1996	Don Hewson (Van.)	68	Old Elm
1998	Glen Seely (Can.)	71	Redtail
2000	Chuck Van Linge (US)	70	The Honors Course
2002	Chuck Van Linge (US)		
	Don Hewson (Can.)	67	Riverside
2004	Patrick Suraj (Can.)	72	Pine Valley

INTERNATIONAL TEAM MATCHES
UNITED STATES – CANADA – GREAT BRITAIN
TRIANGULAR TEAM MATCHES
For the Earl of Derby Cup

Year	Course	USSGA Total	Canada Total	Great Britain Total
1927	Sunningdale	23	19	36
1928	Blind Brook	40	22	16
1929	St. Andrews	16½	13½	32
1930	Toronto	28½	12	14½
1931	Swinley Forest	5	–	11
1932	Apawamis	5½	12 ½	6
1933	St. Georges	18	3½	32½
1934	Royal Montreal	22	19	22
1935	Prestwick	18	4½	31
1936	National Golf Links	24½	9	20 ½
1937	Royal Lytham	16½	6	31 ½
1938	Toronto	27½	16	10 ½
1949	Woking	7	–	5
1953	Mid–Ocean	64½	15½	28
1954	St. Andrews	17½	5½	32
1956	Mid–Ocean	18	3½	14½
1957	Muirfield	24½	4½	25
1959	Pine Valley	35½	13	23½
1961	Woking	24½	6	23½
1963	Royal Montreal	22½	19½	12
1965	Royal St. Georges	19	9	26
1967	Pine Valley	27	10½	16½
1969	Formby	20	16½	16½
1971	London Hunt	23	8½	12½
1973	Royal Birkdale	17	11	26
1975	Pine Valley	27	10½	16½
1977	Sunningdale	24	11	19
1979	Mt. Bruno	29½	1½	13
1981	C. C. of North Carolina	18	25	11
1983	Formby	20½	13	20½
1985	Capilano	17½	22	14½
1987	Shinnecock Hills	28	13½	12½
1989	Muirfield	21½	16½	14
1991	Calgary	22½	17	14½
1993	Pinehurst No. 2	25½	11½	17
1995	Saunton	24	11½	18
1997	Toronto	14½	16½	5
1999	Castle Pines	19	21	14
2001	Royal Liverpool	21	27	24
2003	Essex	43½	32	14½

Founders Cup
Individual Champions, Medal Round

Year	Winner	Gross Score	Course
1934	J. W. B. Pease (GB)	74	Royal Montreal
1935	R. M. Gray (Can.)	77	Prestwick
1936	A. R. Aitken (GB)	78	National Golf Links
1937	Hon. M. Scott (GB)	77	Royal Lytham
1938	R. M. Gray (Can.)	75	Toronto
1949	T. E. Cunningham (GB)	73	Woking
1953	Dr. G. F. Laing (Can.)	78	Mid-Ocean
1954	Brig. W. H. Aitken (GB)		
	H. J. T. Neilson (GB)	72	St. Andrews
1956	F. G. Clement (US)		
	Dr. Wm. Tweddell (GB)	76	Mid-Ocean
1957	J. W. Roberts (US)		Muirfield
1961	E. F. Quittner (US)	71	Woking
1963	N. C. Barnabe (Can.)	75	Royal Montreal
1965	Francis Francis (GB)	71	Royal St. Georges
1967	Curtis Person (US)	76	Pine Valley
1969	R. P. H–C Borgnis (GB)		
	F. W. G. Church (GB)		
	Francis Francis(GB)		
	Gordon B. Taylor (Can.)	74	Formby
1971	David "Spec" Goldman (US)	69	London Hunt
1973	D. A. Blair (GB)		
	F. W. G. Church GB)	74	Royal Birkdale
1975	D. Morey (US)		
	Lew Oehmig (US)	75	Pine Valley
1977	Major D. A. Blair (GB)	72	Sunningdale
1979	F. W. G. Church (GB)	71	Mt. Bruno
1981	Lew Oehmiig (US)	72	C. C. of North Carolina
1983	Ed Tutwiler (US)	71	Formby
1985	George Irlam (GB)		
	Richard Remsen (US)		
	Ed Ervasti (Can,)	71	Capilano
1987	Ed Tutwiler (US)	68	Shinnecock Hills
1989	Glen Seely (Can.)	72	Muirfield
1991	M. Trammell (US)	70	Calgary
1993	J. M. Key (US)	73	Pinehurst No. 2
1995	Harcourt Kemp (US)		
	R. Scott (GB)	74	Saunton
1997	Harcourt Kemp (US)	70	Toronto
1999	John Owens(US)	75	Castle Pines
2001	Mark Dixon (GB)	83	Royal Liverpool
2003	Bruce Brewer (Can.)	68	Essex

KNOWLES–SOMERVILLE CUP
Winners, Age Sixty-five and Older Competition

Year	Course	Winner	Year	Course	Winner
1975	Pine Valley	USA	1991	Calgary	USA
1977	Sunningdale	GB	1993	Pinehurst No. 2	USA
1979	Mt. Bruno	USA	1995	Saunton	USA
1981	C. C. of North Carolina	USA	1997	Toronto	Canada
1983	Formby	GB	1999	Castle Pines	Canada
1985	Capilano	USA	2001	Royal Liverpool	GB
1987	Shinneock Hills	USA	2003	Essex	USA
1989	Muirfield	USA			

THE AITKEN–SALVER
Low Net, Medal Round, Age Sixty-five and Older Competition

Year	Winner	Net Score	Course
1969	J. H. Ackerman (US)	77	Formby
1971	N. Ransick (US)	71	London Hunt
1973	H. G. Bentley (GB)	73	Royal Birkdale
1975	P. H. Strubing (US)	75	Pine Valley
1977	Sir John Carmichael (GB)		
	A. Borthwick (US)	80	Sunningdale
1979	A. Borthwick (US)		
	W. S. Terrell (US)	78	Mt. Bruno
1981	W. S. Terrell (US)	78	C. C. of North Carolina
1983	R. Getliffe (Can.)	76	Formby
1985	R. Giddings (US)	75	Capilano
1987	R. Willits (US)	68	Shinnecock Hills
1989	R. Giddings (US)	77	Muirfield
1991	W. Campbell (US)	71	Calgary
1993	Ed Ervasti (Can.)	74	Pinehurst No. 2
1995	R. Scott (GB)	69	Saunton
1997	D. Cooper (Can.)	68	Toronto
1999	J. Cook (GB)	68	Castle Pines
2001	David Frame (GB)	83	Royal Liverpool
2003	Jack Hesler (US)	72	Essex

T^3 TROPHY
Low Aggregate of Four Cards

Year	Site	Winner
1989	Muirfield	United States
1991	Calgary	United States
1993	Pinehurst	Canada/United States (tie)
1995	Saunton	United States
1997	Toronto	United States
1999	Castle Pines	United States
2001	Royal Liverpool	Great Britain
2003	Essex	Canada/United States (tie)

WELLER NOBLE TROPHY
Low Net, Medal Round, Team Member or Official

Year	Winner	Year	Winner
1981	M. Noyes (Can.)	1993	E. Ervasti (Can.)
1983	J. A. Nezan (Can.)	1995	R. Scott (GB)
1985	J. Thornton (GB)	1997	J. Vickers (US)
1987	E. Tutwiler (US)	1999	J. Owens (US)
1989	G. Seely (Can.)	2001	D. Frame (GB)
1991	M. Rothwell (Can.)	2003	M. Saffran (Can.)

D.

INVITATIONAL TOURNAMENT WINNERS

EKWANOK COUNTRY CLUB
Manchester, Vermont

1962	Weller Noble	1984	Jerry Fitzpatrick and John Poinier
1963	Weller Noble	1985	Moore Gates and Ken Corcoran
1964	Egon Quittner and John Ledbetter, Jr.	1986	Theodore E. Gordon and Edgar Updegraff
1965	Joseph Morrill, Jr. and John Ledbetter, Jr.	1987	Henry G. Hay and Robert Penny
1966	James T. Kirkpatrick and Franklin Mead	1988	James Knowles and J.G. Fitzpatrick
1967	David Goldman and James Miller	1989	John W. Kline and Robert B. Egan
1968	Chester T. Birch and Willis De La Cour	1990	William Maize and Richard D. Frame
1969	Pliny G. Holt and Fritz Pruyn	1991	Allan M. Doyle and J.G. Fitzpatrick
1970	Pliny G. Holt and William Stockhausen	1992	Charles VanLinge and Robert Everson
1971	Chester T. Birch and H. K. Halligan	1993	George O. Holland and Monte Bee
1972	Chester T. Birch and Pliny G. Holt	1994	Edward C. Shotwell and James W. Key
1973	Pliny G. Holt and Richard G. Stevenson	1995	John R. Adams and Edward C. Shotwell
1974	Egon Quittner and William Holt	1996	Patrick Pate and William F. Bogle
1975	Chester T. Birch and M. Pierpont Warner	1997	Harcourt Kemp and C. Adams Moore
1976	Allan W. Betts and Raymond Evans	1998	Pete Parker and Clark F. MacKenzie
1977	Howard L. Clark and Ed Littlefield	1999	B. Kenneth West and Raymond T. Riffle
1978	Chester T. Birch and William Zimmerman	2000	James L. Frost and Donald H. McCree, Jr.
1979	Bing Hunter and Robert J. Shaw	2001	James W. Key and David O. Zenker
1980	William S. Terrell and Ed Ervasti	2002	George H. Bostwick, Jr. and William H. Black
1981	James R. Hand and Robert T. Isham	2003	O. Gordon Brewer, Jr. and Henry K. Wurzer
1982	William Holt and Gerald Lauck	2004	Fairleigh Lussky and Peter J. McLachlan
1983	Gordon Taylor and Robert T. Isham		

COUNTRY CLUB OF NORTH CAROLINA
Pinehurst, North Carolina

1970	Chester T. Birch and Samuel Ellis	1988	James L. Frost and Henry G. Hay
1971	Joseph Morrill, Jr. and Fred Brand	1989	Arthur Snyder and Richard Meister
1972	Pliny G. Holt and Robert J.G. Morton	1990	George Pottle and Edward Marshall
1973	John F. Pottle and Dr. John Y. Howson		Richard Remsen Jr. and Monte Bee
1974	Sidney P. Davis and Louis DeLone	1991	William O. Alden and James B. Hoefer
1975	William S.Terrell and P. J. McDonough	1992	Eli W. Tullis and Richard E. Thigpen
	Frank Lyon and Leonard Raichle	1993	Richard E. Thigpen and Reynolds W. Guyer
1976	Louis DeLone and Robert J. Shaw	1994	Patrick Pate and James L. Garard
1977	John Prestini and Carl Schieren	1995	Eli W. Tullis and Milton A. Barber
1978	William McEwan and Carl Schieren	1996	David U. Cookson and David W. Wiley
1979	Dave MacHarg and George Cavanaugh	1997	Hugh R. Beath and Jack Hesler
1980	Joe Hall and Pliny G. Holt	1998	Clark F. MacKenzie and Edward C. Darling
1981	Dave MacHarg and Howard Ferguson	1999	David N. Hall and M. Hugh Hinton
1982	John Landen and Gen. Francis Roberts	2000	Richard E. Thigpen and James B. Hoefer
1983	Fred Kroft and Erwin Laxton	2001	David W. Wiley and Milton A. Barber
1984	David P. MacHarg and Lewis W. Oehmig	2002	Michael Sanger and William B. Clement
1985	Richard Remsen Jr. and Thomas S. Royster	2003	Clifford W. Perry,Jr.andRichard Remsen, Jr.
1986	Lewis W. Oehmig and Jack Poinier	2004	Charles A. Phillips and Thomas A. Wilson
1987	John S. Griswold and James B. Hoefer		

MOUNTAIN LAKE CLUB
Lake Wales, Florida

1971	Fred Kammer and J. Porter Brinton	1988	Howard Ferguson and Bill Gray
1972	William Holt and Frank Sample	1989	Frederic L. Yarrington and Bill Risley
1973	James Ackerman and Neil Ransick	1990	L. Patton Kline and Walter S. Robbins
1974	Thomas Block and Ken Corcoran	1991	William Heyburn and Ericsson Broadbent
1975	Leon Bishop and Leo Schoenhofen	1992	George P. Swift, Jr. and Ericsson Broadbent
1976	John I. Dean and M. Pierpont Warner	1993	Jerry Smith and L. Patton Kline
1977	William Holt and M. Pierpont Warner	1994	Samuel T. Reeves and John K. O'Loughlin
1978	Chester T. Birch and Robert J. Shaw	1995	James L. Garard and Walter E. Robb
1979	Samuel Callaway and Robert J. Shaw	1996	C. Adams Moore and Bradford R. Boss
1980	Henry Hay and Jack Poinier	1997	L. Patton Kline and David W. Wiley
1981	Walter Brown and C. Ted Krug	1998	Walter E. Robb and David Zenker
1982	Henry Hay and Henry Wischusen	1999	Clark F. MacKenzie and Donald Kohler
1983	Theodore E. Gordon and Samuel Callaway	2000	Arthur M. Rogers and Richard H. Tilghman
1984	Kenneth Corcoran and John Poinier	2001	C. Harvey Bradley and Richard N. Edie
1985	Theodore E. Gordon and Leon Bishop	2002	Arthur M. Rogers, Jr. and Allen N. Jones
1986	Robert J. Shaw and Walter F. Brown	2003	A. Harcourt Kemp and John A. Brabson, Jr.
1987	Norman Boucher and Howard Ferguson	2004	Michael Sanger and Henry K. Wurzer

KITTANSETT
Marion, Massachusetts

1972	William Carleton and M. Pierpont Warner	1989	Theodore E. Gordon and Richard A. Tilghman
1973	Chester T. Birch and Joseph Oliver	1990	Buck Bradly and Robert J. Shaw
1974	Kenneth Corcoran and Arthur Rice	1991	"Hurricane Bob"
1975	Chester T. Birch and A. Stevens	1992	Robert Hart and William L. Rudkin
1976	David Lapham and Henry Wischusen	1993	David U. Cookson and Philip M. Drake
1977	Samuel R. Callaway and Robert J.K. Hart	1994	Walter S. Robbins and Edward C. Shotwell
1978	Eugene Pulliam and Robert J. Shaw		David Zenker and Thomas P. Greeman
1979	Eugene Pulliam and Ray Evans	1995	James R. Hand and J. Woodward Redmond
1980	Samuel R. Callaway and John S. Griswold	1996	Rained Out
1981	Robert J.K. Hart and James Casey	1997	William B. Marx and Paul E. Mersereau
1982	Theodore E. Gordon and Robert Lee	1998	Allan M. Doyle and David R. Gavitt
1983	Robert J.K. Hart and Kenneth Corcoran	1999	Howard A. Halligan and James P. Ingram
1984	Theodore E. Gordon and Skip Carstensen	2000	Allan M. Doyle and James P. Ingram
1985	Samuel R. Callaway and Theodore E. Gordon	2001	Cancelled due to September 11th
1986	Frank Souchak and Everett Jones	2002	Arthur M. Rogers and Edward W. Turley
1987	Francis J. Roberts and Ralph T. King	2003	Thomas M. Wilson and Donald T. Valentine
1988	Howard Ferguson and Ralph T. King	2004	Allan M. Doyle and Richard N. Young, Jr.

LYFORD CAY CLUB
Nassau, Bahamas

1972	James H. Ackerman and Edwin E. Bennett	1989	Thomas Dannemiller and William Evans
1973	Harry F. Stimpson, Jr. and Dick Wightman	1990	Edward C. Darling and Stuart A. Christie
1974	David H. Northrup and James C. Morrison	1991	David Zenker and Skid Livingstone
1976	Harry Jensen and Henry Wischusen	1992	Robert B. Egan and Skid Livingstone
1977	Robert Roos and Preston Dalglish	1993	David Zenker and William C. Ford
1978	John Dean and Lyle B. Ramsey	1994	Paul Hardin and George J. Gillespie
1979	Jack Busby and Richard Semple	1995	David Zenker and James P. Gorter
1980	Bing Hunter and Everett Jones	1996	James H. Dowling and William F. Souders
1981	Edward Clark and Stan Deland	1997	James H. Dowling and James L. Garard
1982	Theodore E. Gordon and Stan Deland	1998	J. Woodward Redmond and Bradford R. Boss
1983	George L. Cornell and William Evans	1999	William H. Black and Edward C. Darling
1984	Lewis W. Oehmig and Lyle B. Ramsey	2000	David N. Hall and J. Woodward Redmond
1985	Arthur Snyder and Francis X. Totten	2001	David N. Hall and Joseph D. Roxe
1986	Robert E. Lee and Richard Miller	2002	Bradford R. Boss and Donald H. McCree
1987	Arthur Snyder and Henry Russell	2003	William F. Souders and Donald H. McCree
1988	John S. Griswold and Clifford M. Kirtland	2004	James L. Garard and William F. Souders

LONG ISLAND
The Hamptons, New York

1973	James Ackerman and Harlan Parks		1989	Marshall Trammell and John S. Griswold
1974	Joseph Stevens and P.J. McDonough (tied for individual low gross)		1990	Marshall Trammell and Howard Ferguson
			1991	James L. Frost and Angus MacLean
1975	Robert B. Gardner, Jr. and David Lapham		1992	Robert R. Hillery and Edward Updegraff
1976	Fred Kroft and John S. Griswold		1993	William H. Black and William B. Caldwell
1977	Robert Roos and Norman Hearn		1994	George H. Bostwick and Raymond Knowles
1978	G. Gunby Jordan and William J. Patton		1995	J. Woodward Redmond and Harcourt Kemp
1979	Richard Remsen, Jr. and William S. Terrell		1996	John W. Kline and Eli W. Tullis
1980	Billy Joe Patton and Jim Paul		1997	William H. Black and Lawrence G. Bell
1981	William H. Zimmerman and Russell W. Billman		1998	Michael G. Conroy and David B. Sloan
1982	Dale Morey and Jack Landen		1999	William H. Black and David B. Sloan
1983	William P. Dougherty and Jack Landen		2000	Fred T. Boice and Robert D. Rogers
1984	Robert J.K. Hart and Henry G. Hay		2001	Clark F. MacKenzie and John R. Adams
1985	John W. Kline and Edward C. Steele		2002	Charles W. Fairbanks and William C. Coleman
1987	Richard Remsen and John W. Morrison		2003	Raymond V. Knowles and E. Maxwell Geddes
1988	Eli W. Tullis and Fred Woodley		2004	Rees L. Jones and John W. Wight, Jr.

PACIFIC COAST–CYPRESS POINT
Monterey, California

1974	Frank S. Souchak (Individual Low Gross)		1989	Richard Remsen, Jr. and Richard J. Giddings
1975	Franklin Mead and Joseph T. Hall		1990	Dean Frisbee and Henry See
	Thomas R. Dwyer and James Morrison		1991	Robert R. Hillery and M. T. Johnson
1976	William S. Terrell and Jack Westland		1992	Patrick Pate and Steve Creekmore
1977	Robert Vaillancourt and Jack Westland		1993	Charles L. Van Linge and John G. Arnold
1978	Richard J. Giddings and Robert J. Shaw		1994	James McKenzie and Patrick Pate
1979	Downey Orrick and Edward Updegraff		1995	Samuel T. Reeves and B. Kenneth West
1980	Frank S. Souchak and Robert W. Willits		1996	Raymond T. Riffle and William F. Souders
1981	Richard Giddings and John Griswold		1997	Paul Spengler and B. Kenneth West
1982	William Colm and Robert W. Willits		1998	Rained out
1983	Richard J. Giddings and Robert A. Roos		1999	William F. Souders and Donald B. Rice
1984	George L. Cornell and Frank S. Souchak		2000	Samuel T. Reeves and Richard G. Rogers
1985	George L. Cornell and John B. Leisure		2001	Leighton B. Ford and Samuel T. Reeves
1986	Jack Landen and Theodore E. Gordon		2002	Raymond V. Knowles and Charles W. Fairbanks
1987	Robert R. Hillery and John I. Dean		2003	Samuel T. Reeves and Richard G. Rogers
1988	Richard Remsen, Jr. and Robert W. Willits		2004	Leland B. Paton and Robert D. Rogers

SEMINOLE–HOBE SOUND
Jupiter Island, Florida

1975	Edward Meister and James Ackerman		1990	Fred Woodley and Eli W. Tullis
1976	Howard Clark and Harton Semple		1991	James W. Vickers and David U. Cookson
1977	John Poinier and Richard Remsen, Jr.		1992	William H. Black and Monte Bee
1978	Howard Clark and Richard Remsen, Jr.		1993	Robert B. Egan and David U. Cookson
1979	William C. Campbell and Walter Brown		1994	William H. Black and Monte Bee
1980	James R. Hand and Richard Remsen, Jr.		1995	William H. Black and Hugh R. Beath
1981	William C. Campbell and William S. Terrell		1996	Thomas G. Cousins and Lynah Sherrill
1982	Tournament rained out		1997	Richard E. Thigpen and Paul T. Wise
1983	Richard Remsen, Jr. and Leo F. Schoenhofen		1998	William H. Black and Richard E. Thigpen
1984	Harry W. Easterly and Robert J. Shaw		1999	Lawrence G. Bell and Richard A. Tilghman
1985	William P. Dougherty and William J. Deupree		2000	A. Harcourt Kemp and Robert R. Hillery
1986	Richard Remsen, Jr. and John I. Dean		2001	Richard A. Tilghman and Arthur M. Rogers
1987	William C. Battle and Harry Easterly		2002	William C. Coleman and George H. Bostwick, Jr.
1988	Thomas G. Cousins and Marshall Trammell		2003	Timothy P. Neher and Edward C. Shotwell III
1989	William H. Black and Joseph A. McBride		2004	Charles V. Moore and William F. Souders

MIDWEST
Lake Forest, Illinois

1977	Samuel Callaway and George Isham	1991	Monte Bee and James L. Garard
1978	Robert T. Isham and Robert Vaillancourt	1992	William Finkenstaedt and William Rudkin
1979	Robert T. Isham and Bob Morton	1993	James B. Hoefer and Philip C. Hughes
1980	G. Gunby Jordan and George Isham	1994	William Finkenstaedt and E. M. deWindt
1981	Robert T. Isham and Jack Landen	1995	Frederick J. Robbins and Lynah Sherrill
1982	Jack Landen and William T. Bacon	1996	Raymond Knowles and David Zenker
1983	Robert T. Isham and G. Gunby Jordan	1997	Raymond Riffle and Robert Wood
1984	John Poinier and William H. Evans	1998	James L. Garard and Richard A. Tilghman
1985	Jack K. Busby and Robert T. Isham	1999	Robert B. Egan and John W. Sullivan
1986	Henry Hay and Warren Carstensen	2000	B. Kenneth West and L. Patton Kline
1987	James B. Hoefer and Gorden H. Ewen	2001	L. Patton Kline and Clark F. MacKenzie
1988	James L. Garard and E. Mandell deWindt	2002	Richard A. Tighlman and James L.Garard, Jr.
1989	James B. Hoefer and John Jackson	2003	S. Bartley Osborn and Stephen M. McPherson
1990	Malcolm Jeffrey and James L. Garard	2004	Peter B. Roby and B. Kenneth West

SEA ISLAND GOLF CLUB
Sea Island, Georgia

1981	David MacHarg and Joesph A. McBride	1993	William H. Zimmerman and Clifford Kirtland
1982	Frank S. Souchak and Thomas S. Royster	1994	David Wilmerding and Robert Rogers
1983	George Swift and Robert Wharton	1995	William J. Deupree and Moore Gates
1984	Hugh Kenworthy and Clifford Kirtland	1996	Wiliam Alden and Frank Stevenson
1985	Richard Miller and David MacHarg	1997	John R. Adams and Stephen McPherson
1986	David MacHarg and Lewis W. Oehmig	1998	William J. Deupree and James H. Dowling
1987	William J. Deupree and Foster Davis	1999	James H. Dowling and Donald T. Valentine
1988	Frank W. Hartmann and William J. Deupree	2000	Paul T. Wise and Gerald A. Stahl
1989	Malcolm Jeffrey and Edward Darling	2001	Milton A. Barber and James H. Dowling
1990	Henry See and Malcolm D. Jeffrey	2002	Thomas C. Dowden and Donald H. McCree
1991	George Cornell and Malcolm D. Jeffrey	2003	Leland B. Paton and Henry K. Wurzer
1992	George Swift and Frank Stevenson	2004	John T. Fogarty and Marvin M. Giles III

Cape Cod, Massachusetts

1986	Warren Carstensen and Edward W. Clark	1996	Richard Remsen, Jr. and Milton A. Barber
1987	Warren Carstensen and Moore Gates, Jr.	1997	Eldon P. Nuss and Robert L. Dewar
1989	L. Patton Kline and David Zenker	1998	Marshall Trammell and George O.Holland
1990	Richard Stimets and Walter S. Robbins	1999	Clark F. MacKenzie and Albert E. Touche
1991	Eli W. Tullis and Charles W. Wallace	2000	John C. Owens and Richard H. Lussier
1992	Lincoln N. Kinnicutt and Richard Miller	2001	R. Woodward Millen and A.G. Wigglesworth
1993	Raymond V.Knowles and George C.S. Hackl	2002	F. Gordon Kraft and William C. Coleman
1994	Walter S. Robbins and Richard Stimets	2003	Kevin K. Carton and Richard J. Fates
1995	James L. Garard and George Frick	2004	Fred M. Filoon and Willis N. Mills, Jr.

INDIAN RIVER
Vero Beach, Florida

1992	Robert Boucher and David Zenker	1999	James L. Garard and Edward N. Dayton
1993	Robert B. Egan and Ralph T. King	2000	James B. Hoefer and Paul E. Mersereau
1994	Thomas V. H. Vail and David Zenker	2001	Michael J. Timbers and M. Gerald Sedam II
1995	Lawrence G. Bell and Richard F. McLoughlin	2002	Michael J. Timbers and Edward M. Prince
1996	Walter E. Robb and Theodore E. Gordon	2003	Thomas M. Wilson and James H. Dowling
1997	Lawrence W. Ward and Anthony D. Carpenter	2004	Richard M. Haverland and Felix C. Pelzer
1998	Frederick J. Robbins and Peter O. Shea		

1997	Robert D. Rogers and Edward C. Shotwell	2001	Raymond V. Knowles and Phil Patterson
1998	Cancelled	2002	Raymond V. Knowles and Raymond
1999	Peter O. Shea and James W. Vickers	2003	Stephen B. Clarkson and Charles G. Rolles
2000	Jack R. Lamey and Frank D. Tatum, Jr.	2004	Bruce C. Richards and Asa G. V. Candler

Discontinued Invitational Tournaments

Point Judith
Narragansett, Rhode Island

| 1970 | Bruce Miller and Tracy Barnes | 1971 | Chester T. Birch and James Murphy |

The Country Club
Brookline, Massachusetts

| 1984 | Edward W. Clark and Charles M. Pyle, Jr. | 1985 | Jack K. Busby and Charles M. Pyle, Jr. |

Somerset Hills
Bernardsville, New Jersey

| 1985 | Arthur Snyder and Howard L. Clark | 1987 | Stuart Christie and Arthur Snyder |
| 1986 | William H. Evans and Robert C. Gunness | 1988 | Lewis Oehmig and Sam Fleming |

Castle Pines
Castle Rock, Colorado

1987	William Rudkin and Jack Vickers	1990	James Garard and Larry Parker
1988	Bradford Briggs and Joseph McBride	1991	Dick Giddings and Monty Bee
1989	Floyd Corbett and Ed Steele	1992	James Garard and Robert Isham

Garden of the Gods
Colorado Springs, Colorado

| 1994 | Gerald Dederick and James Garard | 1996 | David Zenker and William Alden |
| 1995 | David Zenker and Donald Kohler | 1997 | Walter Nelson and Willard Denham |

Valley Club–Birnam Wood
Santa Barbara, California

2000	David N. Hall and William P. Dougherty	2003	Samuel H. Armacost and James W. McKinzie
2001	David N. Hall and Richard T. Love	2004	Alexander MacDougall and Stephen Summers
2002	Howard G. Giles and Charles V. Fairbanks		

PUBLISHING

Q Publishing LLC
Franklin, Virginia
757-569-0929
QPub@mindspring.com

Elizabeth B. Bobbitt, EDITOR AND GRAPHIC DESIGNER

Library of Congress Cataloging-in-Publication Data

Quirin, William L.
  United States Seniors' Golf Association, 1905/2005 /
by William L. Quirin.
    p. cm.
  ISBN 1-931169-06-3 (alk. paper)
 1. United States Seniors' Golf Association--History.
 2. Golf for older people--United States--History. I. Title.
  GV969.U53Q85 2005
  796.352'64--dc22
                                          2004028939

Printed in Hong Kong